SHOWPLACE OF THE NATION

STEEL PIER

Atlantic City

SHOWPLACE OF THE NATION

STEEL PIER

Atlantic City

Steve Liebowitz

With historic photographs from the collections of
Allen "Boo" Pergament and Robert Ruffolo

DOWN THE SHORE
PUBLISHING
WEST CREEK, NEW JERSEY

Box 100, West Creek, NJ 08092
www.down-the-shore.com

*The words "Down The Shore" and the Down The Shore Publishing
logos are registered U.S. Trademarks.*

Book design by Leslee Ganss

Printed in China
2 4 6 8 10 9 7 5 3
Second printing, with revisions, 2012

Library of Congress Cataloging-in-Publication Data

Leibowitz, Steve, 1956-
Steel Pier, Atlantic City: showplace of the nation / Steve Leibowitz.
p. cm.
Includes bibliographical references and index.
ISBN 978-1-59322-036-5 (hardcover)
1. Atlantic City (N.J.)--History. 2. Steel Pier (Atlantic City, N.J.)--History. 3. Atlantic City (N.J.)--Buildings, structures, etc.--History.
4. Amusement parks--New Jersey--Atlantic City--History. I. Title.
F144.A8L44 2009
974.9'85--dc22
2009021277

To Frank Gravatt, George Hamid and George Hamid, Jr., three giants of 20th-century entertainment whose vision and innovation transformed a moribund ocean structure of steel and lumber into a magical place where anything could happen — and usually did.

Steel Pier, Labor Day, 1934.

Table of Contents

Introduction

When traveling to Atlantic City today, slots, craps, or blackjack are usually the main reasons for a visit. Yes, there's the Boardwalk, along with the beach and the grand casino-hotels that have been built since 1980. You can still buy salt water taffy, and gulls still fight over a piece of old pizza lying on the Boardwalk planks. Today when you mention Atlantic City, people will ask, half-jokingly, "How much did you win?" The casinos are the first thing people think about.

This wasn't the case at the turn of the 20th century through the early 1970s. From a genteel Quaker gathering place where folks sat and listened to concert bands, to vaudeville, big bands, and rock & roll, when you thought of Atlantic City back then the first thing likely to pop in your mind was Steel Pier and its famous act, the Diving Horse. *A diving horse?* Today this is a strange concept for generations not old enough to remember.

The Pier closed in 1978 and burned four years later, so how would they know? They never grew up with Steel Pier, as so many others had before them. But from 1898 until 1978 — eight glorious decades — Steel Pier was Atlantic City. It was the heart and soul of the resort. There were glamorous hotels, restaurants and nightclubs full of celebrities; there were other amusement piers. Yet none was so beloved as Steel Pier, which stretched a half-mile out over the ocean. If you go through a stack of old Atlantic City postcards today, Steel Pier will be featured on most.

I was a teenager in 1972, when I went to Atlantic City for a short visit with my family. It was a tough time for the resort. Hotels had been blown up (well, imploded), crime soared and people were staying away. The Steel Pier that I saw at that time still had its old signs and decorations from the 1930s intact, all slowly rusting away. But there was something about this old, decrepit entertainment center then on its last leg that intrigued me.

I never had the opportunity to see Steel Pier before. My family had always vacationed in Wildwood, forty-some miles south on the Jersey Shore, near Cape May. Then a few years later, when the building's ancient signs were replaced with modern billboards heralding the "NEW Steel Pier," I finally got to see the revered Diving Horse act. Sadly, the Pier itself was in its last days.

* * *

How would Steel Pier be presented today? Let's say the Pier is still alive as it used to be — all the buildings are in place and refurbished, and it still has the same policy that it always had. Most of this would be impossible, due to the astronomic costs of booking top acts, but this is a fantasy, so take a look:

The big sign on the side of the Pier would present the large STEEL PIER letters on top. "Now appearing" it would say, and in larger letters, "pop diva LADY GAGA along with comedian CHRIS ROCK". Lady Gaga would perform four shows daily in the Music Hall, the building in the middle of the Pier, which held 2,000 people. It was, in fact, America's first Music Hall, opening more than thirty years before New York's Radio City Music Hall. These performances would last about forty minutes. Chris Rock would also perform four shows daily, at the end of the Pier in the large Marine Ballroom, which could accommodate thousands more. Because the Pier booked only "clean" acts, Rock would have to tame his down. (That in itself would be a fantasy!)

Two motion pictures would also be shown, one in the front Casino building, while the other would alternate between the pop star's shows in the Music Hall. These would be PG-rated films so that the whole family could enjoy them. No R-rated films would be allowed.

In addition to the entertainment, there would be the Diving Bell that would take you to the bottom of the ocean (at the sandy foot of the Pier); the House of the Century, where you could witness exhibits of modern conveniences; a huge showroom on the front of the Pier presenting the latest new vehicles and products from General Motors; and numerous other lesser exhibits of interest.

But wait! There's more! In back of the Marine Ballroom, at the very end of the Pier, is the huge outdoor Water Circus, complete with seating for 5,000. You'll witness clowns, daredevil acts above the ocean, wild divers, and the world-famous horse that will clip-clop up a ramp to a height of forty feet, then dive headlong into a huge pool of water with a female rider clinging to its back!

Needless to say, this spectacle would take you practically all day and night to cover. Shows, movies, exhibits! But the best part is … it would only cost one price for the entire venue! That's right! Today it would probably be impossible to price in a comparison to the few dollars it cost in the old days; perhaps $60 to $85.

But who cares? Look at all the entertainment you would get!

And that was the appeal of Steel Pier. There was nowhere else in the world that would give you so much for so little. "The Showplace of the Nation." "A Vacation in Itself." That's how it was presented. And that's exactly the way it was.

This is the story of that Pier.

Steve Liebowitz

Chapter One

Beginning of The 'World's Playground'

THE STEEL PIER

SEASON 1903

Atlantic City, N. J.

Why was Steel Pier built in Atlantic City? Why was anything built in Atlantic City? Why not somewhere else? The answer lies in the beginnings of what became Atlantic City and how it rose to prominence along the New Jersey Shore.

In 1783, the first white man to live on today's Absecon Island was Jeremiah Leeds, who had explored the area and built a log cabin. The name "Absecon" was derived from *absegami*, which translates as "little sea" in the Leni-Lenape language, the original settlers of the area.

After Leeds died in 1838, his second wife, Millicent, received a license to operate a tavern called Aunt Millie's Boarding House. It was the first business in what was to become Atlantic City. It's safe to say that initially there weren't too many boarders.

By 1850, there were only seven families living on the

barren Absecon Island. Except for a few small buildings, nothing else existed except sand, surf and foliage. The towns of Long Branch to the north and Cape May to the south were already well established resorts when development of the area to become known as Atlantic City was conceived. Cape May, in fact, was already known as a vacation spot for U.S. presidents.

Dr. Jonathan Pitney, a physician, politician and landowner living in the mainland village of Absecon, believed the healthy shore climate could help create a resort that could also attract ordinary working city dwellers if a convenient and comfortable means of travel was available. So, with support from local and Philadelphia businessmen, he obtained a charter for a railroad from the New Jersey legislature. He then sold the idea to Philadelphia investors.

Pitney hired a young civil engineer from Philadelphia named Richard Osborne. Osborne laid out the prospective railroad line, designed a layout for the proposed resort town, and conceived the name "Atlantic City," according to the National Railway Historical Society's account in *The Trains to America's Playground.*

Pitney decided that the streets running parallel to the ocean would be named after the world's great bodies of water: Atlantic, Pacific, Baltic, Mediterranean, Adriatic and Arctic. Streets that ran east to west would be named after the different states.

In January 1853, a plan was presented to a board of directors, which approved the name. Railroad promoters launched an advertising campaign for the proposed resort. Pitney and Osborne knew that for their plan to succeed, a fast, convenient and relatively inexpensive mode of transportation was vital to bring in the working people of Philadelphia, the closest big city, some fifty-five miles away.

On March 3, 1854, the City of Atlantic City was incorporated. Soon after, track was laid eastward from Camden to the still-desolate Absecon Island. The newly-named Camden & Atlantic Railroad cost $1.2 million to build.

On July 1, 1854, the first travelers ventured onto the first Camden-Atlantic excursion train bound for Atlantic City. Dignitaries and newspaper reporters from Philadelphia traveled with other curious passengers, and two and a half hours later, they arrived at the half-completed United States Hotel.

Growing beyond the mere handful of houses that existed when Pitney first conceived his idea, until 1854, when the C & A was completed, several boarding houses were built. Pitney and Osborne envisioned Atlantic City as a healthy haven for everyone, regardless of class. It was their belief that the railroad would make it possible for the working man to travel from the crowded city to the seashore in a few hours to spend a day at the beach, breathing in fresh salt air and swimming for exercise. However, it was the wealthy class

Absecon landowner Dr. Jonathan Pitney thought building a healthy seaside resort would also attract working-class visitors.

that would be the first visitors because they could easily afford to travel by train.

By 1857 there was a lighthouse, three churches, a market, some wood-frame buildings and railroad structures existed along with the boarding houses. It was a sign that a permanent population was slowly growing.

The first railroad to come close to the surf served the Sea View, a combination hotel-railroad terminal that occupied the block between Missouri and Mississippi avenues, from Pacific Avenue to the ocean. The Sea View introduced the first Ferris wheel-like amusement as well as the first "salt-water taffy" booth and the first organized beach patrol in the United States. The wheel amusement, inventor Isaac Newton Forrester's "Rotary Swing," carried sixty-four passengers to a thrilling height of nearly fifteen feet on Mississippi Avenue in 1872.

Two decades later, in 1893, George Washington Gale Ferris built a mammoth wheel at the Columbian Exposition in Chicago, making a name for himself and his wheel. His creation handled 2,164 passengers, taking them to a dizzying height of 263 feet! However, a local man by the name of William Somers took Ferris to court, claiming he had already held the patent on the wheel ride in New Jersey in 1891. Somers lost the infringement case, but the lengthy legal battle went on for years until Ferris died and had diminished Somers' stature as the true inventor of the ride.

Legend has it that salt water taffy got its name when a Mr. Bradley's stock of candy was doused by ocean waves in 1883. It only added to the allure of Atlantic City, and the name stuck.

By the 1880s, Atlantic City evolved into a popular vacation destination, gracing the cover of *Harper's Weekly* magazine numerous times. A staple of traveling acrobats and performers entertained on the beach for curious onlookers while dignified men and women arriving from Philadelphia strolled along the surf, breathing in the invigorating salt air.

The first roadway was built by the Pleasantville & Atlantic Turnpike Company from the mainland of Absecon to the island of Atlantic City in 1870, enabling visitors to arrive via other means than locomotive. It followed the train tracks from the town of Pleasantville to Florida Avenue in Atlantic City.

A problem peculiar to the resort's location led to its most famous landmark. The sand that beach strollers tracked into his hotel annoyed Jacob Keim, owner of the Chester County House, a beachfront hotel near the end of New York Avenue. He and Alexander Boardman, a conductor on the Camden & Atlantic Railroad and a hotel owner, devised a wooden walkway to solve the problem.

It was a temporary structure, built in eight-foot sections and ten

The layout of the railroad line as well as the resort's design was created by Philadelphia civil engineer Richard Osborne, who also named the town "Atlantic City".

feet in width. It was moved according to tides and beach conditions, but it essentially lasted throughout the summer season. These wooden boards were placed on small pillars dug into the sand, allowing people to walk over the beach without actually walking on the sand itself. Strollers loved it, and eventually booths, stalls and pavilions sprouted along its land side, offering snacks, amusements, attractions, and games of chance.

What Keim and Boardman had produced was Atlantic City's first boardwalk. No other resorts in the country, until that time, had an ocean boardwalk or any permanent businesses on any beach; only Atlantic City.

The construction of hotels grew to meet the demand of an increasing number of visitors. Most maintained a luxury lifestyle and demanded comfortable lodging. In 1879, the Lafayette Excursion House was established. A year later, the West Jersey Excursion House was built.

By the turn of the century, Atlantic City boasted a permanent population of over 27,000.

Atlantic City's African-American population also began to swell, due to the need for cheap labor within the hotels. In 1880, the black population stood at fourteen percent; by 1910, it was fully one-quarter of the city's population. Segregation was fully enforced, however. Blacks were to live on the city's Northside, with their own nightclubs, stores and services. The men were not allowed on the Boardwalk except to push visitors in rented rolling chairs.

The rolling chairs became a symbol of leisure and indulgence (as well as racism). Those who were photographed in a chair showed the world that you had "arrived," that you were a part of Atlantic City society — and even if you were almost poor, no one had to know.

Atlantic City's image grew to that of a resort where the average person could enjoy the healthy beach and ocean but also indulge in risqué behavior not accepted at home. Brothels, gambling and other vices were fully known.

The Boardwalk itself was improved. The second Boardwalk of 1880 was fourteen feet wide. The third one in 1884 was twenty feet wide and two miles long. In 1890, railings were first introduced, and the present Boardwalk, built in 1896, was forty feet wide and four miles long. It was declared a street by the city council that year and vehicles were prohibited. With more improvements, the Boardwalk measured sixty feet across its widest point. It began at the Inlet area and continued south to the towns of Ventnor, Margate and Longport, almost eight miles in length.

Large cottages were built on lots facing the water, most with vast fronts of manicured green lawns. Some of these, with names like Traymore, Seaside, Haddon Hall and Shelburne, eventually were rebuilt as large hotels that could hold hundreds of visitors and conventioneers, inviting expansion of railroad travel to Atlantic City. Soon after, trains from New York, Washington, Baltimore, Pittsburgh and elsewhere brought more big-city residents to the shore, leading to the construction of more hotels and entertainment facilities.

Railroad business remained steady until after World War I, when growing automobile ownership and improved roads began to erode railroad traffic. In 1933, the Penn-Reading Seashore Lines offered a one-day, round-trip for $1.25, quite a bit of money for those Depression days. The trains still brought visitors as late as the 1970s, but by then, they ran a distant third to automobiles and buses.

By 1919, Atlantic City had a year-round population of 60,442. (In August, it swelled to approximately 450,000.) There were six ocean piers, thirty-one bathhouses, two large indoor pools, twenty-one theaters, five national banks, eight daily newspapers and three weeklies. A 1924 list of houses of worship included nine Baptist (seven for African-Americans), one African-American Apostolic, two Christian Science, five Episcopal (one for African-Americans), one Lutheran, nine Methodist Episcopal (five African-American), two Methodist Protestant, six Presbyterian, four Roman Catholic and five Jewish congregations.

Housing developments were also springing up all over the area by 1928. Those who were making fortunes in the stock market were also making plans for summer homes.

Thanks to the vision of Dr. Jonathan Pitney, the trains made Atlantic City popular and successful — creating the environment for a structure such as Steel Pier. The city became the most popular resort in the United States, catering to a genteel class of people — represented in part by the Pier.

But it was not the first pier built.

Chapter Two

Amusement Piers: The New Attraction

Steel Pier, built in 1898, was not the first amusement pier in Atlantic City. Others preceded it, and the first was built eighteen years earlier.

The piers were, in essence, a continuation of the Boardwalk. One could explore the attractions directly over the sea, relax and smell the fresh sea air while also observing the action on the beach. It was a novelty for many to dance to orchestras out over the ocean.

The West Jersey Pier, a small extension 500 feet into the ocean, opened on July 16, 1880. The West Jersey & Atlantic Railroad erected it as a portion of its Excursion House facilities. The railroad made its first run that day, dropping off numerous visitors. Located at the foot of Georgia Avenue, the West Jersey Pier was a simple structure with seats and facilities for picnic parties and band concerts. Storms eventually washed away Atlantic City's first pier by 1886.

Howard's Pier opened in 1882 and was Atlantic City's first true amusement pier. The very first carousel in the United States was presented on Howard's Pier.

Howard's Pier

Howard's Pier was Atlantic City's first true amusement pier. Colonel George Howard of Washington, D.C. built the 650-foot pier at Kentucky Avenue. It opened July 12, 1882 and presented the very first carousel in the United States. Gustav Dentzel, a Philadelphia cabinetmaker, was the architect behind this popular ride, which cost only a nickel to ride. One of the carousel's operators was a young man named John L. Young, who later used his knowledge of amusements to become one of Atlantic City's great showman.

Because the pilings of Howard's Pier were not deeply sunk into the ocean floor, a storm that September washed it out to sea. Howard learned from the experience and rebuilt the pier the following year. It stretched out to 856 feet and included three large pavilions, one of which became the first ballroom constructed over the ocean.

But bad luck continued. During a gale on January 9, 1884, the schooner *Robert Morgan* smashed into the pier and destroyed it. Howard rebuilt it once more, but again it didn't last long. In 1889, when the city was preparing to build the fourth boardwalk they condemned and then purchased Howard's Pier; eventually it was torn down.

Applegate's Pier

While Colonel Howard tried to figure out a way to build an enduring oceanside pier, John Applegate, a boardwalk photographer and entrepreneur, purchased land on the beach in front of his gallery at Tennessee Avenue. Applegate's Pier opened on June 1, 1884, as a 625-foot, multi-deck pier that contained an amusement pavilion and a four-level gazebo, called Lovers Pavilion, at the outer end. Applegate was the first pier owner to present multiple amusements to his patrons. He claimed that 10,000 people could be seated on the decks at one time.

Applegate presented concerts and vaudeville, picnic areas, sunbathing pavilions, and a huge ice water fountain in front of the pier that used 3,000 pounds of ice a day to provide visitors a refreshing drink. Women with small children were admitted free.

Applegate can be credited with bringing Atlantic City's true amusement pier to fruition. But it took Colonel Howard's young carousel operator, John L. Young, to take it to the next level.

Iron-Heinz Pier

The 600-foot Iron Pier was the first to be built with iron pilings, hence the name. It was built by the Atlantic City Iron Pier Company and opened on April 25, 1886 at Massachusetts Avenue, near Atlantic City's northern end.

A lithograph presenting another view of Howard's Pier.

Originally the Iron Pier was built straight out to sea, but due to a Boardwalk reconfiguration about ten years later, a long section of the pier's entrance was chopped off and it extended out at an angle. The beautiful white façade entrance was removed from its original location and placed at the new entrance.

It was a simple pier by most standards and featured a large theater at the outer end for presentations and exhibits. In 1889, the small pier was almost lost to the gales and battering surf of a northeaster.

After a dozen years, the owners sold the pier to the Henry J. Heinz Company, the ketchup and pickles producer in Pittsburgh. Renamed Heinz Pier, it found great success with a marvelous promotional campaign that gave away thousands of free pickles and pins advertising the virtues of Heinz products.

Daily organ recitals and community song programs were popular, as well as sundecks and exhibits in the building at ocean's end. A

landmark of the pier was a large neon sign above the ocean building announcing "57" — referring to the slogan "Heinz Famous 57 Varieties".

The problem with Heinz Pier was that it was far removed from the center of action along the Boardwalk. It was also the smallest of the several piers that competed for patrons. The Hurricane of September 1944 destroyed most of the pier, and it was dismantled soon after.

Young's Ocean Pier

John L. Young was born just outside Atlantic City in the mainland village of Absecon on September 25, 1853. A very colorful sort of man, Young started out as a carpenter and worked at his trade until 1885. He then became a lifeguard and policeman in Atlantic City, earning forty dollars a month.

While patrolling the Boardwalk one day in 1887, Young met a retired Pennsylvania entrepreneur named Stewart R. McShea. They

The front of Young's Pier at the turn of the century.

THE SUN PARLOR.

H.J. HEINZ COMPANY
PICKLES AND FOOD PRODUCTS.
57 VARIETIES.

PITTSBURGH, U.S.A.

HEINZ OCEAN PIER, Atlantic City, N.J.

HEINZ PIER, ATLANTIC CITY July 26 1900.

A SNAP SHOT OF *Gail on Snow pond*
AT ATLANTIC CITY

(Top) The drawings on early postcards were sometimes exaggerated, as in this example of Heinz Pier extending almost to Spain. (Left) This 1900 postcard seems more accurate.

decided to go into business together by building and selling homes. They also bought some Boardwalk amusements and a bathhouse at South Carolina Avenue.

In 1891, the partners purchased Applegate's Pier at Tennessee Avenue. Renamed Young & McShea's Pier, it featured an enclosed ballroom measuring 80 by 120 feet, and presented daily concerts, evening dances, a children's carnival, and "Sacred Concerts" every Sunday evening. Extending an extraordinary 1,400 feet out over the sea, it became Atlantic City's biggest amusement center.

Fascinated with the sea and marketing himself as an expert on marine life, "Captain" John Young built an English Tudor cottage for himself and his wife at the pier's end. He claimed to fish from his kitchen window.

McShea retired in 1897, leaving management of the pier and businesses to the Captain, who promptly renamed it Young's Ocean Pier. He spent $56,000 to upgrade, extending the structure outward to 2,000 feet, enlarging the ballroom to provide space for convention gatherings, and presenting various types of entertainment, including the introduction of the "cakewalk," a minstrel dance that became a sensation.

Perhaps the most famous attraction was the twice-daily net hauls that were personally supervised by Young. Giant nets were lowered into the ocean near the end of the pier and brought to the surface full of fish and other sea creatures, whereupon Young would lecture to the crowd about the different species caught. Most became seafood,

(Top) Visitors to the Heinz Pier would receive pickle pins, a popular souvenir. Heinz Pier in all its glory, before the devastating hurricane of 1944.

but some were displayed in the pier's aquarium. Young's Ocean Pier quickly became Atlantic City's premier destination due to the Captain's showmanship and presentations.

The pier brought in European acts for vaudeville, Gilbert and Sullivan operettas, roller-skating, live lions, Punch and Judy puppets, and famous French actress Sarah Bernhardt.

In 1901, Young built one of the first fireproof hotels in Atlantic City, located on the Boardwalk directly across from the pier. Young's Hotel lasted over eighty-five years. It went through various name changes; the Alamac, the Knickerbocker, and finally the Mayflower. It survived the beginning of the casino age, but it could not compete with the newer hotels and was later demolished about 1990.

A major fire destroyed much of the pier on April 3, 1902, but Young immediately rebuilt. The newer Steel Pier had opened by this time and was a hit with the masses, but Ocean Pier still offered a unique variety of entertainment. For instance, in 1904, you could witness an exhibition of infant incubators with living infants, "The Success of the Pan-American Exposition", operettas and vaudeville in the Music Hall, children's carnivals in the Marine Hall, Charlie Grapewin in the play "The Awakening of Mr. Pipp" in the rear theater, an aquarium, net hauls, a bowling alley, a miniature railway, and Lee Schuyler's one-hundred-foot dive.

Sarah Bernhardt, possibly the world's greatest actress at the time, returned to Ocean Pier on June 6, 1906 for one night only, performing in "Camille." Tickets were priced at an unheard of $1 to $3, yet the show was sold out. The great magician Houdini appeared two years later, and then there was the risqué Floradora Sextette, along with live whales, fireworks, motion pictures and Skee-ball alleys.

On July 26, 1906, Young opened his new Million Dollar Pier at Arkansas Avenue. Ocean Pier was renamed Young's Old Pier, so as not to confuse. Although he now owned two of Atlantic City's piers and was estimated to be worth over $15 million, Captain Young focused primarily on his new pier and left management of the Old Pier to others.

On March 29, 1912, fire burned most of the Old Pier down to the pilings. Unfazed, Young charged and admitted 5,000 spectators a day to see the ruins and watch workmen clear away the debris. It was in process of sale to the Absecon Company when the fire hit.

The following summer, with the debris cleared, the remaining structure was renamed Young's Free Ocean Pier. In July, ten cents was charged to witness the Philadelphia Athletics versus the Cleveland Indians on Noke's Electrascore, which showed every detail of baseball games exactly as played, including the motion of the ball and the players in action.

Alfred Painter was the proprietor by 1915, along with Union Adams as manager. The pier presented a new ballroom for dancing, motion pictures and cakewalks.

Primarily wreckage that stood for many years, the moribund pier was totally rebuilt in 1922 to a much shorter length. New owners bought the structure and formed the Central Pier Company, added a new Moorish front and renamed it Central Pier. Office space on the second floor housed the Atlantic City Convention Bureau and Chamber of Commerce.

A fire on January 26, 1929 collapsed the roof, damaging a General Electric exhibit.

Central Pier was never serious competition to any of the other piers, simply because it mainly featured exhibits and, until the 1960s, few amusement rides. From the expanded 2,000 feet of Captain Young's enterprise, Central Pier was a scant 800 feet long by 1954, presenting a model home exhibit and a small aquarium.

Robert and Abraham Schiff bought the structure in 1984 and remodeled the 1922 front building. It exists today but has seen better days — now it is a collection of low-end shops with a few rides and amusements thrown in — but it is notable that the pier has been in use at that same Tennessee Avenue location since John Applegate built it in 1884, the longest such tenure in Atlantic City.

Steeplechase Pier

On August 25, 1899, a little over a year after Steel Pier's opening, competition came in the form of another pier located only some 300 feet away, at Pennsylvania Avenue. Auditorium Pier was built and owned by entrepreneur William Riddle, who had no idea how to market it to the public. In 1902, George C. Tilyou, the showman who built and owned the famed Steeplechase Park in Coney Island, bought it and decided to bring the same New York "anything goes" attitude to the new pier.

The Loop-the-Loop, or Flip Flap Railway as it was called in 1901, was an exciting novelty to visitors on Young's Pier.

The structure was renamed Steeplechase Pier in 1904, although there wasn't a Steeplechase ride, as there was around his building in Coney Island. Tilyou proved he was an expert in showmanship when he brought in "March King" John Philip Sousa for concerts, as well as high-class vaudeville.

From 1914 to 1922, Steeplechase was tagged "The Funniest Place on Earth" as Tilyou pulled out all the stops. There was a Hawaiian Village, including a complete reproduction of the beach at Waikiki, along with sixty other attractions. Visitors could watch a Blue Ribbon Pony Show, have youngsters enjoy Dawson's Dancing Dolls and Children's Carnivals, dance to orchestras, listen to radio concerts, or watch motion pictures three times daily.

Patrons entered the pier cautiously through the ominous mouth of a clown and immediately onto a revolving barrel. After that, it was anyone's guess as to what would happen next. For instance, blasts of air coming from the floor would uplift women's skirts — with exceptional timing.

An advertisement from 1922 stated:

Young's Ocean Pier evolved into Central Pier by 1922, sporting a concrete Moorish façade.

ture of Niagara Falls in woven glass, made by handlers out of 600 pounds of materials.

On its exterior, Steeplechase was proud of showing the world's largest electric sign. Designed and installed by the R.C. Maxwell Company in 1926, the large "Chesterfield" sign had 27,000 electric bulbs on two displays, back to back. It was 215 feet long and fifty-five feet high. At peak load, it used 465 kilowatts and took seventy-five seconds to complete the full circle of animated lighting effects in color. Some consider it the most spectacular signage ever created.

But it all came crashing down on the beach on Valentine's Day, 1932, when a three-alarm fire swept though the pier and destroyed it, a $500,000 loss. The intense heat broke windows of Steel Pier 300 feet away, right after patrons were evacuated from a Steel Pier movie theater.

It took a long time for the remains of Steeplechase Pier to be

Here sports and frolics are offered for everybody, kiddies and elders. There are 51 features included in the one admission with 3 sessions each day. No two are alike and the entertainment is most unique in character. Thrills, surprise and mystery are the order everywhere on the Pier. Every nook and corner contains its quota of pleasant memories. A tour of the Pier is just one laugh after another!

Steeplechase offered a potpourri of entertainment. There was a pony paddock at the end of the pier, ballroom dancing, and a motion picture airdome at the extreme end of the structure, seating 1,200. The "Glass Exposition from the Fair in San Francisco" presented a minia-

rebuilt. In the late 1930s, it was called Calvert Pier, due to a giant sign advertising Calvert liquor. Finally, in the mid-1940s, Steeplechase arose as a shorter, open-air pier with amusement rides.

Mammy's, a pancake restaurant, was located as an anchor on the Boardwalk side, and the pier did well. Steeplechase measured 950 feet long in 1954. It was shortened to 432 feet long in 1967, due to storm damage. The small pier carried on, though, through Atlantic City's rough 1970s, filling a niche for those who enjoyed amusements and rides.

In 1984, the city ordered Steeplechase closed due to its damaged and unsafe wooden structure. Resorts International owned it, but Steeplechase still operated under a lease agreement with the George C. Tilyou family. The pier was somewhat repaired and reopened for a short time, but closed again in 1986. The dilapidated structure burned in December 1988.

A small wooden portion remained near the Boardwalk, the last remains of what was once Atlantic City's "fun pier," but it was finally torn down in the early 1990s. Nothing of Steeplechase Pier remains.

Million Dollar Pier

Captain John L. Young was a master of surprise. He surpassed his Ocean Pier on July 26, 1906 when his new Million Dollar Pier, built by the Sterling Realty Company, opened at Arkansas Avenue and the Boardwalk. Stretching 1,700 feet out to sea and of a Moorish influence, the bright white pier boasted the "World's Largest Ballroom," Hippodrome Theatre, Exhibit Hall, Greek Temple, an aquarium, and a roller skating rink. There was dancing in the evenings with Fauman's Boston Concert Band, Sacred Concerts, and deep sea net hauls, which Young had introduced on his Ocean Pier. Famed millionaire "Diamond" Jim Brady was known to have his own box at the Hippodrome.

Million Dollar Pier was even heated for the winter months, and a ten-cent admission in December 1906 would offer skating, basketball, and Royal Italian Band concerts.

Young claimed the pier cost him $1 million to build, hence its name. Shortly after its opening, Young built himself a three-story, twelve-room Venetian mansion that he addressed as "No. 1 Atlantic Ocean," the "Most Famous Address in the World." Statues from Florence, Italy of Adam and Eve, Diana, Harmonia, and Beauty and the Beast were displayed in front of the house in the Italian Garden. The mansion's concrete construction alone cost $70,000. The interior was a natural oak. The dining room decorations represented the depths of the ocean to the heavens, and the Reception Hall was surrounded by plate glass, in back of which were embedded butterflies from all nations of the world. Over 3,000 electric bulbs at night illuminated the entire exterior of the pier.

Young claimed to fish from his window as he had when he lived on Ocean Pier. He hosted numerous famous visitors such as Thomas

John L. Young, Atlantic City's early innovative promoter, had at times lived on the piers that he owned.

Edison and composer Victor Herbert, and even served President William Howard Taft dinner in 1911.

By 1925, Young was spending his winters in Florida and was also president of Associated Realities Company, owner of the pier and other beachfront properties.

On April 5, 1922, Million Dollar Pier opened for the season with Friday night tango contests, net hauls, aquariums, sun parlors, seal feedings and roofed ocean promenades. Both Jim Shields' Mason-Dixon Seven Orchestra and the Benson Orchestra of Chicago played in the front ballroom. The Hippodrome Theatre, largest on the East Coast with 4,000 seats, presented the Emmett Welch Minstrels and five vaudeville acts. New stars such as Bert Lahr (later to become famous as

Central Pier circa 1940. Though the building's structure is much the same today, the outward appearance is very different.

the Cowardly Lion in "The Wizard of Oz") and George Raft were but a few who appeared at that time.

Million Dollar Pier was called "A World's Fair in Itself" and was prime competition to Steel Pier, the so-called "Showplace of the Nation" at that time. Before Convention Hall was built in 1929, Million Dollar Pier was host to many of Atlantic City's conventions, including the 1925 Miss America Pageant. By 1931, Million Dollar Pier and Steel Pier began a run of true competitive spirit. Both were similar yet also very different in their attractions. At the Million Dollar Pier, there was a rodeo and Wild West show, Jungle Land, dancing with two bands, Princess Yvonne-Psychic Marvel, movies, an aquarium, net hauls, Indians, an arctic seal, and the Royal Midget Band. Admission was also cheaper than Steel Pier, costing twenty-five cents until six P.M., and forty cents for evenings and on weekends.

Only one boardwalk block separated Steeplechase Pier from Steel Pier.

Dance marathons, a common recreational diversion during the depth of the Great Depression, were held in the ballroom of Million Dollar Pier from 1931 through 1933. A young Richard "Red" Skelton was the emcee at one point and held the crowd's attention while he perfected the comic bits that would later lead him to stardom. The winner of the 1932 marathon was one Frank Lovecchio, who later returned to Atlantic City many times as renowned singer Frankie Laine. He and dance partner Ruth Smith kept their feet moving for 130 days!

By the mid-1930s, Million Dollar Pier offered a circus and vaudeville, thrill acts, wild animals, three orchestras in the ballroom, puppets, movies in the Hippodrome, and net hauls. You could see Hardeen the Magician, the Salici Puppets, and eleven-year-old wild animal trainer Manuel King. Young still personally conducted the two net hauls daily, even while in his eighties. He died on February 15, 1938 at age eighty-six in his winter home in Palm Beach, Florida, the end of an amazing life as a showman.

George Hamid, fresh from working under Steel Pier owner Frank Gravatt, thought this was a perfect opportunity to go out on his own, so he signed a ten-year lease to take over as manager of Million Dollar Pier. Hamid, born in Lebanon, came to America as an acrobat and rose from poverty to eventually own one of the biggest agencies for circus and outdoor talent. He overhauled Million Dollar Pier with a new, modern marquee and signs. He repainted and redesigned the theaters and opened a 7,800-square-foot hall for roller skating. He called the dance hall the Ballroom of States, which could seat 10,000 for sporting events and measured 21,800 square feet plus 12,000 square feet of balcony space. Exhibits from *Collier's* magazine were presented, as well as top-name bands such as Artie Shaw, Glenn Miller and Woody Herman among others.

There were circus acts with elephants, lions and other animals. Famed movie cowboy Tom Mix showed up, as did George Jessel, Henny Youngman and other stars of screen and radio. From Hamid's opening

on June 25, 1938 until 1945, competition with Gravatt's Steel Pier was fierce — and sometimes dirty. Hamid knew it was an uphill battle to overcome Steel Pier's marketing prowess.

George Hamid, Jr., in 2003 recalled the two piers' differences:

The Steel Pier had the magic name. They had Goodman, Tommy Dorsey, all of the MCA bands. In the 1920s and 1930s, the Steel Pier had all the big stars, plus the bands. They also had big movies. The Million Dollar only had one movie theater and there were three on Steel Pier. And the Ballroom being out over the ocean on Steel Pier had a little more magic than the ballroom being up front on Hamid's pier, although the ballroom we had was just as pretty. It's like comparing a Cadillac to a Dodge. It was the public image.

Hamid later bought Steel Pier, and he diminished the Million Dollar's role, so as not to compete with himself.

On September 13, 1949, arson destroyed the front of Million Dollar Pier, causing at least $300,000 in damage. It was discovered by a patrolman at 4:29

(Top) Steeplechase Pier in the 1940s. Note the smiling face, a trademark of owner George C. Tilyou. Similar faces were found at Steeplechase Park in Coney Island, N.Y., and Asbury Park, New Jersey. (Bottom) The famous Chesterfield sign on Steeplechase Pier contained 27,000 electric bulbs and was the world's largest sign of its kind.

Steeplechase Pier — "The Funniest Place on Earth"— circa 1920

A.M. and raged out of control for ninety minutes. The blaze undermined the large Four Roses electric sign, sending it crashing through the roof of the Ballroom of States and completely destroying it and a surrounding area of 300 yards from the Boardwalk, according to an account in *The Atlantic City Press.*

The pier was owned by Associated Realties Corporation under Clarence K. Crossan of Philadelphia, who became company president after the death of Captain Young. Eviction proceedings had been pending against the Million Dollar Pier Operating Company headed by George Costello of New York, who had a five-year lease. It was said that Costello's company failed to make agreed improvements to the property.

The blaze spared the Hippodrome and Young's mansion, but the ballroom area was cleared for rides that opened in 1950. The famous net hauls were still held twice daily, 1,575 feet out over the ocean, until they were discontinued in the late 1950s due to the weakening condition of the pier's outer end.

An Italian village was created inside the old Hippodrome, exhibit-

Million Dollar Pier, Atlantic City, N.J.

(Opposite) Young's new elaborate Million Dollar Pier in 1906 presented a tremendous front ballroom and an almost equally large Hippodrome theater. Compare with the 1949 picture on page 35. (Above) Million Dollar Pier at night. Early conventions were held here.

ing Italian foods and products. But Young's famous mansion, in deteriorated condition, was torn down in 1953, bringing an end to the pier's grand years.

In 1969, Milton Neustadter, Maxwell (Sonny) Goldberg and others (all owners of the Howard Johnson Motor Lodge) bought the pier. A year later, as the Golden Dome was erected on the ocean end of Steel Pier, most of the huge Hippodrome building of Million Dollar Pier was demolished for additional rides.

On October 12, 1981, fire destroyed what was left of the surviving Hippodrome. The entire pier was torn down for the building of the 900-foot-long Ocean One shopping mall and food court. Ocean One, with an exterior to resemble a moored ocean liner, opened in 1983. It was demolished in 2003 and replaced with a bigger, upscale shopping complex called The Pier at Caesar's.

GARDEN PIER
BALL ROOM

DANCING OVER THE WAVES

YOUNG and old throng the great concert and dance halls in *Atlantic City* after the day has ended. Magnificent ball rooms, among the largest in the world, are located directly over the bounding waves on several of the ocean piers. These great halls are in most cases beautified with richly colored draperies and vari-colored lights, which give added zest to this form of amusement. All of the larger hotels also have beautiful ball-rooms, as well as unique grill-rooms, for the entertainment of their guests.

(Above) A rare sketch of the Garden Pier ballroom. (Top right) John Young's address for his three-story, twelve-room mansion on Million Dollar Pier was "No. 1 Atlantic Ocean". (Right) Garden Pier in the midst of construction, 1912.

New Garden Pier, looking South, Atlantic City, N. J.

The large theater on Garden Pier underwent many transitions from vaudeville to movies to Broadway shows before the 1944 hurricane badly battered it

Garden Pier

The beach between Steel Pier and Heinz Pier remained vacant until July 19, 1913, when the new Garden Pier opened to the public. Smaller than Steel but larger than Heinz, Garden Pier presented a beautiful array of landscaped flowerbeds and gardens that occupied the center of the structure.

There was a large vaudeville theater built on the ocean end, along with Spanish Renaissance exhibition buildings constructed on both sides. The theater immediately featured year-round, refined, high-class vaudeville that was later presented in 1918 by the famous B.F. Keith circuit. George Jessel, Eddie Cantor, Sophie Tucker, Eva Tanguay, and Will Rogers were just some of the big names one could see at the theater. Houdini hung upside down from the theater's roof in 1917, showing the tremendous crowd how he could escape from a strait-jacket.

The world's largest typewriter was a major draw in 1916. Built by Underwood for the Panama-Pacific Exposition a year earlier, the typewriter weighed fourteen tons, was eighteen feet high and cost $100,000 to build. A person had to stand or hop on each key to type each letter.

By the 1920s, with vaudeville eclipsed by the advent of talking movies, the theater of Garden Pier resorted to live stage plays and musicals, some as try-outs before heading to Broadway. In 1922, Aaron Lebedoff appeared in *"Yoshke Chvat"*, a Yiddish comedy. A year later, "Abie's Irish Rose," the comedy hit of Broadway, stayed all summer, playing seven weeks and seventy-one performances — an Atlantic City record.

Major motion pictures were presented in 1924; "The Covered Wagon" and Cecil B. DeMille's "The Ten Commandments" brought in steady audiences. A year later, "The Student Prince in Heidelberg" was a big favorite.

The dance orchestras of Ted Lewis, Rudy Vallee, Paul Whiteman, and George Olsen appeared. So did Fletcher Henderson and Cab Calloway, offering the rare event of an African-American band playing dances for an all-white crowd.

During the 1930s and early 1940s, stage plays and musicals returned and became Garden Pier's forte. Stars such as Al Jolson, the Three Stooges, Gypsy Rose Lee, Molly Picon, Ray Bolger, and Milton Berle could be seen in a variety of shows, some before heading to Broadway.

However, shows became infrequent, and the huge theater languished because no one really had an idea of how to make money with it. On March 6, 1944, the city took over the structure due to unpaid taxes. Five months later, the 1944 hurricane did enough damage to cause the city to condemn it. As its buildings deteriorated, Garden Pier became an eyesore, and its main building was torn down in 1950.

It was then decided to rebuild the pier using city money and reopen it as a community center. During Atlantic City's Centennial celebration of 1954, the new Garden Pier opened with plenty of hoopla and fireworks. It was a modern structure, 675 feet long with a band shell built on its middle, facing out to sea. Band concerts and sing-alongs were popular for many years thereafter. However, with the downslide of the city during the 1970s, the pier's concerts ceased. People grew wary of being on the

(Top) President Taft visits John Young at No. 1 Atlantic Ocean in 1911. (Above) Young (left) in a rolling chair with John Eveler, owner of the chair concession.

Boardwalk after dark. On October 19, 1981, a fire broke out, damaging a part of the building.

But the city wanted Garden Pier to remain a vital part of Atlantic City. Casinos had now become the main attraction and the city was experiencing a rise in tourism. Garden Pier was remodeled into the Atlantic City Historical Museum and Arts Center in 1985. One building maintains a permanent history exhibition of Atlantic City's golden years, and the other building exhibits art shows. The band shell itself is still on the pier but faces nothing but the open sea, and the seating area is gone.

ℂ ℂ ℂ ℂ

Besides the piers, there were other amusements that competed for

Deep-sea net hauls at the very end of Million Dollar Pier became very popular and were held several times a day. One never knew what sort of sea creature would appear during the net hauls (opposite).

attention and admission tickets. Before the famous Ferris Wheel came along, local businessman Isaac Newton Forrester invented a similar ride about 1872. Its name: the Epicyclical Diversion. Located near the Seaview Excursion House on Mississippi Avenue, the ride consisted of four wheels thirty feet in diameter that rotated simultaneously on a ten-foot high circular platform that also rotated.

Another local man, William Somers, designed the Observation Roundabout, which was located near Kentucky Avenue and the Boardwalk. Made of steel and standing 125 feet high, it had a circular elevator up to 103 feet and carried people to an enclosed platform, which revolved around the tower and was slowly lowered, affording passengers an incredible view.

Jessie Lake of Pleasantville invented and built a revolving observation tower at New York Avenue and the Boardwalk and another at Massachusetts Avenue about 1895. A much later version of an observation tower was built on Central Pier during the mid-1960s.

"The Haunted Swing," created by local inventor Captain Amariah Lake, was built in 1894 at the Boardwalk and States Avenue. A large swing held twenty people and was suspended from a room. As the swing remained still, the entire room flipped, giving passengers the illusion that they were upside down.

In July 1901, the Loop-the-Loop made its appearance at the Board-walk and Connecticut Avenue. Forerunner to the roller coaster, the ride consisted of a passenger car that traveled back and forth on tracks and performed an upside-down loop. It was touted as "the greatest novelty of the season — safe, quiet, easy running."

A similar ride called the Flip-Flop appeared over the ocean on Young's Pier during this same time.

There was also a version of Coney Island's popular Shoot the Shoots in the inlet area near Caspian Avenue and also next to the

(Top left) The beach next to Million Dollar Pier was designated for African-Americans and fondly nicknamed "Chicken Bone Beach". (Top right) Cowboy star Tom Mix made a personal appearance on Million Dollar Pier in August 1940. (Left) From 1938 to 1948, George Hamid directed Million Dollar Pier. Note the "Hamid's Pier" painted on the roof.

Million Dollar Pier after the September 13, 1949, fire destroyed the front ballroom (far right). Young's home, a bit worn and minus its cupola, stands to the left of the surviving Hippodrome section on the left. On the far right, a front portion remains prior to demolition.

revolving observation tower at New York Avenue and the Boardwalk. A block long in size, patrons would ride in little boats on tracks until they ascended a waterslide and splashed down into a tank of water at the bottom. A stand was built near the ride to hold the throngs of amused visitors who came to watch this spectacle.

Although not a pier, Rendezvous Park at the Boardwalk and Georgia Avenue took up much of a city block during the early 1920s and also entered the amusement mix. Nicknamed "The People's Playground," the park opened in May 1921 and offered free admission to "25 big attractions, five big circus acts, and dancing afternoon and evenings." A large dance hall could accommodate a few thousand, and

others could enjoy many rides and restaurants on the property.

In 1923, a young George Hamid, who later booked acts for the Million Dollar Pier and Steel Pier, presented the world's greatest exhibition of freak animals to Rendezvous Park, along with Princess Cleopatra & Company — Egyptian Dancers. Rendezvous Park burned to the ground in 1924.

Building began on the site in 1926, and in 1929 the huge Convention Hall opened. At the time of its construction, it boasted the largest indoor arena in the world. Convention Hall, now renamed Boardwalk Hall, remains an Atlantic City landmark to this day, best known as the former location of the Miss America Pageant.

Chapter Three

Steel Pier's Early Years

Atlantic City of the 1890s was largely a culture of Victorian expectations and manners. There was a tempting combination of amusements, beer gardens, gambling dens and houses of prostitution, but the average visitor was expected to act civilized and enjoy what the resort had to offer without embarrassing themselves or others.

Men were expected to wear proper clothing, usually a bowler or straw hat and a suit. Women wore long dresses and extravagant large hats, the fashion of the day. On the beach, skin was not to be shown and that protocol was strictly enforced. Until 1928 women had to wear stockings that covered their legs and feet. Men had to wear tops on the beach until 1940, when that ordinance was finally lifted.

Large wooden cottages and ornate hotels dotted the Boardwalk with proper names like Seaside House,

The Entrance to the Steel Pier, Atlantic City, N. J.

Steel Pier's original façade had windows, open-air lobbies, and minimal signage, designed exclusively for a refined clinetele.

Haddon Hall, The Chalfonte, The Dennis and the Hotel St. Charles; expansive, manicured lawns divided them from the sand of the beach that lay in front. The upper crust usually stayed in the larger beach-front hotels, like the 250-room Dennis with its available fifteen private bathrooms, while the middle and lower classes rented guesthouses lining the side streets where shared bathrooms were the norm. Porches for relaxing and social viewing were a necessity for all lodging, how-ever, even on side streets.

"Diamond" Jim Brady, the famous and extravagant millionaire of this period, stayed at the Shelburne and spent a fortune on lavish dinners with Broadway star Lillian Russell. Brady and Russell were considered "America's first couple," and they spent considerable time together, though they never married. The opulent restaurants in the Boardwalk hotels usually offered orchestras or Hungarian violin music as guests enjoyed the featured delicacies.

Wheelchairs used by invalids on the Boardwalk evolved into the famous Atlantic City rolling chairs. Philadelphia wheelchair manufacturer Harry Shill set up Boardwalk stands renting out a modified wicker basket chair that held usually two people and was pushed to one's destination by an African-American man. A tradition was born.

Victorian Atlantic City was lively and full of frolic. Minstrel shows were the rage. Guvernator's Theater and Fortesque's Pavilion, both at Arkansas and the Boardwalk, presented high-class vaudeville. The Hotel Rudolf's Grotto Café showcased Fulton's Famous New York

THE STEEL PIER·ENTRANCE PAVILION.

The original Casino building would remain underneath remodeled exteriors until the Pier burned in 1982.

Band. A marionette theater on States Avenue charged ten cents to see something titled "The Myriad Dances."

If you wanted choice wines, liquors and cigars, you would have ventured over to O'Neill's Pavilion at Boardwalk and Florida Avenue, or dined at the first-class café at the Inlet Pavilion.

The 1,000-seat Academy of Music on the Boardwalk at New York Avenue presented "Uncle Tom's Cabin," while at the Japanese Tea Gardens and Village at Connecticut Avenue, there were three acres of magnificent grounds that contained hundreds of Asian performers. Or you could watch a baseball game between the Atlantic City Collegians vs. the Century Wheelmen at Inlet Park. Sand sculptors designing intricate scenes on the beach passed around a hat for donations.

Before 1898, the only piers that existed in Atlantic City were Iron Pier, which was the smallest, and Young's Pier, which carried more amusements and was the favorite precisely for that reason. Young's Pier featured vaudeville, aquariums, fish net hauls, seals, presentations and shows — certainly a variety of entertainment that became popular in Victorian Atlantic City. Young's was a very awkward and boxy-looking pier, however, as its buildings lacked any decoration or cohesion.

So when visitors in 1898 saw the massive Steel Pier being built at the Virginia Avenue Boardwalk, the skeletal beauty taking shape mesmerized them.

❦ ❦ ❦ ❦

The architects of Steel Pier were influenced by the pier structures of Great Britain. The British had built multiple piers in their beach towns, some with ballrooms, theaters and arcades, and others just simple piers for strolling, perhaps with a covered pavilion for occasional band concerts.

Today, the longest pier in Britain is in Southend-On-Sea, Essex, which juts out an astronomical 7,080 feet into the water! Steel Pier, in comparison, was only 2,000 feet. Out of the top ten in Britain, seven are over 2,000 feet.

However, piers likely to have most influenced the design of Steel Pier were those in the town of Brighton.

Built in 1866 and designed and engineered by Eugenius Birch, West Pier stood high above the ocean in Brighton, mounted on dozens of cast iron, threaded columns screwed into the seabed and strengthened by a lattice of ties and girders. Originally it had an open deck with six small, ornamental houses of Oriental design, two tollhouses, and glass screens to protect visitors from the wind and sun. A large pavilion had been erected in 1893 with seating for over 1,000, along with an area that provided bathing accommodations. In 1903, the pavilion was converted into a theater for 1,000 people. In 1914-1916, the covered bandstand was demolished, and the pier was widened and an oval concert hall seating 1,400 was built — the final expansion. With an unrivaled architecture in its seaside entertainment buildings, it was considered the "Queen of Piers."

The 1920s featured an eclectic assortment of paddle steamer excursions, high divers, military bands, recitals by the pier's resident orchestra in the concert hall, and a year-round program of plays, pantomimes and ballets in the theater. In its heyday, over two million people visited each year, very comparable to Steel Pier at that time.

When West Pier closed in 1975, it was essentially that which existed architecturally in 1916. The modern day West Pier, despite its decay and destruction from fire, is 1,115 feet in length — mostly a ruin. In April 2003, a major fire thought to be intentionally set destroyed the ornate pavilion building at the end of the pier. The concert hall, partially collapsed, was untouched. Officials are still hoping to restore the West Pier, a task that is proving to be extremely difficult as time goes on.

The other showcase at Brighton's waterfront in England was the Palace Pier. Opening in 1899, a year after Steel Pier, Palace Pier illuminated the sky nightly with over 3,000 electric light bulbs. In 1901, the Oriental Pavilion opened, housing a concert hall for 1,500, in addition to a dining hall, a private dining room and a kitchen.

Brighton Pier closed during World War II, then reopened in 1946, as popular as ever, for nearly five more decades. By the 1980s, however, it was deteriorating and its popularity waning. It was renovated in 1984 with two amusement arcades, three bars, sideshows and retail outlets, and a fish and chips restaurant that seated 250 people. Some original kiosks remain. The 1,722-foot-long Brighton Pier still hosts 3.5 million visitors a year. Sadly, West Pier, with its ornate buildings, did not share the same good fortune.

The Palace Pier and beach in Brighton, England, clearly shows the inspiration for Steel Pier.

☾ ☾ ☾ ☾

Steel Pier was to be built on land that was originally owned by the state of New Jersey. When bathhouse operator George W. Jackson purchased the land and signed the easement deed in 1896, he and his newly formed Atlantic City Steel Pier Company owned up to the high water line. Jackson and his partners decided to build a pier over the beach to offer the public a place to relax and enjoy the vista of sea and sand. Philadelphia architect John T. Windram was hired to design the $200,000 structure; Atlantic City contractor Frank A. Souder would build it. The Steel Pier Company's first president was Kennedy Crossan, a Philadelphia businessman whose family was later involved with the building and operation of Million Dollar Pier.

Steel Pier was built on iron pilings dug forty feet into the bottom of the ocean, and utilized a concrete understructure with steel girders — hence its name. It was one of the world's largest amusement piers. The *Atlantic City Daily Press* presented glowing reviews before it even opened to the public:

The pier, which is now in a state of erection, extends into the Ocean 1,621 feet from the Boardwalk and is built of iron piles and steel girders and varies in width from 150 feet to forty feet and will be the most magnificent and complete and thoroughly up-to-date Pier on the Atlantic seaboard. The Main entrance will be a handsome two-story building in Italian Renaissance, covering an area of 150 feet by ninety-five feet, which will serve the purpose both as an entrance and casino. It will be luxuriously furnished and will contain lounging, smoking and reading rooms, parlors, lavatories, etc. A feature of this building will be the Auditorium, which can be used for entertainments or dances.

Three hundred sixty feet beyond this building will be a dance pavilion, seventy feet by 150 feet in area, one-story high and connected with the entrance by a promenade deck, seventy-five-feet wide on either side of which will be covered walks. The dance pavilion will be a perfect gem, differing from anything of its kind in this part of the country. The floor will cover a surface of 105,000 square feet. A thoroughly equipped stage and band shell, with all necessary dressing rooms, etc. for giving theatrical performances will be found complete. Prof. Sol Asher and Son of Philadelphia have been engaged to take charge of the dancing and all social functions.

The Aquarium of fifty feet in diameter will be located on the Pier between the dance pavilion and the sun parlor and will be filled with all the denizens of the deep, rare and attractive marine specimens and sea lions.

On the end of the Pier, the sun parlor will be located, 50 square feet, giving a magnificent view of the ocean and Atlantic City Boardwalk, beautifully furnished with rockers, lounging chairs, etc.

Extending out 400 feet beyond the sun parlor to the extreme end of the Pier will be what is known as the "fishing deck," where bait and lines will be furnished by courteous attendants.

Many novel entertainments and delightful features will be introduced during the season, which will be announced later on.

The June 13, 1898 edition of the *Daily Press* reported:

There are three buildings on the structure facing the esplanade — the Casino, the Dancing Hall, located about midway between the shore and the outer end, and the Sun Parlor, 350 feet from the end. There is another small circular building between the Sun Parlor and Dancing Hall in which there is a huge tank for aquarium purposes.

The Casino has a frontage on the esplanade of 150 feet and a depth of 120 feet. In architecture, the Casino and all the other buildings follow the Colonial style. The entrance on the walk is flanked on either side by ticket offices. Great white pillars in stately rows serve as supports to the upper stories.

The floor is laid with octagon shaped tile, the side walls are ribbons of glazed white tile and the stands and other fixtures are of pure white marble.

Upstairs is the auditorium or Casino proper. The ground floor will be the great lounging place, where visitors can watch the throngs as they move to and fro on the walk. It will easily accommodate several thousand seated people.

The Casino — There is a grand stairway leading up to the Casino's auditorium or dancing hall. It is built of highly polished cherry stained wood. Halfway up, the stairway divides at a landing. A combination hallway and balcony is at their head. From them and also two sun balconies, a commanding view is had of the sea and surf. Rockers, lounges

and easy chairs will enable patrons to enjoy in comfort the breezes always to be found on the pier and at the same time watch the bathers. There are smoking and reading rooms, the latter being provided with a fine library of books. There are two square balconies of considerable dimensions, one on the east and one on the west of the building, which overlooks the esplanade.

The Music Hall is a vaulted chamber, 30 feet in height. The walls and ceiling, finished in rough sand, are painted buff. There are a half a dozen heavy arching wooden girders ...

☾ ☾ ☾ ☾

Steel Pier opened for the first time on June 18, 1898. From 9 to 11 A.M., the Pier was open for public inspection. General Superintendent Thomas R. Dibble took the liberty of embellishing the Pier with 500 potted plants. In the arcade there was an open-air concert at 10:30, featuring Kendle's First Regiment Band.

From the *Washington Post* on opening day:

The weather, always the divinity to which the people at the seashore pray to, turned out after a moderately warm beginning to be at Atlantic City's most favorable. Cool breezes, water which has become warm enough to tempt bathers to begin the best of summer's sports, have combined to make the city by the sea an ideal place for those who get away from the heat of the city streets.

The summer tide of visitors has begun to run in earnest. It is one of the best parts of the season to enjoy Atlantic City. Not too crowded, the wide sweep of the Boardwalk still a comparatively free promenade, but with that zest added which comes from the presence of fellow-beings. Excursions have not yet set in, and for those who enjoy that happy medium between a crowd that is too large and solitude, it is the most enjoyable time of the year. People you know are here, people whom you don't want to know have not yet come.

The big hotels are well filled. That insane war fear which for a time did injure the season has subsided. The Brighton, Arlington, Garden, St. Charles, Haddon Hall, Windsor, Rudolf and other big houses are all doing a splendid business. The Windsor has been especially fortunate in that it has been the headquarters of two conventions, that of the International Hohnemannian Association and the United States Brewers

Association.

From a purely local standpoint, the opening of the new Steel Pier today at the foot of Virginia Avenue was the event of the week. Music by the First Regiment Band of Philadelphia, which has been engaged by the proprietors for the season, and by the Hungarian Band during the morning and afternoon, combined with a formal opening in the evening with addresses by prominent men from three States.

The pier runs 1,600 feet, one-third of a mile out to sea. At the entrance is a casino, 120 feet deep, 150 feet wide. In the middle rises an auditorium with a stage and dancing floor, and at the end, right in the path of any stray breeze which might not reach shore, is a sun parlor, where the invalid can feel health returning with the cool swell of each incoming curling wave. This is the second pier at the resort, and the old and the new will vie with one another with consequent advantage to the public. Atlantic City is now so very far ahead in those practical and varied forms of aids in recreation that comparison with other resorts is now almost impossible. Numbers of resorts have features that attract certain classes. Atlantic City, cosmopolitan and pleasing to all, has become differentiated enough in its attractions to please anyone and everyone.

ℰ ℰ ℰ ℰ

The first Sacred Concert on the Pier was held on a Sunday evening, on June 19, featuring Madame Emma Suelke, soprano soloist, with music by Verdi, Rossini, Mascagni and Victor Herbert.

The Steel Pier illuminated the night with 3,500 white bulbs, which wasn't a problem since the Steel Pier Company had its own electrical plant nearby on Virginia Avenue.

The Pier's first newspaper advertisement simply said, "The New Steel Pier — on the beach at Virginia Avenue — Atlantic City's newest and greatest attraction."

The opening was described by the *Atlantic City Union* in its June 20, 1898 edition:

The Atlantic City Steel Pier, which is the adopted title of the new structure on the oceanfront, was formally opened on Saturday, when more than 10,000 people examined and admired its graceful architecture and rich furnishings.

In the evening, President Crossan presided and faced the largest audience that he has assembled in this city for a long time. He spoke briefly of the enterprise and the spirit that had inspired the erection of the pier, modestly refraining from any allusion to his own connection with the affair and paying a deserved tribute to his co-workers.

Mr. Crossan introduced Mayor Joseph Thompson, who expressed his admiration for the structure, which he said would be an inspiration for a higher order of oceanfront architecture.

Judge Allan R. Endicott spoke eloquently of the new structure. He paid a glowing tribute to the men of brains and money who had placed so much faith in the future of the city. The energy of President Crossan in watching every detail connected with the pier, from its inception to the driving of the last nail, was complimented.

John K. Anderson, Esq. of Philadelphia, closed the speech-making program with a clever address in which he reviewed the men and measures employed in the construction of this beautiful adornment to the oceanfront.

The floral decorations and the brilliant illumination at night were only a small part of the pier itself, yet they were appreciated in their place and lent a charm to the foot of Virginia Avenue far beyond anything ever attempted at this section of the Boardwalk.

There will be a hop in the dancing pavilion tonight, inaugurating the summer pleasures of this character. There will be dances every Monday, Wednesday and Saturday evening. Sea lions are fed 11 A.M. and 4 P.M. and there is good fishing on the outer pavilion. The admission is 10 cents, children, 5 cents.

ℰ ℰ ℰ ℰ

Steel Pier's schedule of September 1, 1898 presented a very refined lineup: Elite Operatic Minstrels, First Regiment Band, Grand Cakewalk, Children's Novelty Ball, Promenade Concert and Dance, Plantation Cakewalk, Concerts and Hops, and Sunday Sacred Concerts. There wasn't a hint of bawdiness anywhere.

The only apparent problem was that of the inability of the management, through legal technicalities, to sell refreshments on the Pier. A law was in effect that wouldn't allow the sale of food on the beach side of the Boardwalk. This was long a source of disappointment to the public, who might have stayed the entire day if food were available. The result was that patrons had to bring their own lunches. It wasn't until the 1930s that the Pier could sell snacks and drinks, by way of an

THE STEEL PIER.

In Victorian Atlantic City, relaxing on the beach and people-watching was a popular pastime. In the 1920s, the open areas shown here proved too valuable and were enclosed, widened, and extended downward into the sand.

interesting loophole in the law that argued the public was only "renting" the products, not buying them.

In 1899, William Jay Turner, vice-president of the Philadelphia Orchestra Association, succeeded Kennedy Crossan as president of the Steel Pier Company. Directors of the company were George W. Jackson, Max Bamberger, A. Ogden Dayton, Jeremiah Sullivan & Morris Pfaelzer, and Louis, Alfred and Henry Burke.

From Steel Pier's 1905 program:

Perhaps this great city of pleasure seekers never appears to be better advantage than on a night in July or August, when the season is at its height. Then, when the great Steel Pier is outlined in a blaze of electric lights and the people are seeking refreshments for mind and body, when the breezes waft the strains of orchestras and bands from a dozen directions, when the Boardwalk is ablaze with light and aswarm with promenaders, when the moonlight touches with silver sheen the spray of the waves breaking upon the shore, when everywhere is music, mirth and merry-making, then it is that Atlantic City looks like a veritable fairy-land of the night, reared on the sand by the waving of a magician's wand.

☾ ☾ ☾ ☾

Under the direction of its new general manager, Jacob R. Bothwell, Steel Pier continued to lead in popularity even when other piers were built. Bothwell would last as GM until the 1930s.

Local transportation also brought more people directly to the foot of the Pier. The Shore Fast Line trolley service opened August 24, 1906 at Virginia Avenue and the Boardwalk. It followed a speedy route that would take patrons to Somers Point on the mainland and then directly to the boardwalk in nearby Ocean City. The Fast Shore Line unfortunately ended its run on January 18, 1948, making it more difficult to travel directly to the Pier.

Historian Adrian Phillips, born in 1898, remembers the wicker rocking chairs on the Pier. "It was always a scramble at the beginning of the day for the choice seats. That was great entertainment for the

---

The Pier continued with its genteel format for some time, generally presenting military-type bands as its main attraction, with a grand hop once a week. This was a typical schedule of 1899:

Music Hall concerts every Aft. & Eve. 4.30 & 9 — *F.N. Innes (musical director)*
Casino Auditorium — *rocking chairs, leisure, side balconies*
9/8/1899 — "An Evening with Richard Wagner";
9/19/1899 — 1812 Overture — Tchaikovsky

Schedule:

11 00 A.M. — Hungarian Band Concert	Dancing every night 9 — Innes & his Band
11:15 — Farce & vaudeville	
12:30 — Seals Fed	
3:30 — Minstrels	Ballroom theatre — 11:15, 4:30, 7:30
3:30 — Hungarian Band	Prof. Hampton's dog, cat & monkey circus with boxing cats & high-diving donkey
4:30 — Innes & his Band	
4:30 — Farce & vaudeville	Adams Sisters
7:30 — Hungarian Band	Master Walter Morgan (clown)
7:30 — Seals Fed	Jas. R. Adams — Emperor of Stilts
7:30 — Farce & vaudeville	George H. Adams Comedy Troupe
8:15 — Minstrels	
8:30 — Cakewalk, Tues & Fri.	
8:30 — Children's Carnival, Thurs.	

Because the entire structure was built on hundreds of pilings, Steel Pier in its early days looked as if it were floating above the ground.

ladies, to see the styles and fashions of the people strolling by in a constant procession.

"Those ladies were corseted; they would wear a heavy flannel suit, a corset, and stockings. And the gentlemen were vested, even on the hottest days. None of this casual dress. Employees in the Ballroom were lectured that if the dancers 'spoon' too acquaintedly, they must be asked to leave."

And even though it was a more refined age in Atlantic City, the reality was that it was a care-free resort that was viewed by visitors as a place to get away from the confines of city life and experience the things they couldn't be caught doing at home.

The 1909 Baedeker tourist's guide summed up Atlantic City during this period: "Atlantic City is an eighth wonder of the world. It is overwhelming in its crudeness — barbaric, hideous and magnificent. There is something colossal about its vulgarity."

And that included the new Steel Pier.

OFFICIAL PROGRAMME
-1911-

STEEL PIER ATLANTIC CITY.

Chapter Four

The Minstrel Shows

The very name now conjures a myriad of perceptions, most of them negative. In today's world, it is hard to comprehend how and why minstrel shows were allowed at all in the United States.

The sight of white men wearing black makeup on their faces and singing Southern songs about Dixie and plantations is puzzling. For many white audiences, watching these performers displaying physical embellishment and laughing hysterically in a stereotypical way became what they perceived to be the black folk's way of life.

Not only was it racial, but it spun a culture alien to most Americans into a grotesque mockery. Although the white men in a minstrel troupe were immaculately dressed, wore white gloves, played banjos and sang sentimental songs, they nonetheless donned fake, close-cut Afro wigs, and exaggerated their lips by encircling a large white or red ring around their mouths.

Performers had blackened up since the 1790s, but the first so-called minstrel was Thomas Rice, who invented a song and dance act between 1828 and 1831 by impersonating an old, crippled black slave whom he named "Jim Crow." The act became a major sensation that launched a long line of minstrel troupes that would last over a century. Later in the twentieth century, the term "Jim Crow" came to symbolize the laws of segregation, particularly in the South, as blacks were forced to embody their existence separately from whites.

Dan Emmett's Virginia Minstrels was the first troupe to appear in public, and in 1843, it made its debut in New York. Many troupes followed, such as the well-known Lew Dockstader Minstrels, which introduced to audiences a young Al Jolson in 1911 as he ascended to super stardom.

Entire families came to see a minstrel show. The Interlocutor, usually a white man, sat in the center of the row, bantering with the two end men, called Mr. Tambo, a derivative of tambourine, and Mr. Bones, named for chicken bones. The program contained songs, dance, and comedy skits, all showcasing what was presented as the African-American way of life. The performer's dialect was an exaggerated form of Southern, African-American speech patterns. Stereotypes such as eating watermelon and stealing chickens were common, as were exploits of the corner dice games.

Blackface minstrels can be understood in the context of the times in which they appeared. It was such an accepted way of entertainment that there were even African-American troupes that also blackened up, stereotyping themselves. One of the most famous was that of Bert Williams, light-skinned comic of the famed Ziegfeld Follies, whom audiences expected to see as a stereotype.

Most of the white performers would claim that they were not racist and that becoming black was just a part of theatric interpretation. Just how much of this is believable is open to speculation. It's tough to accept that many of these performers didn't know they were making fun of an ethnic group.

But Germans, Jews, Chinese, Swedes, Dutch and other nationalities were also commonly referred to in derogatory slang in vaudeville during the late 1890s, when America's "melting pot" grew dramatically due to vast immigration. It was a common practice that was widely popular and accepted. In fact, if some ethnic group were not part of a program, the audience would have thought that something was amiss.

Therefore, when Steel Pier opened in 1898, it was only natural to have its own minstrel troupe for the refined clientele. The Murphy & Gibson Minstrels, led by producers John Murphy and Alf Gibson, became the yearly stock company for the new Pier. W.C. Fields, a young unknown performer who was known to fake drowning in the ocean for the purpose of luring curious customers back to Fortesque's Pavilion at Arkansas Avenue and the Boardwalk, joined the cast for a brief time in June 1899.

But Fields didn't really care for the minstrels, and soon tried his luck in other shows, billed as "The World's Greatest Comic Juggler" before attaining worldwide recognition as one of the all-time film comedians.

A Steel Pier ad of May 30, 1908, announced:

Fun for old and young will be provided in the Casino Hall tonight where the Murphy & Gibson American Minstrels have their regular summer engagement. The performance, which will include 'first part' and an interesting enlivening 'olio,' begins promptly at 9 P.M. In the company are all the old favorites, among them Mat Wheeler, Frank Tinney, Emmett Welch and others. (Welch later led the Million Dollar Pier troupe.)

By 1910, John Murphy, the troupe's first interlocutor, took over the entire minstrel production at Steel Pier. He oversaw a growth in his cast and even featured future stars of the Broadway stage. Famous minstrels and actors such as Tinney, Raymond Hitchcock and George "Honey Boy" Evans got their start on Steel Pier.

Tinney, who was earning twenty-five dollars a week, stayed on the Pier for eight years as the star of the troupe until Broadway showman Flo Ziegfeld discovered him and offered him a part in his "Ziegfeld Follies of 1913."

Murphy's Minstrels would regularly perform in the Casino theater, located at the front of the Pier, twice daily at 3:00 and 8:30 P.M. They were also a part of the very popular evening cakewalk dances that were held in the Ballroom three or four times weekly.

The cakewalk, which came out of the ragtime era, became a sensation in the same manner that "The Twist" took over America in 1960. It consisted of an exaggerated African dance in which performers would bend back the body, drop the hands at the wrist and high-step around

A troupe from Murphy's Minstrels poses on the Pier, circa 1915.

revues titled "Military Cadets" and "Vacation Days," and they now shared the Casino theater with motion pictures.

In 1934, the minstrels were described as "a new show, modernized, but retaining the volume of laughs created by old timers." In other words, there would be more of a vaudeville flavor than a Southern one, proven by the fact that by this time only the end men in the skit wore blackface.

In 1936, Elliott, the troupe's production manager and talent scout, discovered a new comedy team trying out new bits in the Republic Burlesque Theater on 42nd Street in New York. The two comedians had honed their skills in the "girly" shows of the era, showcasing a genuine chemistry that left audiences in stitches.

Elliott signed the two new talents separately and billed them as "Lew Costello and Buddy Abbott." The team turned old vaudeville routines such the now classic baseball skit "Who's on First" as their own, with their impeccable timing. They played three seasons with the minstrels but never blackened up.

the floor, mimicking high society. The male minstrels would wear tuxedos and top hats, while the females would wear gowns. It was the first dance crossover from black to white society.

In the early years, one could see the "Grand CakeWalk" on Monday evenings and the "Plantation CakeWalk" on Wednesdays. Amazingly, the cakewalk lasted into the mid-1920s, proof of the longevity of the minstrel fascination.

🎵 🎵 🎵 🎵

In 1926, Frank Elliott, who had been performing with the Steel Pier troupe, took over the operation after the beloved John Murphy passed away. By then, there was a huge cast of thirty-five minstrels, plus the Jimmy Jones Orchestra.

When Frank Gravatt bought the Pier a year earlier, he slowly shaped the Pier to his vision. Yes, there were minstrels, but a watered-down version. Now the minstrel show changed every Sunday, with

Bud and Lou slowly inched their way up the show business ladder. Known as Abbott and Costello by the time they were headlining the troupe in 1938, they were billed as the "comedy stars of Kate Smith's radio hour," earning $500 a week. One review boasted they "bring roars of laughter that stop the show with their new line of rapid repartee at the baseball game." When they returned to Steel Pier in 1941, they were the country's biggest movie stars.

Another member of the minstrel cast at that time was Pinky Lee, another product of burlesque, who went on to host a kiddie program on television in the early 1950s.

Author Russell LeVan, in *Atlantic City Boardwalk and Beach*, quotes James P. Kenney, an employee on the Pier at that time: "Abbott and Costello had a feud with Pinky Lee. They stole his tap shoes so he couldn't go on stage and do his act. They also threw him out on the stage and threw him an old pair of shoes. Bud Abbott sometimes had medical seizures and one time they had to lower the curtain and take

him off."

The minstrels moved to the Music Hall by 1937, bringing in guest dance acts such as the Four Step Brothers and Tip, Tap and Toe. Elliott was still director, and singer Ben Yost and his Varsity Singers took up a top billing in presentations titled, "Jitterbug's Revue" and "Join the Navy."

The August 30, 1941 issue of *Billboard* describes the show during its last years as a pier attraction:

A skit from the blackface minstrel show has good comedy fodder in team of Ryan and Benson, working with comic Pinky Lee. They manage to get plenty of laughs out of the old breaking-egg-in-hat bit of magic tomfoolery.

In its last incarnation, the Steel Pier Minstrels, as they were finally called, featured Dick Dana as M.C., along with still another burlesque comic, Joey Faye, who later went on to do television and movies. The minstrels gasped their last breath in 1943, in the midst of World War II. It was tough booking name acts during the war, so management decided to combine what was left of the minstrel revue with other vaudeville acts and put them all together in the Music Hall.

The minstrels had run their course. They were dropped entirely, probably due to the war, diminished crowds and public indifference.

But shows like these didn't stop overnight in America. Minstrel shows continued until the mid-1950s on the Pier in Tony Grant's "Minstrel Daze" revues in his "Stars of Tomorrow" shows. In November 1948, the Atlantic City Fire Department held minstrel shows on the Pier that sold out for three straight nights.

It wasn't unusual to see Mr. Tambo and Mr. Bones yuk-yuk it up at charity shows in many towns and cities as late as the 1960s. Even Philadelphia's famed Mummers, who wore faces of all colors, didn't ban blackface until 1966, in response to heightened civil unrest.

The Steel Pier Minstrels, a fixture from 1898 to1943, represented an era that was both popular and a disgrace to American entertainment. In the context of a theatrical representation of a stereotype, they were a product of their time.

STEEL PIER
ATLANTIC CITY
1912

Frank Gravatt, Entrepreneur & Innovator

Who was Frank P. Gravatt and how did he transform Steel Pier into the greatest entertainment spot in the world? No one had the slightest inkling that Gravatt's plans would transform not only the moribund pier, but also all of Atlantic City.

Called "a salt water Barnum" by the *Atlantic City Press*, the shrewd businessman took chances that no one else would take.

Born April 26, 1890 about thirty miles from Atlantic City in rural Lower Bank, on the Mullica River, Frank Gravatt didn't grow up in a privileged childhood. His father was an upholsterer in Philadelphia but moved the family to Atlantic City.

In 1897, when he was but seven years old, Gravatt was helping his father carpet rooms in the Seaside Hotel near the Boardwalk. Looking out a window, he saw the construction workers putting the last touches on the soon to be opened Steel Pier, not knowing that one day he would own both the Pier and the Seaside Hotel.

Gravatt had little formal education. When he was eleven, he delivered the local *Press-Union* newspaper, serving four routes. Leaving school, he gave up a boyhood ambition to explore the sea and took a job as clerk in a grocery store. He then went into business for himself, dealing with wholesale coffee and then making and selling ice cream cones.

He married Flora Somers of English Creek, New Jersey, and soon after, Gravatt, a budding entrepreneur at age twenty-one, met Alvah Hall. Hall had money and Gravatt had ideas, and as the two men quickly became a business team, they looked for ways to advance.

In 1911, as the motorcycle became a popular toy in the East, the entrepreneurs sought a way to profit from the fad, and the firm of Hall & Gravatt became agents for Indian Motorcycles. By 1917, however, they realized automobiles had a brighter future. They acquired a local Buick dealership, then landed a lucrative contract to supply limousines, which came to be known as "jitneys", for Atlantic City's public transportation company. By 1922, four out of every five jitneys in Atlantic City were Buicks from Hall & Gravatt Buick on Atlantic Avenue.

During an explosive real estate market in the 1920s, Gravatt's found a new gold mine. He made large sales and purchases, including vast acreage on the mainland and beachfront properties. He soon began making so many real estate deals that he would be in and out of the bank completing up to four transactions a day.

The Chelsea Bank was so impressed with Gravatt that they made him a director. His buying and selling continued at a rapid pace. During his travels, he learned in late 1924 that Steel Pier was up for sale by owner Louis Burke, a well-known Philadelphia wholesale meat packing distributor.

On June 16, 1925, the Pier was sold by the Alfred E. Burke estate to Frank P. Gravatt & Assoc., operating as the Atlantic City Realty Company, for $2 million. Louis Burke had reached a verbal agreement with Gravatt a month earlier and he kept it, despite receiving more attractive offers for the Pier. After a down payment of $50,000 of his own money, Gravatts' partners in the proposed acquisition backed out,

Frank Gravatt , former paper boy and grocery clerk, was a self-made man.

leaving Graval responsible for the remaining $450,000 that was due at settlement. In a bind, Gravatt sold off his entire real estate portfolio to get the needed funds.

The sale included the properties of the Steel Pier block from Virginia Avenue to Presbyterian Avenue, each store with a boardwalk frontage of 150 feet. On August 5, 1925, a new incorporation of the

Harry C. Volk was the marketing genius who managed to put promotional signs everywhere and anywhere, including New York's Times Square

Atlantic City Steel Pier Company and Trust — now called the Steel Pier Company — was formed with principals Frank P. Gravatt, Alvah J. Hall and John H. Krimm.

Gravatt had taken over a mortibund open-air facility known for its concert bands and its rocking chairs. He knew nothing about show business, so he immediately went out and bought *Variety* and *Billboard* trade magazines to locate the country's biggest attractions in enter-tainment. He had one goal in mind: to have visitors enjoy themselves and feel good about Atlantic City.

There's a strong possibility that if Gravatt hadn't bought Steel Pier, the rival Million Dollar Pier would have been Atlantic City's hub for entertainment. Million Dollar Pier was booking name vaudeville acts, and it also held the Miss America Pageant in its ballroom in 1925.

Gravatt was a genius at marketing and promotion, so when Steel

Pier opened for the first time under his ownership, on June 18, 1926, more than 11,000 people were on hand for the spectacular event. The Lounge Room, flanking the Main Entrance, was massed with flowers. Large pipe organs were installed in the lobby and all the theaters. There were card rooms, sun decks with steamer chairs and blankets, a library and one of the first indoor miniature golf courses in the country.

Gravatt received congratulatory telegrams from around the country. After speeches by officials, Steel Pier Secretary Raymond P. Read moved everyone into the Casino to introduce Frank Elliot and his Minstrels. Moving again to the Arcade, Bandleader Guiseppe Creatore was introduced, as was soprano soloist Pauline Talma and the Royal Mountain Ash Male Chorus of Wales. The audience joined Creatore in a song titled "The New Steel Pier," which Creatore dedicated to Gravatt.

In the Ballroom, the Morris Guards, who had marched in formation from the Armory on South New York Avenue, staged a drill. The Ted Weems Orchestra played for dancing, and 800 newsboys and boy scouts were guests of the management.

Secretary Read also presided over the opening of the new Marine Studio of radio station WPG, making it the only ocean pier broadcast studio in the country. Station Director Edwin Spence and announcer Norman Brokenshire joined the festivities. WPG was a city-owned station that originally went on the air in January 1925. Its call letters were chosen to promote Atlantic City as the "World's Play Ground." But it was never a real moneymaker, finally calling it quits in 1939. The next year, Gravatt founded WFPG, "World's Famous Play Ground" (or, coincidentally, "W. Frank P. Gravatt"), utilizing the Pier as home base.

Only those men wearing jackets and ties were allowed on Steel Pier, as it was considered the most conservative of all the Piers. Evelyn Off, Gravatt's daughter, recalled in the *Press of Atlantic City* in 1988: "I remember taking all my friends there for free. We wore dresses and short white gloves. That was the sign of a lady. We didn't wear jeans — there was no such thing."

And no shows were presented on Sundays, either — only concerts. There was no questioning, however, after that grand re-opening day, where the best quality entertainment was presented in Atlantic City.

Gravatt's first coup was signing famous march composer John Phillip Sousa to a "lifetime contract" in 1926. Unfortunately, it rained eleven of thirteen weekends that first summer, and Sousa's band played to only half-filled auditoriums.

Also beginning in 1926 were performances by the Steel Pier Grand Opera Company, comprised of nationwide talent. The operas

Novel roadside advertisements, built in the 1930s, reminded motorists to visit Steel Pier.

were directed by Jules Falk, violinist and musical director. But what was absolutely unheard of at the time was that all the operas were translated and sung in English — even "Pagliacci" in 1928! The nation-wide publicity for this sort of novelty was enormous. Operas in English lasted on the Pier until the end of the 1930s.

☾ ☾ ☾ ☾

It took Gravatt about two years to come up with the marketing formula for the Pier's success. The mantra became "Low Admission, Lots of Attractions," offering something for every taste. He bought huge billboards along the highway and railroad lines leading into Atlantic City, advertising Steel Pier with one, catchy sentence: "A five dollar show for fifty cents." Almost two million people spent that fifty cents each year.

Harry C. Volk had run the advertising and publicity department on the Pier since 1926. Originally from Philadelphia, Volk had worked on various Philadelphia newspapers and later spent stints as advertising manager of the *Camden Courier* and *New York Post*. His job was to get Steel Pier's name out: on billboards, buildings, roadside stands and Atlantic City jitneys. Large billboards in Philadelphia at 16th and Market streets and at 18th & Chestnut streets carried the name. Steel Pier used more billboards in Philadelphia than all of the theaters of the city put together. Gravatt also paid for thirty full-page ads in the Philadelphia newspapers that said simply, "Visit Steel Pier."

Two contracts were signed with the R.C. Maxwell Company, totaling $100,000, to display Steel Pier and Atlantic City signs in every train station from Boston to Pittsburgh, and also maintain a sign on Broadway in Times Square. In 1929, a large, animated letter sign on the corner of 42nd Street and Broadway announced the virtues of the Pier.

Perhaps topping all that were the nationwide radio broadcasts of dance bands that played nightly in the Ballroom. Steel Pier was every-where.

Businessmen were dubious and some didn't think Gravatt could make it work. But he proved himself to be a master showman, and he demanded nothing but the best. On August 2, 1926, famous movie star Rudolph Valentino appeared and gave his last public interview in the WPG Marine Studio before his untimely death on August 23.

In September 1926 the song "On the Pier" by bandleader Edwin

Goldman was described as "a characteristic novelty description of a summer evening on the great Steel Pier at Atlantic City." It was dedicated in a public ceremony to Gravatt and Raymond P. Read of the Steel Pier Company.

Gravatt went to his friends at General Motors and offered a display area for GM products. The auto company had used the Pier before, but this time GM agreed if only Gravatt would build an exhibition hall for them. A half-million dollars later, GM had its year-round space at the front of the Pier facing the Boardwalk and paid Gravatt $156,000 a year for the lease.

Gravatt hired Richard Endicott as general manager in 1927 to con-trol, coordinate and organize the operation. Endicott's career had been in real estate, and he had been an official of Gravatt's Atlantic City Realty Company. Gravatt invited him to manage the Casino theater for the summer and Endicott agreed to help his friend. After that, he decided to get back into real estate. Jacob Bothwell, who had been the original manager, returned from convalescing in Florida and took over his previous position. But Endicott was to return.

The dance hall was enlarged and renamed the Marine Ballroom in 1929. Gravatt contacted Texaco that same year and offered to build a sign atop the Ballroom a half-mile out to sea that would be seen by Boardwalk strollers and on ships. Texaco rented the space for $80,000 a year, and the oil company's sponsorship of the Pier lasted until 1935. In 1930, Gravatt hired a young man named George Hamid, who had a reputation as one of the country's top bookers of exotic circus acts. If he was good enough to book acts for the Ringling Brothers Circus, he was good enough for Gravatt.

A large outdoor circus area was built at the back end of the Pier, along with a stadium that could hold thousands of people. Hamid developed the circus with novel acts that included high divers, aerial-ists, acrobats, trained elephants and bears, and a soon-to-be-famous diving horse.

In 1932, Gravatt purchased a one-time yacht of Florida developer Henry M. Flagler called the Miami and converted it into an upscale passenger steamer for promotional sightseeing. The used million-dollar ship had been transporting cargo and passengers between Key West and Havana and cost Gravatt only $100,000 from the Peninsular and Occidental Steamship Company. Rechristened the *S.S. Steel Pier,*

Even a blimp advertised the Pier in a 1933 promotion.

In 1932, Gravatt purchased a yacht from Florida developer Henry Flagler, renamed it the S. S. Steel Pier, and turned it into an excursion ship for Pier patrons.

municipality six miles south of Atlantic City, and weekly trips to New York Harbor. In September 1932, the yacht headed to New York with 200 passengers. A storm arose and when the vessel tried to return to Atlantic City, the ocean became so rough and a wind storm raged so fiercely that it was impossible to dock the boat at the Pier. The ship had to steam around the entire state to dock in Philadelphia. A train then returned the passengers to Atlantic City.

Perhaps that misadventure was the primary reason the *S.S. Steel Pier* was soon considered expendable. In 1934 it was sold at auction in Florida to a New England steamship company that put it to use in the Cape Cod area.

❧ ❧ ❧ ❧

"Frank Gravatt, President of Steel Pier Amusement Co., does not believe in the Depression when it comes to offer attractions to the amusement-loving public," observed the September 9, 1932 *Atlantic City Press.* "And he believes in giving the public the best in every field of entertainment, thrilling or otherwise. This week the guiding hand of the gigantic amusement center is piling attraction upon attraction on the program in order to fittingly celebrate its thirty-fifth anniversary. Featured will be bandleader Ben Bernie and singer Kate Smith."

Gravatt remade the Pier as a place where there were attractions for everyone. There were name dance bands, vaudeville with top stars, three movies, exhibits, opera, shows for children, a huge water circus, minstrels, stunts and much more, all for just one price. More than 20,000 could be entertained at the same time without crowding, and more than 12,000 could be accommodated in its four theaters, ballroom, outdoor stadium and lobbies.

And yet Frank Gravatt himself would climb up on a ladder and replace burned out light bulbs, or go beneath the planking to check on the underbelly. He was a very meticulous and neat man and wanted a pristine Pier that reflected on him and his tastes. From 1927 through 1937, Gravatt spent more than $3 million for improvements. He was constantly looking for ways to upgrade the Pier.

He was proud that no objectionable feature was ever on Steel Pier, and that it had hosted fifty million people from 1898 to 1938. In 1936, he hired two unknowns named Bud Abbott and Lou Costello, who later

Movie idol Rudolph Valentino appeared on the Pier in 1926, just weeks before his untimely death.

the 240-foot, 1,741-ton yacht was lavishly remodeled for dining and dancing and held up to 1,148 people. Huge steel reinforced pilings were installed onto the Pier alongside the Ballroom to prevent damage to the Pier when the yacht was moored. Because of a sandbar at the Pier's end, the ship couldn't dock except during high tide.

The *S.S. Steel Pier* made daily excursions to Longport, a beachfront became the number one box office attraction in Hollywood. Bud and Lou were always grateful for the break in show biz given to them by Frank Gravatt and returned to perform on a regular basis.

❦ ❦ ❦ ❦

Gravatt's relationship with George Hamid deteriorated in the late 1930s. Radio broadcaster Ed Davis told *Atlantic City* magazine in 1981 that he thought the antipathy grew out of their different business styles. "Gravatt was more of an entrepreneur," Davis said, "and Hamid was a real showman". When the opportunity arose to lease the rival Million Dollar Pier in 1938, Hamid jumped at the chance. But Gravatt congratulated his one-time employee just the same, with an ad in the *Press* announcing, "Welcome! George Hamid and Sam W. Gumpertz — May you have oceans of success in your new undertaking."

Collier's magazine sent writer Kyle Crichton to cover Memorial Day 1938 in Atlantic City. His description of Gravatt's Steel Pier is fascinating:

The facts about Herman Eichelman of Frankford, Pa. are very simple. He bought a ticket for Steel Pier at nine o'clock on a bright Sunday morning, and at 1:48 the next morning, approximately 17 hours later, while trudging doggedly through something known as the Haunted Castle, he suddenly gave forth a noise … and collapsed. The guards dragged him forth in a state of prostration.

The nurse on the Pier took one look at Herman and made a slight movement of the hand which meant that it would be well to notify Herman's folks. She had him rushed off to Atlantic City Hospital.

Herman had left home with just enough money for his train fare from Philadelphia and for admission to Steel Pier. He had eaten no lunch nor dinner; no hotdog or frozen custard. In that seventeen-hour period, he had seen two motion pictures, a minstrel show, a performance of opera in English, a complete vaudeville show (headliners Willie and Eugene Howard and Helen Morgan), had danced in the Ballroom, afternoon and night, to the music of Benny Goodman's orchestra, and sat through a complete show of circus acts, including diving Hawaiians and diving horses, had listened to two Hawaiian and Filipino orchestras, had marveled at the Fish Bowl illusion and had finally been wandering his way desperately through Laughland and the Haunted Castle when

unconsciousness crept up on him.

The fault lay, as Herman might have discovered, with one Frank P. Gravatt, owner and manager of Steel Pier, the world's largest amusement attraction. Mr. Gravatt is the ex-motorcycle salesman, ex-automobile dealer and still real estate promoter who maneuvered himself into a spot about thirteen years ago, when he found that he had signed a paper that obliged him to pay 2 million dollars for the privilege of owning an amusement pier. The nine other gentlemen who had originally been on the deal with Mr. Gravatt had gracefully withdrawn, knowing a white elephant when they saw one, even if it happened to be sticking out into the Atlantic Ocean.

Gravatt found that he had a pier that was 2,298 feet in length and affording a nice place where the old folks could sleep while listening to a band concert. Vessella's band had been playing on the Pier for twenty-six consecutive seasons and this made an impression on Gravatt. He felt that nothing was needed but a better-known band and engaged John Philip Sousa's. Sousa arrived during 1926 and played there every summer till he died in 1932.

With that accomplished, Gravatt proceeded to spend approximately $550,000 in altering the premises to make room for the General Motors exhibit and since has spent $1.75 million for extensions, new theaters and new attractions.

But by the end of two years, the Pier was making money on the Gravatt theory that if a Woolworth store can pack them in by keeping prices low and offering something for every taste, an amusement pier can do the same. He bought every act that was foolish enough to venture into South Jersey. He had men being fired out of cannons, gentlemen jumping from autogiros.

Amos 'n' Andy played fourteen performances the day the Pier did its biggest business in history — 84,000 paid admissions in one day at seventy-five cents, making it the biggest single amusement attraction in the world. In its best year, 1930, it handled 1,800,312 people. Thousands of people sleep overnight in deck chairs and on benches on the Pier on important weekends when hotels and boardinghouses are jammed to capacity.

There are unusual statistics about Steel Pier: an estimated 2,250 pounds of gum a month or about 75 pounds a day is taken off the seats

Gravatt shrewdly struck promotional deals with big companies. Texaco is prominently advertised above the Marine Ballroom in this 1930s image.

and floors (this includes sticky substances such as salt water taffy), and about 50 pounds of waste paper is sold every day by the Pier during the season. The Pier hires an average of 350 people, including the acts, and there are 48 on the payroll year-round.

One favorite story is of the lady who bought a ticket and proceeded to lead her flock of nine children through the gate. When stopped, she pointed to the sign that said: "All for the price of one admission," and insisted on her rights. When informed of this, Mr. Gravatt laughed very

heartily and said let them in, the joke was on him. But it would be well to warn others to refrain from repeating the jest, lest his sense of humor become strained.

On an average day during the season, the Pier has around 12,000 customers, amounting from $6,000-$9,000 according to the price of admission on that particular day. It is estimated that 50 million customers have used the Pier since it was built in 1898.

Things will undoubtedly be stirred to a pitch this summer because, after some years of quiet existence, the Million Dollar Pier has now become Hamid's and the billboard battle will soon be superseded by the attraction battle, with both Piers conducting a rather similar policy and the customers being in a position to risk TWO admissions in one day. Gravatt is known as a sucker for any advertising scheme and Mr. Hamid gives indications of being one who will stop at nothing.

Because of a city ordinance, nothing can be sold on the ocean side of the Boardwalk. Hence there are no eating booths, restaurants or the like on the Piers, although Mammy's opened in April on Steeplechase. Both Steel Pier and Million Dollar people go to strange lengths to get around this. There are soft-drink booths, but you don't buy the beverage; you simply rent the container for a small sum. Most people bring brown bags of lunches that they check in or leave on picnic benches to be eaten later for lunch or dinner.

But say what you want, the Gravatt gentleman has been a success. All his life he has been a trader, buying an apartment house and swapping it for a hotel, swapping the hotel for a vacant lot on the Boardwalk, swapping the lot for a golf course. With Steel Pier, he got himself into it in a burst of enthusiasm and couldn't trade his way out. Consequently, he has made a fortune out of it on the theory that if you give the customer more than he expects, you can't keep him away. If you think it's all mercenary business, you overlook the case of Amos and Andy, who had an iron-clad contract saying they would not work more than four shows a day and eventually did fourteen without extra pay because they "got into Steel Pier spirit of things."

Mr. Gravatt appreciates this spirit and hopes it will be a lesson to others.

☾ ☾ ☾ ☾

In June 1939, the Pier underwent a financial reorganization and escaped being sold at public auction. Several years before, mortgage holders had started foreclosure proceedings, but mortgage of $975,000 was issued and the old mortgage of $1,446,000 was cancelled.

A profile in the June 7, 1941 *Press* said:

Frank Gravatt is known as the "Salt Water Barnum." He transformed Steel Pier from an open-air pavilion filled with rocking chair

ladies to a seagoing World's Fair providing 18-hours of top-flight entertainment. Gravatt attached himself to Steel Pier when it was a place where old people assembled to gossip and rock in time to the "oompa oompa" music of brass bands. That was in 1925, when a syndicate of ten Atlantic City businessmen walked out on Gravatt in his attempts to negotiate a deal. He refused to back down and carried the deal through alone.

He put his signature on the dotted line, taking unto himself the jumbled mass of Pier buildings a half-mile out into the ocean and obligations amounting to some $2 million — possibly more.

From the beginnings of Gravatt's "New Deal in Entertainment," the Pier began to have its face lifted. His first official act was to institute "name attractions" — the first show under the Gravatt banner being headed by John Philip Sousa, at that time the idol of America's music loving public.

☾ ☾ ☾ ☾

Atlantic City became a training ground for the war effort in spring 1942 and was turned into "Camp Boardwalk" as the military turned many Boardwalk hotels into hospitals. Bandleader Glenn Miller was even stationed at the resort before starting up his Air Force Band. It was tough for Steel Pier to book name acts and bands during this time as many of the entertainers were drafted or used for the war effort in Hollywood. Difficulties also arose for construction and expansion due to fewer supplies. Military men stayed in Atlantic City until 1946, just after the war ended, enjoying special prices for Steel Pier and Atlantic City movie theaters.

Steel Pier had always been open throughout the year since its inception, if only for movies or dances in the Marine Ballroom. After 1939, however, it opened in spring and closed in the fall. Gravatt announced plans in July 1942 to once again keep the Pier open year-round, and he provided special recreation rooms for soldiers. The Pier was open every weekend until October 1943.

John Berglund was only fifteen when he supervised a Boardwalk cleanup crew in front of the Pier in the early 1940s. In the Rutgers University Oral History Archives of the war years, he remembered: "The owner of the Pier was a man named Gravatt, and he'd look out

Twin-Screw Ocean Liner "STEEL PIER" leaves on frequent trips daily throughout the summer season from end of Pier.

THE STEEL PIER

extending seaward one-half mile from the famous Boardwalk is one of the outstanding features of Atlantic City. Its leadership rests in the remarkable extent of its varied entertainment throughout the year— for the enjoyment of all ages and for less money than may be had anywhere—and in an appeal different from anything else on the American continent.

★ First showings of feature Motion Pictures in its three large theatres; Dancing to nationally known orchestras in the glorious Marine Ballroom; the Stadium Carnival of Water Sports and thrilling acts at the ocean end of the Pier; headline Vaudeville in the Music Hall; good old-fashioned Minstrel Shows in the Casino Theatre; performances of Grand Opera in English and superb Operatic Concerts; interesting and educational Exhibits brought from many lands; Singers and Players from the Mid-Pacific; Tinytown Village; the Wild Animal Nursery and many other attractions hold constant interest.

★ An imaginative Voyage at Sea—Steamer Chairs on the Ship-Deck Promenades, in the Solariums and under the Vita-Ray Glass invite rest and relaxation.

★ ADMISSION—a single reasonable charge at the Steel Pier entrance admits to all attractions on the Pier.

STEEL PIER   ATLANTIC CITY

Under Frank Gravatt's ownership, one could attend the Grand Opera, visit the little people of Tinytown Village, take a trip on a former yacht, or gawk at wild animals — all in the same day.

of his office over Fralinger's. He'd see a cigarette butt, and he'd call Dick Endicott, who managed the Pier. Endicott would call the front manager, Jim Rock, and then I had six or seven guys that I could tell to go get that cigarette."

By 1945, the last year of the war, the pressures of running the Pier began to get to the fifty-five-year-old Gravatt. Because of the war, profits were not as plentiful as the years before. But Gravatt didn't want to sell to George Hamid, his rival with whom he had been in a running promotional battle for seven years.

In April 1945, Gravatt sold the twelve-story, 420-room Chelsea Hotel for $1 million. Then on May 8, as newspaper headlines across the nation bannered the news of V-E Day, the unconditional surrender of the Nazi Third Reich in Europe, the *Press* also had a significant local story:

Steel Pier has been sold to a syndicate of prominent Boston and New York theatrical men, it was announced by Frank Gravatt. The purchasing group is headed by Abe Ellis, owner of the Essex House in Newark and the Manhattan Center, the largest auditorium in NYC.

The Pier changes hands by virtue of the group's agreement to buy all the capital stock of the Atlantic City Steel Pier Company, which owns the Pier property. Settlement will take place later this month.

The new owners will operate the Pier this summer, Gravatt said. He added the buyers were all experienced showmen and the public could be assured of continued high-class entertainment features in the future. Negotiations have been underway since February.

❦ ❦ ❦ ❦

The *New York Times* reported that Gravatt signed an agreement for the sale of all the capital stock for $1 million, which is exactly what

---

GOOD FOR AN ADMISSION TO
Atlantic City STEEL PIER

Admit Mr. J. C. Cumming, A.G.F.
Union Pacific System,
921 Southwest Washington
1936 Portland, Oregon.

Subject to U. S. Gov't Amusement Tax

FRANK P. GRAVATT,
President

---

happened. It was $1 million less than what he had paid for it years earlier. On May 17, 1945, Gravatt's sale of Steel Pier for one million dollars went to the Abel Holding Company.

But what Gravatt didn't know was that the Abel Holding Company and Abe Ellis were fronts for the real buyer: George Hamid!

Hamid had tricked Gravatt and had bought the Pier right under his nose.

Obviously, Gravatt was initially incensed, but what could he do? Hamid wanted it and Hamid got it, creatively. Finally, Gravatt smiled, shrugged his shoulders and congratulated Hamid. "Well, George, you put one over on me," he said, according to George Hamid Jr. And the Gravatt years were over.

On February 15, 1946, Gravatt bought the Traymore Hotel for $3.5 million. As a co-owner of the Shelburne Hotel, he built a new Boardwalk Lounge in August 1946. Only five years later, the tremendous fourteen-story, 638-room Traymore was sold to Gravatt in June 1951 for about $5 million. It was like the pre-Steel Pier days for Gravatt, only with more millions.

He sold the Golden Gate Motel on Absecon Boulevard in 1960, only to buy it back again five years later. In December 1961, Gravatt bought the nine-story, 227-room Lafayette Hotel and spent $2 million to build a motel addition and to modernize the older building. In November 1963, he built an eighty-foot-tall replica of the Eiffel Tower, made of gold aluminum, placed on top of the building.

"Since the Lafayette is named after the French hero of our Revolution and our motif is generally French," he was quoted in the *Atlantic*

City Press, "I don't know of anything more French than the Eiffel Tower. Margate has its elephant as a landmark and now Atlantic City will have an Eiffel Tower as a landmark."

The now demolished Lafayette has gone down in history as the hotel where the Beatles held a press conference and stayed during their appearance at Convention Hall in September 1964. Gravatt sold the Lafayette for $3.5 million in April 1965.

With all of his wheeling and dealing, Frank Gravatt was long respected as a courageous developer with a great commitment to Atlantic City. "If I had my life to live over again, I would want to live it in Atlantic City," he stated in 1970.

He was not happy about the demise of Steel Pier, but social changes in Atlantic City and competition from other vacation spots were almost impossible to stop at that time.

Frank P. Gravatt died at his home on Fredricksburg Avenue in Ventnor, just down the beach from Atlantic City, on January 28, 1979 at the age of eighty-nine. Surviving him were his wife, Flora, and his daughter, Evelyn.

The accolades were many, as the *Atlantic City Press* reported from his memorial service: "He was the model gentleman — never pretentious," said the Rev. Karl Kraft. "He seemed most comfortable being in the background."

Dr. Andrew Braun, a longtime friend of Gravatt's, remembered, "He always talked of the sea. He was very fond of the grains of sand. He said they were like acres of diamonds to him."

"Everything that he advertised, he delivered," said Ed Davis, former newsman at the Pier's WFPG radio station. "He was an honest and fantastic man."

Historian Adrian Phillips later summed up the man in *Atlantic City Magazine*: "He was a great believer in innovation. If word leaked back to him about a very novel act or some new method of lighting, he'd go wherever necessary to become informed about it and secure it if he could. He had the ability to gather a staff of people of extraordinary talent."

Gravatt built the first escalator in town, placing it in Gray's restaurant, across from Steel Pier. He had the first air-conditioned hotel — the Lafayette. He revived the Miss America Pageant. And with all his holdings, he had more than 2,000 people on his payroll.

Besides owning the Pier and numerous hotels and property, this astute investor owned real estate companies and the Chelsea National Bank. Gravatt was a founder of radio station WFPG and the Atlantic County Improvement Authority.

In the 1970s, Gravatt still could size up the business world. "I see where the food stores and appliances stores are going 'discount' today and think it's something new," he once told the *Press*. "I went discount on the Pier nearly fifty years ago."

"Believe in work, " he said, and that was the secret of his success.

Remnants of early Steel Pier marketing might still be found occasionally on the streets of Atlantic City.

Chapter Six

George A. Hamid, Top Showman

They couldn't have been more different. One was an entrepreneur, born not far from Atlantic City, working his way up the financial ladder through his real estate investments. The other was born in the Middle East and came to America as a young boy who couldn't speak English, but worked hard to become one of the greatest circus and entertainment promoters of the twentieth century. These were the two men who shaped the legacy of Steel Pier.

If there was anyone who deserved to win the Horatio Alger Award (and he did), it was George A. Hamid. His was a classic story, of a poor immigrant with the odds stacked against him.

In his neatly pressed, white flannel suits, the five-foot, four-inch Hamid was hard to miss on the Pier. The close-cropped mustache, the twinkle in his eyes, the ever-present smile and perfect, near-white hair made him a familiar face in the crowd. An outgoing, warm and energetic man, he had an uncanny ability to never forget a face.

Atlantic City was his life, but it began as far away from New Jersey as can be imagined.

Puabla Hamid was born in Broumana, Lebanon, with an unrecorded birth date but a christening date of February 4, 1896. He was the third of five boys who lived in a stone hut within a diverse neighborhood evenly shared by Muslim, Jewish and Christian residents. When Puabla was three and a half, his mother died giving birth to her fifth son.

In 1906, after only four years of formal education, he joined his Uncle Ameen Ben Hamid, head of the "Abou Ben Hamid Tumbling Arabs" act, touring then with Buffalo Bill Cody. Young Hamid was earning forty cents a week from his uncle and performing with his cousin Shaheen and friend George Simon. The three boys appeared in Europe with Uncle Ameen, and they temporarily joined a show in Marseilles, France, where Puabla also had a job as water boy for the livestock. It was young Hamid's first experience with a traveling amusement show.

From his autobiography *The Acrobat,* Hamid remembers: "Uncle Ameen was a slave-driver whose brutality was open and undisguised. When I pleased him, he rewarded me a little, if at all. When I crossed him, or he thought I did, punishment was swift, sure and strong. Yet, in his own bitter, twisted fashion, Ameen respected me, maybe loved me."

Hamid took over Million Dollar Pier in 1938 and quickly turned it into a viable entertainment center, rivaling Gravatt's Steel Pier. Huge advertising signs covered most of the original 1906 buildings.

The troupe traveled to the United States in 1907. From Ellis Island, the boys took a train to a fairground in New Jersey where they would await orders from Uncle Ameen. Their first night in America was spent in a horse barn on the fairgrounds, trying to get comfortable in the piles of straw.

Puabla (now known as George) became top mounter in acrobatic formations known as *tukul.* Uncle Ameen would hold eight acrobats and young George, being the smallest, had top position. He improved his tumbling and added the European (forward) and Irish (back) flips.

George, his cousin Shaheen and George Simon wound up in Atlantic City in 1908 as beach tumblers. They were so poor they hardly ate and spent their first night in Atlantic City sleeping under the Boardwalk. It was George Hamid's first taste of the Jersey Shore.

In 1909, at the age of thirteen, Hamid competed against the best tumblers of the Barnum and Bailey Circus, Ringling Brothers' Circus, and Buffalo Bill's troupe at Madison Square Garden in New York City — and won. Now that he was considered the top tumbler in the world, his salary doubled from $5 a month to $10. In Buffalo Bill's "Congress of Rough Riders of the World," Hamid rode as one of the fierce Bedou in the "Marauders in White Hood and Cloak" act, and appeared in chaps for the famous burning-of-the-stagecoach scene.

Hamid, then a mere 130 pounds, was also the perfect sparring partner in the offseason for Stanley Ketchel, the 1910 middleweight boxing champion. Buffalo Bill Cody always shut down his show for a few months before the next tour, freeing up some down time for his performers.

But Cody's once-popular show was failing by 1913, and financial problems forced him to close the show for good after a final run in Denver, leaving Hamid, his cousin and his friend broke and stranded. They decided to seek work in Chicago, walking halfway across the continent and performing for food and money along the thirty-four-day trek.

Within a week in Chicago, they were booked to tour with vaudeville star Eva Tanguay's burlesque show. After five weeks touring the midwest, the company traveled east. That summer, they played the Globe Theater in Atlantic City. But the boys' troubles soon returned. One night, Tanguay fought with her manager and packed her bags, leaving the act high and dry. Once again the boys had to sleep under the Boardwalk, a memory Hamid never forgot.

As they tumbled and performed on the beach for food money, they were noticed by John Murphy of the Steel Pier minstrel troupe. Murphy offered them a job to play on the Pier for a week. Ironically, the future owner of that very pier once performed there in a tumbling act, as a poor Lebanese teenager.

With his back against the wall, Hamid became the booking agent for his own tumbling troupe. Meanwhile, he managed nine other acts with other indigent performers, mostly immigrants hoping, as he was, for a lucky break. In 1915, Hamid, now nineteen, was learning the business aspects of a traveling circus, where he also worked as the equestrian director and supervisor of all the acts in the ring.

While he was on tour in the east, Hamid met Elizabeth Raab of Jersey City, and soon fell in love. Though they would later be married, he had to first prove himself worthy to Elizabeth's parents.

They had nothing to worry about. With his increasing list of contacts, he was beginning to advance in the business world. Booking vaudeville headliner Eva Tanguay — whom he first met in Chicago — and magician Howard Thurston were milestone achievements. Next came bookings with producer Alex Pantages, who was later to develop "Hamid's Oriental Circus, Wild West and Far East Shows, Combined."

The road wasn't all paved with gold. A decision to invest $19,000 with a Texas company drilling for oil came up dry.

There was cause for celebration, however, when son George, Jr. was born in 1918. Three years later, things finally began to pay off. Hamid opened the Wirth & Hamid Fair Booking Company with two vaudeville agents, Frank Wirth and Herman Blumenfeld, concentrating on furnishing acts to county fairs. At age 25, Hamid began traveling to every state capital in the east to convince those interested to book his acts.

His first business venture in Atlantic City took place around this same time. He leased Rendezvous Park, an amusement area that stood where the present Convention Hall sits. Hamid presented his side-shows and unusual acts until the park burned to the ground in 1925.

The following year, John and Charles Ringling brought Hamid to Sarasota, Florida, and offered him an exclusive booking job for their circus. Hamid sought out the major circus acts around the world and brought them to the top circus in the United States. As official booking agent for Ringling Bros. Circus, Hamid could also buy many of the top European acts.

ℂ ℂ ℂ ℂ

In 1927, Frank Gravatt, who was methodically reinventing Steel Pier as a vast entertainment center, decided that Hamid was the man he needed.

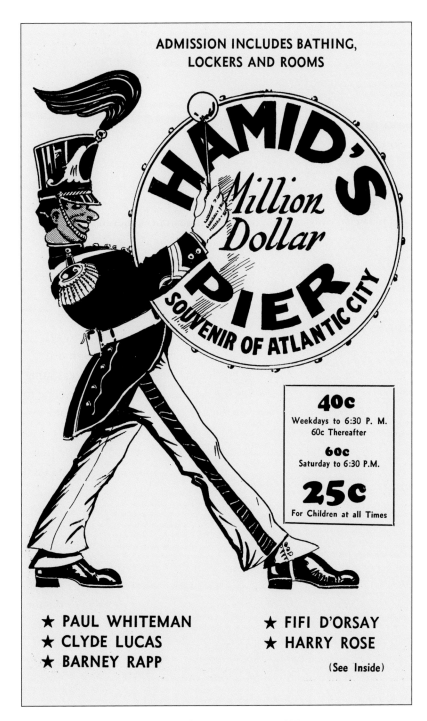

Million Dollar Pier program, 1938

"Gravatt chose me to create an over-the-ocean stadium circus," Hamid recalled. "Our bookings mounted — hundreds of fairs, dozens of amusement parks, plus four or five circuses. We branched to London, Paris and Berlin to scout European acts. We imported more than the remaining American offices combined.

"Our name became synonymous with circus and thrill acts as we discovered the Zacchini family of human cannonballs, the Wallenda high-wire walkers and hundreds of others. For Steel Pier, we perfected Carver's high-diving horse and a dozen more circus features."

By 1928, Wirth & Hamid had agents in every world capitol, scouting the far corners for acts. Hamid then bought out Wirth and other partners in 1931 and became sole owner of the agency, bringing many spectacular and thrilling acts to Steel Pier and developing the outdoor circus.

Hamid signed on to run the North Carolina State Fair in 1933 and clean it up from gypsies and scam artists who were giving the fair a bad reputation. Hamid's no-nonsense approach finally drove the riff-raff away and made the fair a presentable outing for the whole family. Also in that same year, most of Chicago's "Century of Progress" stunts were his acts, furthering his reputation as a leading booking agent.

In 1936, he was asked to take over the faltering Trenton State Fair in New Jersey. Hamid bought the fair grounds, almost 100 acres, including the grandstand, barns and exhibition buildings. In a surprising twist of fate, he discovered that the horse barn on the fair grounds was the very place he had slept on his first night in America, almost thirty years before.

"In Buffalo, I decided to bid on a major indoor circus. My only real competition came from Bob Morton, who had an outdoor circus in Texas," he recalled. "We got together and conceived of a year-round tour for a circus-indoors. I was to organize and put on the shows and Bob would tour them." Known as the Hamid-Morton Circus, it was one of the first circuses to specialize in producing shows for the Shriners throughout the United States. When Bob Morton passed away in 1957, ownership of the circus passed into the hands of the Hamid family.

Meanwhile, in Atlantic City, Gravatt was interested in leasing Million Dollar Pier — ostensibly to minimize its competition with his own Steel Pier — and in 1938, he decided to go forward on that venture with Hamid as a partner. Hamid went to Gravatt's office on Steel Pier to sign the papers and it was then, Hamid recalled later, that he secretly wished he were dealing for Steel Pier, rather than for the far less showy Million Dollar Pier. Before the meeting ended, however, Gravatt had a change of heart and opted out of the partnership, saying he already had his hands full with one pier.

Hamid was undeterred. He later met with the Million Dollar Pier owners and took out a ten-year lease, with a purchase option, on his own, immediately raising a challenge to Gravatt's enterprise.

"I'll run it the way he runs Steel Pier," Hamid said to newly-hired Million Dollar Pier manager Sam Gumpertz. "Bands, vaudeville, pictures. He's proved the formula." Gumpertz, an old friend of Hamid's, was a circus legend, having been the general manager of Dreamland Park in Coney Island from 1909 to 1911, and also in charge of the Ringling Brothers Circus from 1932 to 1937 in Sarasota, Florida..

It was head-to-head competition: Hamid versus Gravatt, with two piers that suddenly began to offer the public almost the same exact type of attractions.

The Hamid family moved into #1 Atlantic Ocean, the late John Young's famous mansion

Left to right: (unknown) George Hamid, Jr., George Hamid, Steel Pier General Manager Richard Endicott, a holdover from the Gravatt years.

on Million Dollar Pier. "They forgot to put in a subfloor and the floor was right on the Pier structure, and under that there was dampness and you could hear the waves all the time. If there was a crack, you could see the ocean. I called it our citadel of darkness and ocean chattering. He thought it was a great house," Hamid's son recalled years later for a *Philadelphia Inquirer* interview. "And despite the fact that Young spent a fortune on the most beautiful woodwork and stuff that he got from Italy, he couldn't fight the dampness on it out there,

and of course, we were never on there in the winter. We stayed there mostly July and August and lived there until 1948. We were running both piers then."

The *Atlantic City Press* reported the following on April 8, 1938: "Ever since it was announced that George A. Hamid, the amusement king, had taken over the Million Dollar Pier, the pier has been besieged by inquiries concerning the now world famous net hauls originated by the late Captain John L. Young. Hamid announced they will still be carried on at noon and four, just as always."

As the summer season began in full swing, *The Press* commented on Hamid's Million Dollar debut:

There will be a special invitation preview for invited guests only; ceremonies will go out over the two major networks and more than a dozen announcers will be kept busy from numerous parts of the Pier introducing honored guests. The Million Dollar Pier has been streamlined at more than $250,000 with new theatres, arenas and attractions added.

At the "Mightiest Amusement Armada," everything is new except the roof, pilings and famous sea net hauls. Hamid achieved the impossible from May till now. There's a modern marquee and lobby — a grand lounge inside the lobby — facing the grand lounge is a new concert stage; next is the Ballroom of States, called because of the seals and flags of each state hung around the front of the balcony.

The Ballroom is totally refurbished and consists of two bandstands. A ceiling of more than 25,000 lights change color with the tempo of the music being played and three huge revolving globes on the ceiling will throw out a spectrum of colors.

The Fun Foundry offers reminders of old Steeplechase — ten acres of the Pier are devoted to amusements such as the Human Roulette Wheel and Crazy Houses.

Atlantic City's first newsreel theatre is on the Pier, as well as a kiddies theatre and an old-time movies theatre. Aquariums are at the ocean end of the Ballroom and a diving buffalo and diving elk will perform towards the ocean end. A huge amphitheater seating several thousands is constructed on the extreme end where there is the water carnival and aerialists. Also featured is an Eskimo Village along with huskies and sleds. Captain Young's house is now a museum featuring his and Hamid's curios from around the globe.

☾ ☾ ☾ ☾

The curious act of the diving buffalo and elk was a direct attempt to replicate the diving horse act on Steel Pier. The animals were trained in Montana but unlike the horse, they did not have riders. Their tank was about two-thirds of the way out on Million Dollar Pier, compared to the ocean-end location of the diving horse tank at Steel Pier.

Along with the popular net hauls at the pier's end, where live sea creatures where brought on shore to show the crowds what lived below, the Million Dollar also presented a motorcyclist who dove into the ocean from a sixty-foot tower, male and female champion log rollers competing in the ocean, and an orchestra of Cuban girls playing rhumbas in the lobby.

On Easter day, 1939, Hamid promoted a Monster Egg Hunt that started at 9 A.M. and offered $100 in prizes. The Isham Jones and Paul Whiteman orchestras played, and crowds were thrilled by animal tamer Clyde Beatty and his circus, which stayed for the entire season.

Starting in July 1940, per Hamid's orders, "God Bless America" was played each morning and the Eddy Morgan Band played the "Star-Spangled Banner" at closing. Hamid felt that with the war looming, Americans should be encouraged to be patriotic, a marketing move that also secured his own position as a staunch American citizen.

Hamid's other ventures were not forgotten. The Hamid-Morton Circus performed at the 1940 New York World's Fair and continued to travel throughout the country. The Million Dollar Pier booked and presented many newcomers to the national entertainment scene — the Andrews Sisters and the bands of Woody Herman, Artie Shaw, Glenn Miller and Vaughn Monroe. In fact, Miller's orchestra broke the all-time attendance record at Million Dollar Pier.

But in 1945, the option to buy Steel Pier once again presented itself. Gravatt wanted to buy two hotels and to do so, he had to put Steel Pier up for sale. Gravatt would never have sold it to Hamid, though, because he thought Hamid was a low-class carnival man. In his book, Hamid later recalled how he got what he wanted:

Frank would never sell to his opposition, me. So my attorney worked on the deal, totally avoiding mentioning my name. For two months, he maneuvered the terms with no success. I had someone buy the Pier as my stooge, and then it was mine.

On a May afternoon, 1945, my lawyer called me. "Come to Steel Pier right away, George." The Million Dollar Pier was a mile up the Boardwalk, so I decided to walk. I looked at the sand under the Boardwalk, where Shaheen, George Simon and I slept (years ago).

I looked ahead at the gigantic structure of Steel Pier, with its four theatres, mammoth ballroom and its circus stadium half a mile over the ocean. I climbed the ramp, nodded to the gate man and entered the office.

I bid my attorney hello, sitting across the desk from him. To my surprise, we were alone. "Over 30 years ago," I told him, "I sat in this very office, in a bathing suit, dead broke." I looked around the room. "Where are the others?" I asked.

"They've gone. They left these papers for you."

"What are they?"

"They're exactly what you wanted. Sign them. It's yours now."

❧ ❧ ❧ ❧

George Hamid, at fifty, was flying high. He was still living in the twenty-room mansion at #1 Atlantic Ocean, and had an office near Radio City Music Hall in New York. He was head of the world's largest outdoor and high thrill act agency, booking upward of 250 features for circuses, fairs and movies. He owned the Hamid-Morton Circus as well as White City, an amusement park in Worcester, Massachusetts. Since 1936, he was also president of the New Jersey State Fair Association in Trenton. And now he had Steel Pier for $2 million.

On June 23, 1945, the *Atlantic City Press* reported: "When, after many 'near-ems,' Steel Pier was finally sold. The co-buyer with Abe Ellis, New York businessman, was revealed as none other than that outdoor amusement mogul in acrobat's tights, George A. Hamid."

Surprisingly, Gravatt didn't fume for long. When he found out that Hamid was the principal, he was incensed but then merely laughed. They had been friends for years until they became competitors. "Well, George, you fooled me on that one," he was quoted in the *Press*. "Take good care of my Pier."

Hamid's son recalled the monumental event:

We didn't change anything when we had the Pier. You see, the 1944 Hurricane took away the end part of the Pier. Gravatt had had two horrible years and lost a lot of money in '43 and '44 and he wasn't sure if Steel Pier would ever come back again. I remember in 1940-1941 we would look from Million Dollar Pier to Steel Pier and see tens of thousands of people crammed into the place and we would have maybe three or four thousand people. And we wanted Steel Pier very badly.

But I was in the war, and when I came back in '45, my father was secretly negotiating — without Gravatt knowing about it — to buy the Pier. Because Gravatt had not rebuilt the end of the Pier, he didn't know

what to do. So my father, through a very fine attorney in New York, arranged to buy it, but the guy who was backing him pulled out. He asked me, "You think we should do this? I can get the money from the bank; we won't have a sound partner. It's going to be a much tougher deal, and if Steel Pier doesn't come back, we have problems. We're going to lose it."

I said, "Dad, we wanted it all these years. Now we have a chance to get it. I'll be out of the Navy soon and I'll be there with you. Steel Pier is what we want."

One person had to own both piers because we were killing each other with prices for bands and movies.

When we took over in '45, we opened the Pier on Easter Sunday, we played weekends until Memorial Day and then we played through most of September. In the '50s, we did Easter Sunday and then we closed until Memorial Day. We opened then until June and in the '60s, we only operated weekends in June and opened a week before July 4th and ran through Miss America Pageant Week, which was Labor Day Tuesday. The Pageant was on Saturday and the winner always played Steel Pier on that Sunday. And it was always a big day for us.

❧ ❧ ❧ ❧

While continuing to operate his own Hamid's Million Dollar Pier, Hamid also acted as managing director of Steel Pier, which made him the amusement czar of Atlantic City, at least on the ocean side of the Boardwalk. It was also additional responsibility for George Hamid, Jr., as he became more involved with the day-to-day operations of Steel Pier as vice-president and assistant general manager. George Hamid, Jr. had become quite a scholar, something his father never had the chance to experience. Enrolling in private school in 1932, Hamid, Jr. was admitted to Princeton University in 1936. After playing with the Princeton football team and graduating with honors in 1940, he ran the Arizona Cliff Dwellers-Hopi Indians Exhibit at the New York World's Fair. He then served five years in the Navy during World War II, took part in the battle at Guadalcanal and came out of the service as a full lieutenant.

Both Hamids shared an office. From January through June, George Sr. traveled with the circus, while George Jr. contacted the agents for the next season's name attractions, looking for acts that might be hot out of his pajamas for days.

In order to relax, he was known to execute a few tricks with the acrobats he booked at the piers, a talent he never seemed to lose.

❦ ❦ ❦

Because of the city's long-standing ban on food sales on the east side of the Boardwalk, none of the piers could sell refreshments. The trick to bypassing this law was to take advantage of a loophole that allowed patrons to pay a fee to "rent" cups and plates. Patrons often brought their lunches in brown bags and ate them at picnic tables on Steel Pier.

In 1945, however, Hamid's piers were selling snacks and drinks. The master businessman negotiator had reached an agreement with the city's restaurant association to serve only fast food items on his Steel Pier, an agreement that also extended

Hamid introduces children to entertainer Victor Borge at the Hamid-owned Warner Boardwalk theater, 1955.

in July — at February prices. The summer policy required a dozen weekly features, plus shorter presentations on the two holiday weekends — a total of fourteen headliners.

A tireless worker and man of action, George Sr. installed a corps of secretaries and typists at each of his piers, with the inevitable extra telephones for his own personal use. He often carried on conversations or negotiated deals on three or four phones while simultaneously tossing off dictation, memos and suggestions. He went to bed late and awoke early. Legend has it that during some of the rush months of summer, he was so busy on the telephone that he was unable to get

opportunity for the Boardwalk's other piers. It opened the door for popular concessions like hot dogs, soda, birch beer and ice cream. The public was happy to have this privilege and cooperated by keeping the Pier litter-free.

"People respected the Pier. They would throw their soda cups away. You wouldn't look down and find junk on the floor or thrown onto the beach. We were happy to let people bring their lunch. We knew we could always sell them the sodas they'd drink with it," George Hamid, Jr. told the the *Press* in 1998.

Steel Pier's publicity department, which had been run by Harry C.

Jane Russell plants a kiss on Hamid while promoting her controversial motion picture "The Outlaw" in August 1946.

Volk since 1926 under Frank Gravatt, was expanded. Hired by Hamid were Mark and Maud Wilson as directors of Philadelphia and Pennsylvania publicity, and Bert Nevins of New York City to run the national promotions.

Aggressive advertising included billboards everywhere, including Times Square in New York. There was even a sign in Long Beach, California that said, "Go East, Young Man. Visit Steel Pier, Atlantic City."

Running two piers, Hamid initially competed with himself, although the bigger names were reserved for Steel Pier. Sometimes the piers shared the talent back-to-back. For example, Gene Krupa and his band played Steel Pier at the end of June 1945, then went right over to Million Dollar Pier for the July 4 holiday.

The year 1947 brought Steel Pier's fiftieth anniversary, and it was celebrated in grand fashion. On June 18, the exact day of the Pier's opening in 1898, a parade on the Boardwalk began at 3:30 P.M. at Convention Hall and proceeded north to Garden Pier. Large crowds enjoyed bands, floats, three dozen gigantic inflated comic balloons — some more than fifty feet in height — and the famous Mummers string bands from Philadelphia.

Hamid as grand marshal led the festivities, which included stage and screen stars Roy Rogers and Trigger, Ed Sullivan, Mitzi Green, June Havoc, and Ginny Simms.

Steel Pier's front facade was painted in gold. Free passes for the Pier were attached to 100 balloons that were released as the parade passed by. The parade lasted more than three hours and cost more than $75,000 to produce.

The celebration concluded with a banquet in the "Victory Home" near the end of the Pier, where dignitaries and celebrities enjoyed a large birthday cake.

The next year brought a prestigious honor for Hamid, when the American Schools and Colleges Association invited him to New York City in May to receive the Horatio Alger Award, honoring his rise from poor immigrant to successful circus promoter. Hamid proudly displayed it in the Steel Pier lobby, along with many other awards.

On November 11, 1948, Hamid's Million Dollar Pier lease concluded its ten-year run. He and his staff could now devote their full attention to the operation of Steel Pier.

"It was very tough because we decided that we would no longer use Million Dollar Pier as a competition to Steel Pier. We put exhibits on it, but it finally became a ride Pier," George Hamid, Jr. explained.

In 1950, Hamid expanded his entertainment empire. He purchased six Atlantic City movie theaters, plus leases of properties of the Stanley-Warner Company. A year later, he wrote his autobiography, *Circus* (later revised with his son and published as *The Acrobat*), primarily covering his life prior to his purchase of Steel Pier.

Just as Frank Gravatt had done, Hamid steadily improved upon the Pier's infrastructure without disrupting its smooth operation. A staff of 200 highly trained guards and ushers kept pedestrian traffic flowing smoothly, with safety always a primary concern in all areas. There were several first aid rooms with nurses and attendants. For fire protection, a new interior sprinkler system was installed.

In 1957, the Hamids opened a tropical entertainment attraction called "Aquafair" on Biscayne Boulevard in North Miami, Florida. It presented porpoises, monkeys, birds, and alligator wrestling. It was also an off-season venue for the Steel Pier high diving horses. More endeavors followed, such as a water spectacular in 1959 at Flushing Meadows, New York, titled "Hellzasplashin'," starring comics Olsen and Johnson.

Richard Endicott, Steel Pier's general manager since 1927, retired in 1958. William Morgan, district manager of Hamid Theaters, became the new general manager at the Pier, staying until 1975.

Steel Pier's top executives during this period were: George Hamid, Jr., secretary and treasurer (1960-64), vice-president and secretary (1965-71) and president (1972-75.); Richard Endicott, general manager (1949-57); William Morgan, general manager (1958-71) and treasurer (1972-75); Joseph Corrado, assistant manager (1960-61); William Duffy, assistant manager (1962); Joseph Laltrello, Jr., general manager (1972-75); and James M. Hamid (George Hamid, Jr.'s son), director of advertising and publicity (1972-75).

George Hamid, Jr. also became executive vice-president of "Freedomland" in 1961, a newly built amusement park in the Bronx. In July 1961, *Time* magazine profiled the Hamids and Steel Pier, noting that the Pier's typical customers were "high blue-collar types. To keep them coming, Hamid gives them much more than corny carny fare. He pays top fees for entertainment headliners."

☾ ☾ ☾ ☾

The decade of the 1960s became a major challenge for the Hamids, the Pier and Atlantic City itself. It became a struggle for city officials to keep the image of Atlantic City intact as a tourist destination. The city thought it had landed a major plum as host of the 1964 Democratic Convention, where Lyndon B. Johnson was nominated for president. But national media coverage turned out to be a disaster, showing the country the deterioration of the resort.

George Sr. was trying to bring tourists back to a city that had deteriorated and grown poorer throughout the 1960s. Racial strife was now a daily event, and crime was prevalent along the Boardwalk. Hamid described the Boardwalk to the *Philadelphia Inquirer* in 1968 as a place with "scantily clad strollers, people walking barefoot, men without shirts."

The *Press* of May 16, 1968, stated that Hamid "wanted to add a big zoological garden with seventy-five animals, which would combine entertainment and education at the back of the Pier. He also planned to build a full-sized ice-skating rink and wanted middle-class values to return. What Hamid couldn't do was build a theme park like Disney or Sea World in San Diego."

By no means did Atlantic City have the Hamids' full attention. In 1965, they opened an attraction called "Aquarama" at 3300 South Broad Street in Philadelphia, where today's stadium complex exists. It was an enclosed structure operated by George Hamid, Jr. and featured aquatic shows with porpoises, seals and other sea animals.

In November 1968, Hamid announced that he was relocating Aquarama from its quarters in Philadelphia to the space that had recently been vacated by the General Motors Exhibit. Aquarama closed in 1970, and the acts were moved to the front portion of Steel Pier. But he was still concerned about what he saw in Atlantic City.

Hamid was an outspoken citizen who fought for the city's betterment.

"The city should not be exposed to rowdyism whether it is done by long-haired hippies or Negro gangs or Mexicans, Asians, Indians, or whatever. If these groups reigned over the city, the beach, Boardwalk and streets would never be safe and decent and there will be no tomorrow," Hamid wrote in a June 5, 1969 letter to *The Press*.

According to Pauline Hill, head of the Atlantic City Housing Authority and Urban Redevelopment Agency, the Inlet area located near the pier represented one of the city's most valuable and least commercially developed sections. So during 1965 and 1966, properties were condemned and the city began tearing down the Inlet neighborhood, an area that for years was a vibrant mix of Jewish, Italian and Irish residents and consisted of houses, stores, delicatessens and rooming houses. Hill planned a new neighborhood that was to become a "suburb" for the middle-class. However, progress on the project was slow, and the Atlantic City renewal area didn't interest developers. An eighty-acre section of the Inlet became known as "Pauline's Prairie" because of the endless vacant lots that now stood barren after buildings had been razed.

Steel Pier, unfortunately, sat at the edge of this no-man's land. Most of the old boarding houses on Virginia Avenue, down the street from the Pier, were torn down. Ten full city blocks lay empty, a "vast wasteland" that Hamid blamed for a twenty percent loss in the Pier's business. "Where is this going to end?" Hamid complained in his letter to the *Press.* "This is the third year that Atlantic City looks like Berlin after the destruction of World War II."

With increasing pressure due to her mishandling of the urban renewal project, Hill reluctantly announced her retirement as the housing authority's executive director in 1973. But the damage had been done.

Hamid promised only "family-type movies" in 1969 and "no seedy rock groups, no smut, no sexed-up gimmick to draw crowds" — only clean and wholesome entertainment. He promised the *Press* on October 9, 1969 that "if Steel Pier received the support of the merchants and hotel/motel people, we will add attractions like Disney does."

Even though the Hamids were Republican, there was no politicking on Steel Pier. Comedian Pat Paulsen was booked in 1969 after running for president on the liberal CBS television "Smothers Brothers Show." Rock bands played regularly, but couldn't cross the line of bad taste.

Hamid was clearly opposed to what he called "long-haired hippies" and the drug culture. He saw them as only another deterrent to bringing back families. He also wasn't too enthusiastic about the music that appealed to young audiences during those years.

In the *Philadelphia Inquirer* of June 3, 1970, he was quoted: "The Canadians saved us from complete disaster last summer. They still come with their families and stay for a week or two and spend money all over town." He then opened an office in Montreal.

🍂 🍂 🍂 🍂

Diagnosed with cancer, Hamid underwent surgery on his lower intestine on January 19, 1970. On May 28, 1971, he re-entered Atlantic City Hospital. Less than three weeks later, on June 13, the former czar of Atlantic City seaside entertainment was dead of cancer at the age of seventy-five. Within a week, at age seventy-four, his wife, Elizabeth, also died.

In his last years, George Sr. had lived with Elizabeth in the Vassar Square Apartments in Ventnor, just down the Boardwalk from Atlantic City, and in Fort Lauderdale, Florida, during the winter. They were survived by George Hamid, Jr. and their daughter, Zyne, who also lived in Fort Lauderdale.

The *Atlantic City Press* stated:

Until his death, he worked too swiftly for his secretaries as he stood with the telephone clenched in his strong hands, arranging aerial acts, animal thrillers and beautiful extravaganzas for circuses, fairs, shopping center openings and charitable events.

In his steel-trap mind were catalogued the addresses and telephone numbers of his far-flung contacts. He spoke to proud and daring performers with a respect that was part of his inbred love for the world of vaudeville.

Writers searched for new superlatives to describe Hamid in features across the nation. His many experiences and achievements, however, dwarfed all attempts to fictionalize his legend.

"He possessed a personal drive, a verve for life, and the ability to retain a small boy's enthusiasm for show business," added an editorial from the *Press.* "He was a forceful and volatile man, whose presence was quickly evident in any group. He knew what he wanted and he did not hesitate to say he wanted it now. Yet, through it all, he was a warm human being who took pride in his family and was deeply disturbed about the deterioration of family life in America."

Within forty-eight hours after his death, George A. Hamid was inducted into the Circus Hall of Fame as a performer, producer and owner.

Pinky Kravitz, a local radio host who worked on the Pier in his youth, told Camden's *Courier-Post* in May 2004, "He was a tough boss, exacting and business-like. But at the same time, he would always greet the employees and ask questions about patrons' concerns and complaints."

"My father had twenty-five of the most exciting years any human being ever had in show business," George Hamid, Jr. remarked in a 1978 interview with the *Press*. "I think he gave the city the same thing. From the day he took over, there was always excitement at the Pier. It was the place every act wanted to play, and, because of that, it was the place everyone wanted to go. People never wanted to leave the Pier. In 1954, we had a fire in the front that damaged the casino theater and the marquee. As the people were evacuated, they were putting up a fight. They all wanted pass-out checks so they could get back in that night."

"Hamid was the greatest showman in the world," added Tony Grant, who for years ran the "Stars of Tomorrow" shows of young performers. "He was much more than a businessman. The man was real. The Pier was his love. You could have given him ten million (dollars) and he wouldn't have sold. He really cared, and I think the Pier was great because of it."

With his sons and grandchildren, George Hamid, Jr. concentrated on the Hamid-Morton Circus, playing state fairs and Shriners' conventions across the country. Having no fixed acts, Hamid put together a completely new circus every year. He also headed the Circus Producers Association, an organization dedicated to preserving the American circus as a vital part of the nation's heritage.

In 1995, the New Jersey State Fair, which had been owned by the Hamid family since 1936, was sold. Two years later, control of the circus (now named Hamid Circus, Inc.) went to James M. Hamid, George Hamid, Jr.'s son.

"My father started out as a tumbler in Europe and worked his way up to the point that he booked the Ringling Brothers circus," George Hamid, Jr. told the *Princeton News* in 1997. "Through him, I got to know every cat act in the country. I know every high-wire act, every acrobatic team. I know anybody that has an elephant.

"I'm still involved, but I'm more of a theatrical guy. My kids look at the ticket prices and grosses. I think about the people in the audience."

When *Billboard* magazine celebrated its 100th anniversary in 1994, it selected ten American "Showmen of the Century," honoring the live entertainment industry. Included on that list were Hamid's old boss, Buffalo Bill Cody; the Ringling Brothers; Walt Disney; and George A. Hamid, who was now as American as apple pie.

Chapter Seven

Entertainers Hit the Stage

Every year, from Memorial Day until Labor Day, a scant twelve weeks, Steel Pier's schedule was packed full with entertainment. For comedians, singers and specialty acts, playing Steel Pier was like playing the top clubs in the country, such as New York's Copacabana or Chicago's Chez Paree. It was almost as important as being seen on "The Ed Sullivan Show," then the top variety show on television.

If you were headlining Steel Pier, you had made it. Some acts were well known, while others were a hot item of a particular summer, only to fade away after their fifteen minutes of fame. To "play the Pier" was a goal of all the great entertainers. And the reason for the Pier's prominence and cachet was owner Frank Gravatt, "The Salt Water Barnum."

Before Gravatt, there were no big-name stars on Steel Pier. It was Gravatt who transformed the Pier into the famous entertainment mecca it became.

The entertainers, however, didn't have the luxury of the huge concert halls of later years. They performed in the Pier's Music Hall, small by some standards because it held only 2,250 people. Movie theaters in larger cities, such as New York's Roxy or San Francisco's Fox, could hold 3,000 or more. With a vaudeville format, it was also expected that these stars would perform a grueling four shows a day, five on weekends — no exceptions.

Famous Jewish cantor Josef Rosenblatt performed at the Pier in concert on June 11, 1922 at a benefit for the Hebrew National Orphan Home of New York. Rosenblatt was so well known that he appeared regularly in vaudeville as a headliner.

After Gravatt bought Steel Pier in 1925, the transformation from the cultured Victorian years to the vaudeville-circus years began. Ironically, it was a swimmer named Gertrude Ederle who was the first "hot" personality to appear, breaking all attendance records on September 12, 1926. Ederle was in vogue at the time because she had just swum across the English Channel and had been featured prominently in the news.

Major stars first came to the Pier in 1930 as vaudeville headliners, including stage and screen star Belle Baker, comedian George Jessel, and entertainer Eddie Cantor. During that period the stars were booked for single nights; in later years they would usually play a full week.

A rare site: a sparsely populated beach on Labor Day weekend, 1933.

In 1930, the Pier began the policy of presenting big-name stars along with vaudeville. Entertainer Eddie Cantor performed Labor Day of that year.

In 1931, the Pier presented Baby Rose Marie, who later starred in TV's "The Dick Van Dyke Show"; entertainer Gus Van; Borrah Minevitch and his Harmonica Rascals; Helen Kane, the original "*Boop-Boop-a-Doop*" girl; and George Jessel again.

Gravatt also brought in stars from other musical venues. Irish tenor John McCormack was paid $7,500 for a fifty-minute concert, and Metropolitan Opera star Marion Talley received $5,000 for her appearance.

The first act to really cause commotion was that of Rudy Vallee and his Connecticut Yankees in August 1932. Vallee was, along with Bing Crosby, one of the nation's favorite crooners, and for him to appear on the Pier was considered a great coup that helped elevate the status of the Pier. He and his band appeared on the stage of the Music Hall at 2:40, 4:50, 8:10 and 9:40 P.M., and then traveled to the Marine Ballroom at the end of the Pier for dancing. Vallee always drew large crowds on Steel Pier, and he appeared fifteen times during the 1930s — more than any other performer.

❧ ❧ ❧ ❧

Easter weekend was one of the biggest weekends in Atlantic City. The town was usually packed with tourists. Steel Pier would open that Saturday and Sunday with special entertainment.

Easter, 1933, the Pier presented radio stars Amos 'n' Andy, radio stars whose program was one of the top-rated in the country. It was a daily fifteen-minute serial focusing on the lives of two African-American men and the people surrounding them. The program was not to be missed, and even President Franklin Roosevelt was a fan. In fact, during the summer of 1930, a series of outdoor loudspeakers was installed along the Pier for the specific purpose of making Amos 'n' Andy available to early-evening patrons.

Amos 'n' Andy were Freeman Gosden and Charles Correll, two white men who later faced controversy over their portrayal of blacks in their comedy routine. Their 1933 contract on the Pier called for five shows a day, but they drew such tremendous crowds that they gave fourteen performances in one day. Russell LeVan, who worked on the Pier for Frank Gravatt, remembers it a little differently. "They did twenty-six fifteen-minute appearances," he said, "mostly at the Casino, then Music Hall, then Ballroom."

Their Steel Pier engagement broke attendance records and it proved that radio stars could become as big a draw as stage singers and comedians. People had not seen radio performers in person, so it was somewhat of a curiosity. Gosden and Correll appeared in blackface during their appearance, leading many whites to believe that they were African-American. On Labor Day 1933, Amos 'n' Andy returned, setting a one-day Steel Pier record of 39,000 customers.

Others who appeared in 1933 were George Burns and Gracie Allen; Hardeen, a magician and brother of Houdini; Milton Berle; movie star Edmund Lowe; tenor Morton Downey; and, once again, Rudy Vallee. But the schedules were grueling, even to those performers who were used to the hardships of vaudeville. Milton Berle remembered, "Mama was with me all the time. She traveled everywhere with me, made me do my homework on the road, and sat in the audience for every show. Two a day, four a day — even when I did ten shows a day at Steel Pier in Atlantic City."

The 1930s were the heyday of Steel Pier, with top names now booked on a regular basis throughout the summer. Just some of the entertainers who appeared were fan dancer Sally Rand, directly from the Chicago Exposition; movie cowboy Ken Maynard; the entire cast of radio's "The Goldbergs," starring Gertrude Berg; comedians Joe Penner and Bob Hope; kid star Jackie Coogan, who was later Uncle Fester of TV's "The Addams Family"; and Betty Grable.

"The Goldbergs" appearance in August 1934 consisted of the radio cast recreating a play just as they would before the microphone in a New York studio, but with an audience for the first time watching the players in action. Overflow audiences demanded encores and attended all of the many performances throughout the day and evening.

Largely forgotten today, Joe Penner was a big star on radio with his nonsensical question skit "Wanna Buy a Duck?" He appeared on the Pier on May 4, 1935, and tried to accommodate all who came for this one-day appearance. He had children as his special guests during his matinee performance, when he would award a live duck and other prizes to the winners of a coloring contest that had been held that week.

Steel Pier became nationally known through radio programs that broadcast from the facilities, such as the "Major Edward Bowes'

Amateur Hour," which broadcast live from the Casino lobby 8 to 9 P.M. on December 23, 1935.

In July 1936, Moe, Larry and Curley — "The Three Stooges" — made the first of many appearances on the Pier. One show also headlined Ed Sullivan, then a well-known Broadway columnist, along with the zany Ritz Brothers and harmonica whiz Larry Adler.

"When we were starring at Steel Pier in Atlantic City, Abbott and Costello were appearing there in a minstrel show, and at every opportunity, they would come backstage and watch us perform from the wings," recalled Moe in his autobiography, *Moe Howard and the 3 Stooges.* "I always felt there was much of Curley — his mannerisms and high-pitched voice — in Costello's act in feature films."

Comedians Joe E. Lewis, Red Skelton and Henny Youngman; comediennes Judy Canova and Molly Picon; banjo virtuoso Eddie Peabody; actors John Boles and Bruce Cabot; movie comedy stars Ben Blue and Hugh Herbert; British actor Arthur Treacher; the Andrews Sisters; "Wizard of Oz" tin man Jack Haley; and singer Tony Martin rounded out the late 1930s on the Pier. Maxene Andrews remembered one hectic Labor Day when the Andrews Sisters did eleven shows, each twenty-five minutes long with only a fifteen-minute break between shows.

Henny Youngman, who was booked ten times between 1937 and 1958, was considered a regular on the Pier. "I booked him so many times I could do his act," George Hamid, Jr. once said.

Many unheralded workers behind the scenes helped the name acts run smoothly. In his history of the resort, author Russell LeVan remembered one in particular. "James P. Kenney worked on the Pier for fourteen years. To Jim, working on the Pier was like living in a circus family. Working his way up the ladder from turnstile boy, he became the soundman for the Music Hall. His job was to make the stars sound as beautiful as they looked."

By the late 1930s, Edward Sherman in New York became the exclusive booking agent for Steel Pier. Gag photos showcasing Steel Pier talent were the norm for publicity. In one photograph, Arthur Treacher, Hollywood's famous butler, serves a giant lobster, prepared by local chef Harry Hackney, to Steel Pier owner Frank Gravatt and Rudy Vallee on the ship deck at the luncheon given by Gravatt to mark the opening of the forty-second season in 1939.

☾ ☾ ☾ ☾

Step'in Fetchit, the African-American comedy star whose stereotyped lazy antics angered many blacks, broke racial barriers in July 1937 with top billing at the rival Million Dollar Pier. This was the first time an African-American entertainer had headlined on any Pier in Atlantic City. Steel Pier's first African-American headliner was the popular singing group The Ink Spots, debuting on July 16, 1939. The comedic Eddie "Rochester" Anderson from Jack Benny's radio program followed on August 11.

The Ink Spots became regulars at the Pier. The show business newspaper *Variety* observed of their act on June 27, 1942, "Held over for a day when crowds were so large, Steel Pier had to stop admitting patrons — added a midnight show — could not accommodate fans." The Ink Spots also were the first African-American group to play New York's Copacabana nightclub, in 1943, firmly establishing themselves as a crossover act for white audiences.

Howard Sprow, who handled dissatisfied customers on the Pier as an attendant at the information desk, remembers that the job was not always pleasant. Russell LeVan recorded his remarks for *Memories of Atlantic City, New Jersey — The Queen of Resorts*:

Sometimes the crowds became angry because a theater was sold out. At moments like those, the advice to smile was often effective for me. But as with any crowd, there were always people who would become increasingly boisterous and threatening. Although there were times when we could have called the police, we never had to do it.

The Pier was a small community that operated with great harmony. Despite differences in ages and backgrounds, employees were loyal to each other and to the Pier. The network of friendships was thick and seemed unique and lasting. My friendships with my former colleagues are still strong. And, of course, my closest friend of all, Mildred, became a cashier during my last summer there. We married in 1945, and are still together fifty-six years later.

The Pier as I knew it is no more. But the memories, ah … the memories will remain with me for the rest of my years. Memories of color and light and excitement. Memories of warm breezes and music and romance.

In June 1940, comedian Bob Hope brought his radio show featur-

80

Comedian Bob Hope is being told why he has to wear a top on the beach, 1940; while comedic actor Hugh Herbert (right) is sporting a suit on the beach, 1936.

A contest in July 1941 invited, "Boys, win a date with the Andrews Sisters — winners [will be] guests of the "Round the World' room [at the] President Hotel for a special dinner, on stage with the girls, then to a show at the Paradise Club." It's hard to imagine a promotion like this today with press agents, handlers and entourages encircling today's most popular acts.

Abbott and Costello appeared in August 1941, coming back to the place where they had their first success in 1936 as members of the Pier's minstrel troupe, each then earning $75 a week. Now they commanded $7,500 for an eight-day stay. In conjunction with the opening of their movie

ing Jerry Colonna and Brenda and Cobina to the Pier. His favorite spot between shows was at the extreme end, looking back at the famous Atlantic City skyline. Following Hope were singer Dennis Day of "The Jack Benny Show," dancers Vilma and Buddy Ebsen (later of "Beverly Hillbillies" fame), Eddie Cantor with his radio show cast, singer Dinah Shore, burlesque queen Gypsy Rose Lee, screen comic Billy Gilbert, and comedienne Martha Raye.

The magic of the Pier sometimes led to unexpected surprises. For instance, Dinah Shore saw the George Montgomery movie "The Cowboy and the Blonde" while performing at the Pier in July 1941 and fell in love with the handsome actor's screen image. She pursued a chance to later meet Montgomery, and then married him in 1943.

"Hold That Ghost," the team appeared first at a "Midnite Jamboree and Ghosts Ball" in the Marine Ballroom, where patrons dressed as ghosts had a chance for $250 in prizes.

Bud and Lou were America's top movie comedy team, but they never forgot that it was Steel Pier and Frank Gravatt that gave them their first big break. And their fans certainly didn't forget them.

"It was in the '30s, and we went to a restaurant nearby. They were as funny as they were in public. They were very delightful people, and they took the time to talk to a little girl," Evelyn Off, Gravatt's daughter, recalled some fifty years later for the *Press of Atlantic City*.

Larry Braverman and John McCullough are among many who posted their memories on *I Love AC.com*:

The lights are bright in 1941 with the latest Abbott & Costello movie and Jack Benny's comic valet Rochester, who was the Pier's first solo African-American headliner.

I used to pray for rain, because my grandmother with whom I stayed with would only let me go to Steel Pier when it rained, recalled Braverman. *I even received a phone call from Bud Abbott and Lou Costello on my seventh birthday because the General Manager of the Pier was the landlady's son.*

My father's uncle by marriage, Harry Volk Sr., was advertising manager of the Pier in the '30s and into the early '40s, wrote McCullough. *I was ten in 1935 and was allowed to spend the day on the Pier with older cousins for free. We were allowed to visit the deck where the current entertainers would rest between sets. I remember Lou Costello inviting me to sit on his lap, chatting with Al Jolson, the Nicholas Brothers and many others.*

As a very young child, I remember Abbott and Costello weren't speaking, they didn't like each other, related Jeannemarie (Volk) McGowan, whose grandfather, Harry Volk, was the Steel Pier publicity director in the 1930s. *Lou Costello had grown up with my uncle in New Jersey and would come for dinner when he appeared at the Pier. And I remember very clearly he taught me how to make knots in people's shoelaces under the dinner table, so when they tried to get up they would fall down. And my grandfather would get so upset with him. He*

said, 'You're never coming back here again!' And of course he always came back. It was a party all the time! And Bud Abbott would be there the next night! They never came at the same time.

((((

Jeannemarie's grandfather was her unique, insider link to many celebrities of that era. In 2004, memories of those experiences, and her grandfather, were like yesterday:

He came in contact with everyone who played there. His favorite person was Perry Como. He said he was the greatest gentleman he ever met and treated everyone like a prince. He never asked for anything.

He said the biggest pain was Frank Sinatra when he was with Tommy Dorsey. He was demanding, full of himself, and a complete pain-in-the-ass who never treated anyone well.

Harry Volk was responsible for all of the billboards you saw everywhere. His wife had a rooming house in Atlantic City, and he would bring home all the vaudevillians, magicians and crazy people who were on the road all the time. A lot of these people were down-to-earth nice people, but once in awhile you'd find someone who was full of themselves, usually a young male crooner.

The rooming houses would have these big, long tables where everyone could have dinner along with a room. That was a part of the deal. These were just very lonely people who were on the road all the time, only ate in restaurants and would never get a home-cooked meal. My grandmother was this Irish woman that would cook from morning until night.

They didn't care if they were stars. They just wanted to sit back and tell funny stories. Harry knew that these people needed tender loving care and that they were special. I can't remember that table having less than eight bowls of vegetables. It was like Horn & Hardart's. We had everything from soup to nuts.

There was an act called Willie, West, & McGinty. They were carpenters, and they would whack each other with the ladders — it was total slapstick. And to a child, this was so funny. They would be at the table and knocking things down, doing tricks.

My grandfather brought in the newsreels press when the Diving Horses first started. But when you (later) saw the film that showed the end of the Pier, the words STEEL PIER were nowhere to be seen! And they realized what an absolute disaster that was, and my grandfather said, "That's my fault. I didn't see that coming." After that, you could not go to the end of the Pier without seeing Steel Pier signs everywhere.

When I was in high school, my brother and I were involved in singing lessons. Something came up that one of Frankie Laine's back-up singers got sick and they needed someone to go in and help out. So I was hired, but it was a grueling schedule, with five or six shows a day. I was sixteen years old, but they were desperate and needed someone to go in there. And if I were to tell my mother that I was doing this, she would have killed me. So I told her that I was staying with a girlfriend, helping her while her mother was away and not to worry. So I went in and auditioned. And Frankie Laine said, "You're great! After this we go to Connecticut. We're on the road." And I said, "Really?!"

So I came home to my mother and I said, "I've got to tell you the truth. *I've been singing with Frankie Laine the last couple of days and it looks like I'm on the road with him. I'm leaving." And she said, "Over my dead body!"*

That was the end of my career! But it was a great experience and a lot of fun.

❝ ❝ ❝ ❝

Singer Lynn Roberts was a child singer who appeared in vaudeville acts. "I remember Steel Pier very well. I was eight years old and the memory is very vivid. I played with Abbott and Costello. They were feuding, but they were really, really big. There were some newsreels, a couple of cartoons, some shorts and then the show. They did a little shtick with me. I had the Shirley Temple curls and that was quite a highlight for me."

In LeVan's book *Memories of Atlantic City*, there were some notes Pier employee James P. Kenney recorded about the stars he saw:

Betty Grable — a very hard person to get along with — a little on the upside.

Milton Berle had his mother backstage coaching him at all times.

George Jessel liked to gamble at the 500 Club or a place across from the Ambassador Hotel.

Morton Downey, John Boles and Dennis Day were all gentlemen.

Ed Sullivan, then a sports writer for a New York paper, would talk baseball with Whitey LeVan, manager of the Music Hall.

Bob Hope accepted his pay, at his apartment in the Claridge Hotel, from Arthur Virtue, then a bookkeeper for Gravatt.

A customer standing by the stage called up to Rudy Vallee and called him a big sissy. Vallee then jumped off the stage and knocked the fellow down for the count.

❝ ❝ ❝ ❝

With World War II firmly on the minds of Americans in the early 1940s, entertainment was needed for the armed services and the USO, and to help the homefront morale. Top name stars had become scarce as many were drafted.

The Pier could not book many big names during this period, so instead, revues featuring an array of stars and show girls were brought into the Music Hall, such as Billy Rose's New Diamond Horseshoe

Abbott & Costello never forgot their days in the Steel Pier Minstrel show and returned regularly. Hanging out near the Water Circus, they are apparently discussing where they should change into their bathing gear and who should jump into the ocean first (Facing page).

Revue in July 1944. Another revue, titled "Tars and Spars," featured talent from the military and film star Victor Mature. There were three shows nightly.

Singer Perry Como, comic Jackie Gleason, singing group The Merry Macs, and comic Benny Rubin appeared as the war drew to an end. New acts began cropping up as Americans packed nightclubs and theaters, clamoring for entertainment that had been stifled during wartime.

On August 7, 1947, you could have a free, autographed, eight-by-ten-inch photograph of heartthrob Perry Como if you arrived on the Pier before noon.

"In 1947, Dick Haymes was the hottest single attraction in the country. And he played for us at the Pier and was hotter than Sinatra and Perry Como," George Hamid, Jr. told *Atlantic City* magazine in May 1991.

The lobby of the Pier was the scene of Eddie Newman's radio program, broadcast seven nights a week over station WFPG. From midnight to 1 A.M. during the late 1940s, Newman played host to many entertainers and bandleaders appearing on the Pier.

Entertainer Danny Kaye made an appearance over July 4, 1950, along with songstress Georgia Gibbs. By the early 1950s, pop singers were predominately featured, showcasing their top hits that were currently sweeping the country. Fran Warren, Eddie Fisher, Mindy Carson, Denise Darcel, Mel Torme, Frankie Laine, Guy Mitchell, Rosemary Clooney, Al Martino, Patti Page, Tony Bennett, Johnnie Ray, and Billy Eckstine all made at least one appearance. Eckstine's appearance on July 14, 1951, marked the first time a black solo singer headlined on the Pier. (In August 1956, singer Sarah Vaughan would be the first black female solo headliner.)

Frank Sinatra had been on the Pier as Harry James' and Tommy Dorsey's singer, and returned as a solo act in June 1949 and headlined Labor Day weekend, 1950. Although his career was going through a rough time, and he had become less popular than singers such as Laine and Eckstine, you wouldn't have known it from his appearance in Atlantic City. He set a new Steel Pier record of 41,000 people in one day, breaking the record Amos 'n' Andy held for seventeen years.

In Nancy Sinatra's 1995 book, *Frank Sinatra — An American Legend*, Frank Sinatra remembers trying to catch a quick bite between shows. He began eating a sandwich on stage as soon as the curtain came down, and suddenly it was time for his next show: "They were so fast that they brought in a whole new audience, seated them and everything. The band starts up and I'm standing there, expected to sing, with a sandwich in my mouth!"

Sinatra's tender side was recalled by Paul "Skinny" D'Amato in the 2004 book *The Sinatra Treasures*. D'Amato was owner of the resort's famous 500 Club. "There was a girl from around here (Atlantic City), she was paralyzed in a wheelchair, and she sent Frank a letter saying she was dying to see him. He was coming to Steel Pier, so he called

The post-war years also brought in singer Allan Jones, whose son Jack, also a singer, would appear some fifteen years later. It also brought in buxom actress Jane Russell, who stayed on the Pier for a record three weeks while promoting her risqué, Howard Hughes-produced western "The Outlaw," which was a huge smash and made her a star.

Other late-1940s appearances were made by child star Roddy McDowall and singers Bob Eberly, Connie Haines, the Mills Brothers, Kitty Kallen, Peggy Lee, and Dick Haymes, along with Atlantic City's own Helen Forrest. Comics included Olson and Johnson in a wacky revue, Henny Youngman, and Jerry Colonna.

me and asked if I knew who she was. I knew the family well, so I made arrangements for her to see him at Steel Pier. They brought the wheelchair right up on stage, in the wings, and nobody ever knew she was there. That's the kind of thing he did."

George Hamid, Jr. remembered the day he hired Sinatra to sing virtually all day long. "The Pier and I gave Frank Sinatra the most expensive sore throat in history. In September of 1950, Frank appeared in our Music Hall theater, which at that time held 2,000 people. The power of Sinatra was coupled with a cloudy day, which closed off the beaches. Forty-one thousand people crammed the Pier and Frank wound up doing eleven shows. Unfortunately for him, he awakened the next morning with no voice at all and a $30,000 engagement at the Michigan State Fair the next day. He had no choice but to cancel. At least it prompted us to rebuild the theater and double its capacity.

Ray Eberle

Morton Downey

Marion Hutton; Eddie Cantor

Eddie "Rochester" Anderson

Happy Felton

Ted Lewis

Perhaps more great stars of stage, screen and radio have dazzled audiences at the Steel Pier than at any other amusement center in the world. A list of their names would read like a roster of show business. To present them all photographically would require a book of hundreds of pages, and to describe their great talents and achievements would require several hundred more. The pictures presented here, however, will serve to establish the high calibre of entertainers and entertainment offered at the Steel Pier.

☆☆☆ **STARS** that have glittered at the great STEEL PIER

Abbott and Costello

Gypsy Rose Lee

Borrah Minnevitch and His Harmonica Rascals

Some of the entertainers that appeared at the Pier during the late '30s and early '40s.

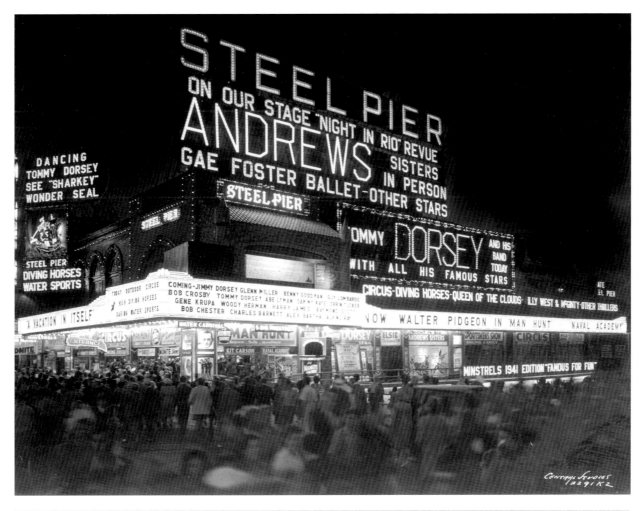

his audience. "The highlight in our lives was singing 'Goodnight Irene' with Frank at Steel Pier back in the '50s," a fan remembered years later.

"The acts didn't have much of an option," said George Hamid, Jr. "At that time, there weren't many places where they could go and get green money for working. After the war, Steel Pier and Las Vegas were the only places in America that had a big-name booking policy.

"During the Depression, the Pier was a light at the end of the tunnel for many desperately poor people. They could come, spend a day, and for fifty cents see the best entertainment in the world."

Comics such as Jack E. Leonard, Chico Marx of the Marx Brothers, and Robert Q. Lewis appeared, as did a young Alan King. King was a part of the bill with singer Billy Eckstine in July 1951, but he

A nighttime scene in summer 1941 that couldn't be equaled anywhere—a packed Boardwalk, the Andrews Sisters, and Tommy Dorsey with Frank Sinatra and Buddy Rich.

"We were still too close to the vaudeville era to think in terms of Sinatra as an individual playing in the Ballroom," he told the *Philadelphia Inquirer* in 2004. "By the time we got to the last show, I said, 'Frank, three songs. Just go out there and do three songs.' We almost put him out of business by ruining his voice."

"He swore he wouldn't come back again," remembered Paul Steinberg, who was a concessions operator that night in 1950. As rough as it was for Sinatra, however, it was an unforgettable night for

had worked at the Pier years before in a different capacity:

George Hamid gave me a job in front of the Pier on the Boardwalk. I was a barker for the people who were waiting on line to go in. Hamid was very good to me. I auditioned for him. I was working in Philadelphia with another guy in a very bad two-act, and we took the bus to Atlantic City. He met me and said I had a lot of guts. He gave me the job, and then two years later I was booked in. I used to play there quite frequently.

I opened for Sinatra on a Labor Day weekend during the early 1950s. It was the first time that I met Frank. I ran over a little bit, and he came to me and said, 'Next show, try ten, kid,' meaning minutes. On the last show of the engagement, there were so many people on the Boardwalk that Sinatra decided to go to the Ballroom in the back. We had been in the Music Hall. The Ballroom was packed with people standing up, and I got out there ... did a little bit of jokes and then I introduced him. It was incredible!

☾   ☾   ☾   ☾

In August 1962, while appearing on Broadway in "How to Succeed in Business Without Really Trying," Rudy Vallee took a week off and headed back to Steel Pier, his first appearance there in twenty-two years. "I was offered a lucrative figure for the week's engagement," he admitted to the *New York Times.* His act consisted of twenty-three minutes and followed a dance team, a comedian and a fire-eater. "This is child's play," he said. "I'd even do it for two weeks."

"I don't want to go back to that 1930 stuff," Vallee continued. "No megaphone. No raccoon coat." His 1962 act included political jokes, comic numbers and a medley of his song hits. Nearly all the seats were filled in the Music Hall for a 4 P.M. show. "To the younger generation, I'm the Pat Boone of the Stone Age," he said.

The Lafayette Hotel, where he was staying with his wife, proudly hung a blue banner across its entrance that read: "Welcome Rudy Vallee." The owner of the Lafayette in 1962 was Frank Gravatt, who originally brought Vallee to Atlantic City when Gravatt owned Steel Pier in the 1930s.

☾   ☾   ☾   ☾

There were also "hidden" perks that not every visitor knew about. Were the locals

Singers of the early 1950s appearing at the Pier.

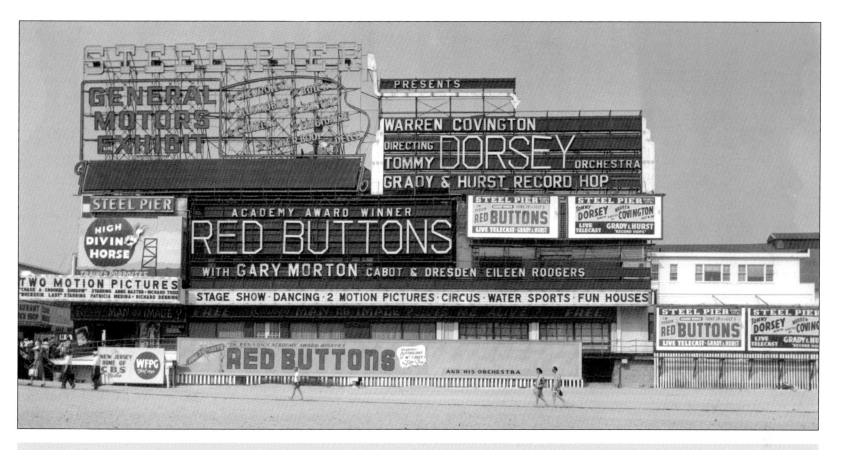

Comedian Red Buttons, hot from his Academy Award winning performance in "Sayonara", headlines in 1958.

the only ones who knew about the Music Hall's seating rules?

"If you wanted to sit in the reserved section of the Music Hall (near the stage), it cost twenty-five cents. But it was worth it if it was Abbott and Costello, Eddie Fisher, Johnny Ray or the Andrews Sisters," recalled one customer.

Movie stars Gloria De Haven and Frances Langford showed up, as did early TV sex symbol Dagmar. Musical acts included The Three Suns, Les Paul and Mary Ford, and the Four Aces. Singer Al Martino appeared twelve times from 1953 until 1976. And Louis Armstrong, the legendary "Ambassador of Jazz," first appeared in August 1953.

Joey Bishop was another young comic to make it to the top playing Steel Pier. A native of Philadelphia, he had visited Atlantic City often. When he returned in June 1953 on the bill with singer Fran Warren, he

knew he was on his way up. In August of that same year, he headlined, along with Vic Damone, at Atlantic City's 500 Club and met Frank Sinatra. He ultimately joined Sinatra's so-called Rat Pack, along with Dean Martin, Sammy Davis, Jr. and Peter Lawford.

"Did you know in 1936 at Steel Pier I won the 'Benny Goodman Jitterbug Contest'? We got free admission for a month," Bishop said in May 1998. "Later on, I worked there with Dagmar. I did very well and when I bowed off, I said, 'I'm sorry, folks. I can't do anymore. I'm also the diving horse.' It was like an honor to work there."

☾ ☾ ☾ ☾

In the early rock and roll years, singers and vocal groups were prominently featured. The Four Lads, the Crew Cuts, Eydie Gorme, the

The Music Hall was the scene of vaudeville and big-name stars throughout the Pier's history. Singer Julius LaRosa stands in the aisle of the Hall in the early 1960s, surrounded by an audience of thousands. Note the pit musicians down front.

Lennon Sisters, Steve Lawrence, Andy Williams and the McGuire Sisters were but a few.

"In June we played the names that hadn't really hit yet," explained George Hamid, Jr. "We played Totie Fields, Steve and Eydie, Andy Williams in June when they were just barely recognizable. We didn't take in enough money in June to pay the big guys. We played Tony Bennett in June, but when he got hot, we sure as hell didn't play him in June."

Such were the advantages of being a venue for both established stars and the up-and-coming acts.

"I once got Tony Bennett for $2,000, and I was being generous," said George Hamid, Jr. "He did thirty shows a week, as most did. Our policy was four shows on weekdays and five on Saturday and Sunday. They did it because there weren't that many other options. You have to remember, it followed vaudeville, and that was the same type of thing. You'd go into a theater for a week, you'd have a movie and then a vaudeville show. It disappeared in the early '30s, but not on Steel Pier. We kept up the vaudeville policy.

"I remember so many of those shows. When Frankie Laine sang, it used to send shivers up and down my spine. And there wasn't a sexier singer than Helen O'Connell. But all anybody ever asks me about was the diving horse."

There was more to booking the name acts than just dialing the telephone.

Steel Pier in 1964. You can see flag-pole sitter Dixie Blandy just above the letter "T" on the Steel Pier sign.

"I'd go to New York all the time and I'd spend two or three days at my favorite hotel. I'd spend one day with GAC (General Artists Corporation) one day with William Morris, one day with MCA [Music Corporation of America]," Hamid said of the big talent agencies. "I had spies in each one of them. The guy who booked my account was my spy, and he would whisper in my ear what's going to be hot. The year we booked Johnnie Ray, we booked him for $7,500 in February, and I said, 'You guys are absolutely crazy! I can't pay that!' He said by summertime, he would be hot ... take him. So I did. And by summertime, 'Cry' and 'The Little White Cloud That Cried' were hits, and he was the rage!"

Al Alberts, who grew up in Philadelphia and found fame as lead singer of the Four Aces, tells of a time in 1958 when he helped a rising star: "Our last show at Steel Pier was a September show, which was the show where I gave my notice to the guys that I was leaving. I sat with a boy who was the star of the next week's show who didn't know where the hell he was going, or what he was doing, what songs to sing, in what sequence. And I sat with him there for an hour after our show closed, advising him. His name was Paul Anka."

Alberts also related the experience of performing on the Pier. "When you go to a place as a kid when you were twelve, fifteen, seventeen years old, and you're sitting in the audience watching all these great performers, and all of a sudden, *you're* the performer — is that exciting? And I remember saying that at every show — 'I don't believe I'm standing here' — because every time I was in this house up to this point, I was sitting where *you* sat!"

☾ ☾ ☾ ☾

The last years of the Pier in the 1960s and 1970s were a curious blend of old acts and new faces that were hot at that particular moment. The 1960s featured familiar names such as Dorothy Lamour, Xavier Cugat and Abbe Lane, Louis Armstrong, Mickey Rooney, Milton Berle, and old favorite Rudy Vallee, who had come out of retirement.

Then there were comics and singers who were in a popular TV show, only to fade away a few years later. The Hamids had their finger on the pulse of entertainment, and they booked these names at their peak, such as Phyllis Diller, Troy Donahue, Joe E. Ross from TV's "Car 54, Where are You?", Allan Sherman of "Hello Muddah, Hello Faddah" fame, Frank Fontaine of "The Jackie Gleason Show," and TV's "Hawaiian Eye" star Poncie Ponce, who returned quite often. Then there was Vaughn Meader, the hot comic whose portrayal of President John F. Kennedy had lifted him to the top, only to see his career end with Kennedy's assassination.

This potpourri also included singers Jack Jones, Wayne Newton, Ray Charles, Frank Sinatra Jr., Trini Lopez, trumpeter Al Hirt, Philadelphia TV host Mike Douglas, the Doodletown Pipers, the New Christy Minstrels, Sandler and Young, O.C. Smith, and kid faves The Banana Splits, as well as comics Soupy Sales, Don Adams of "Get Smart," Totie Fields, Bill Dana as Jose Jimenez, London Lee and Pat Paulsen. The

strange and unpredictable singer Tiny Tim first announced his engagement to Miss Vicki on Steel Pier in 1969. Their wedding was held live on Johnny Carson's "Tonight Show" shortly after.

"Tiny Tim performed two shows and accidentally broke his ukulele on stage. His anger was palpable," according to K. Rippin, who posted his recollection on *ILoveAC.com* in 2002. Tiny Tim set yet another attendance record, drawing almost 130,000 paid admissions (most of whom came out of curiosity) for the week that he performed.

"We stopped trying to buy expensive comics because they didn't draw like the singers did," said Hamid.

Special Forces Staff Sgt. Barry Sadler, whose "Ballad of the Green Berets" was then topping the charts, was booked into Easter weekend 1966, probably becoming the most surreal booking of all time, given the increasing protests against the Vietnam war.

But there were also unforgettable entertainers who weren't a household name. Patron Dom Arruzzo related, "We used to go to the shows, and there was a comedian I saw many times named Jack Durant. His show always started with the announcement 'And now, from the Metropolitan Opera in New York — Jack Durant!' He would come out and try to hit a high operatic note but end up falling downstage. He would then get up and would start his act while panting. His first joke would be: 'I went to the doctor the other day and said, 'Doc, I haven't been feeling myself lately.' The doctor said, 'I'm proud of you.' After we had seen his act a few times, we knew that he was always introduced the same way, and my Dad and I would watch other people in the audience cringe when they heard the word *opera*. I never got tired of his act!"

"Four shows a day, and back in those days if you didn't keep moving, you didn't make it," Durant later told *The Press of Atlantic City* "Everybody had their gimmicks. Me, I'd do a few jokes and if they didn't work out, I'd shift to a (Clark) Gable imitation and then I'd do a somersault.

"The key was to keep moving. That was vaudeville. That was what it was all about. People loved that stuff."

☾ ☾ ☾ ☾

By the 1970s, with the Copacabana, the Latin Quarter and other big rooms closing, Steel Pier was the only place still getting big names, with the exception of Las Vegas. But it was becoming exceedingly hard to find family-oriented acts in an increasingly expensive and explicit environment. Until George Hamid, Jr. left the Pier after 1975, bookings included singers Enzo Stuarti, Glen Campbell, and Buddy Greco; and comics Marty Allen, Shelley Berman, and Pat Cooper. Music groups included the Pat Boone Family, Dean Martin's the Golddiggers, Doc Severinsen and his Now Generation Brass, stars of "The Lawrence Welk Show," and Johnny Mann's "Stand Up and Cheer" singers.

Barry Williams of TV's "The Brady Bunch," and David Cassidy and Danny Bonaduce from "The Partridge Family" also appeared. The mentalist The Amazing Kreskin was there, and Hi-De-Ho legend Cab Calloway, whose orchestra, ironically, could never appear in the Marine Ballroom during its peak years because of its segregationist policy.

Dean Scarpa was an usher in the Music Hall in the 1970s. "I met everybody ... Oliver, Enzo Stuarti, Shelley Berman, Freda Payne, Woody Herman, B.J. Thomas ...

"I remember going to rehearsals early Sunday mornings, and on Friday hawking tickets for reserved seats in front of the Music Hall. Also, having to walk the movie cans across the roof of the buildings, to be picked up by the agent. What a place! It was the best job I ever had and the greatest place I've ever been to."

Comedy team Fisher and Marks, originally from Philadelphia, played the Casino theater in 1976 and 1977 in the twilight of the Pier's existence. Lou Marks remembered, "I played the part of an usher seating the people and two guys came and threw me out. I was doing the show and they locked the door on me. I was trying to get in! My partner was yelling, 'Where the hell is he?! I've gotta find that guy!' And the two guys apologized — it was bedlam! They must have thought I was a heckler!"

❧ ❧ ❧ ❧

By the early 1970s, George Hamid, Jr. knew that his Pier and Atlantic City were in dire trouble. The crowds were diminishing as the city's deterioration and subsequent racial unrest sent visitors to more exotic places for vacations. He could do only so much to stop the bleeding, and when that failed, there was only one thing left to do: sell.

In January 1973, Hamid sold Steel Pier to a group of Atlantic City investors who tried to improve the Pier's image and bring it up to date. Hamid then leased the Pier back and ran it until 1975.

There was an aggressive effort under the new ownership of Milton Neustadter, Maxwell Goldberg and Albert Gardner in 1976 to bring back top stars as in years past. Ella Fitzgerald, Jerry Lewis and others came to the Pier, but the crowds were just not in abundance anymore. Atlantic City had ceased to be a major tourist destination.

Ironically, aging singer Eddie Fisher appeared on Steel Pier on May 26, 1978, the first official day of casino gambling in Atlantic City. As the Pier struggled to continue on its last opening day, huge lines formed a block away on the Boardwalk outside Resorts International's new property, as thousands lined up for slot machines and roulette in the former Haddon Hall hotel.

Steve Lawrence and Eydie Gorme, Resorts' first headliners that day, had appeared on the Pier some twenty years earlier when they were rising stars. Now the scene was reversed.

There is no question that over the years, Steel Pier brought Atlantic City the best in live entertainment. But the times had changed. Vaudeville could not continue; television and Las Vegas — and the casinos in Atlantic City — were now the kings of entertainment.

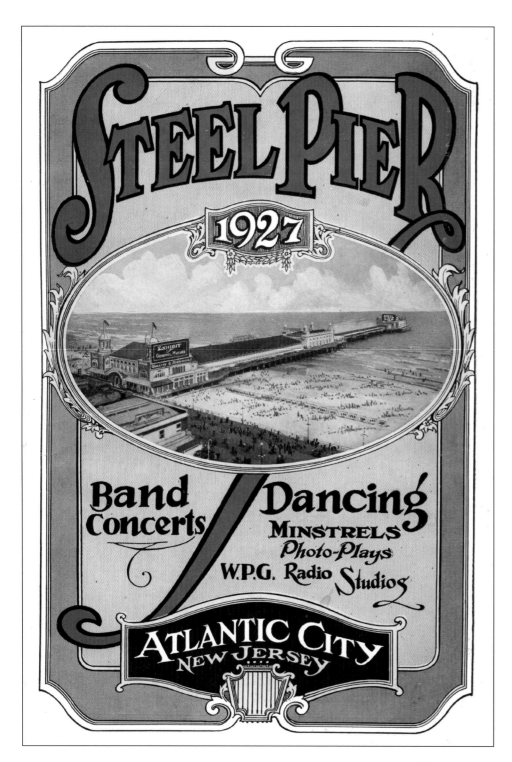

Chapter Eight

Orchestras And the Big Bands

"Good evening, ladies and gentlemen! From the beautiful Marine Ballroom at George Hamid's Steel Pier, a half-mile at sea in Atlantic City, the world's famous playground, CBS Radio presents, for listening and dancing around the nation, music by Vaughn Monroe and his orchestra, with vocals tonight by the Moon Maids … ."

That was the way Atlantic City veteran radio broadcaster Ed Davis would announce a name-band over the nation's airwaves from Steel Pier's WFPG. He filled that role from 1946, when he joined the WFPG staff, until twenty years later, when remote broadcasts of big bands became a relic of the past.

In the early 1950s, an average August night began at about 11:30 P.M. in the Marine Ballroom, with a top name band swinging away on stage. The brass was loud, the saxophones were smooth, the bass thumped and the drums rocked. The Ballroom was packed with thousands, from teenagers to those in their forties. There were locals from Atlantic City, along with visitors and vacationers in the resort. Some came for dancing; others just wanted to find a temporary date. Many stood by the stage and just listened and watched their idols in awe.

One didn't have to mingle with the large crowd. There were 500 seats in the balcony for those who didn't want to dance, but enjoyed just listening, and watching the people below.

It was a romantic evening. A popular orchestra was playing right in front of you, on a coast-to-coast national radio broadcast, while you danced to a sultry ballad — almost a half-mile out to sea, near the end of the Pier, with a cool breeze wafting through the open Ballroom windows and the lapping Atlantic Ocean just below.

This was what made the Pier a bigger attraction that the rival Million Dollar Pier — both featured famous bands, but the Marine Ballroom was at the "romantic" end of the Pier, overlooking the ocean. That alone made a tremendous difference.

The bands that played the Pier during its early years were devoted to an entirely different class of audience compared to the later big-band era. Italian and Hungarian concert bands performed light classics, which segued into the marches of John Philip Sousa. Then, early dance bands were the norm, followed later by swing and jazz bands, and then finally the trend returned to dance bands.

In 1899, concert orchestras were headlining regularly and played in the open arcade area of the Pier, where visitors would sit and listen to light classics and marches. Evening dances usually took place in the ocean-end ballroom, which at that time was named Music Hall.

Giuseppe Creatore and his Royal Italian Band first appeared at Steel Pier in 1901. With his mop of unruly hair, the egocentric conductor would, during heavy passages of certain classical pieces, dramatically drop to his knees in front of a solo player. Creatore freely boasted he was "the greatest," long before heavyweight boxing champion Muhammad Ali made that line famous.

Another Steel Pier favorite, Oreste Vessella, with his Banda Davoia, arrived in 1902. Vessella had to employ a bodyguard to keep over-enthusiastic females from snipping his wavy locks. He played only Italian composers, unless pressured otherwise.

Now Playing–Steel Pier

Lieutenant-Commander
JOHN PHILIP
SOUSA AND HIS BAND

Lieutenant-Commander John Philip Sousa, who opens his 39th annual tour with his famous band on the STEEL PIER, September 2 to 8, has written five new marches, all at the invitation of patriotic, public and educational organizations in America and abroad. Following his custom of many years, these new numbers will all find places in Sousa's program during his concerts on the STEEL PIER.

John Phillip Sousa, America's "March King", played Steel Pier every summer from 1926 thru 1931.

Sousa and his band draw a large crowd in the Marine Ballroom for the last time, September 1931.

The Johnny Johnson orchestra poses in front of the entrance in 1931 while resting on the famous rolling chairs.

Vessella's Farewell Concert for the season on October 26, 1912 featured the potpourri of a march by Mendelssohn, an overture by Jubel, "Othello" by Verdi and ballet music from Gounod's "Faust." Vessella's band played often and was featured every year from 1906 to 1917, and again from 1920 to 1926.

❧ ❧ ❧ ❧

The *Atlantic City Press* proclaimed in May 1907: "The ever-popular Steel Pier Promenade Dance Concert was a largely and brilliantly attended social event Saturday evening. Many members of the summer social set were noticed upon the dance floor, while dainty and summery gowns were worn by the women, who took advantage of the first warm May night."

The report from September 1915 was: "The Promenade Concert

Dance, as has been the custom of Steel Pier, will be the attraction to the thousands. … Many will come down from Philadelphia and various other points to take advantage of the dance offered at the cool end of the city's immaculate pier," said the *Press*. "Martini's Orchestra will play the dance music."

"At that time, the Pier was very sedate," distinguished local businessman Adrian Phillips remembered decades later in the August 1981 issue of *Atlantic City* magazine. "People were very well dressed and they enjoyed the bands, which played some classical music and on Sundays had sacred concerts, with the audience sitting around the bandstand. People also gathered under the Pier to hear the concerts as well.

"The Pier was very conservatively conducted. More so than the Million Dollar Pier, which had more progressive music. On Steel Pier, everybody was well-behaved, and there was no boisterousness or loudness permitted."

The greatest name during this period was that of "The March King," John Phillip Sousa. With his flair and his original compositions, Sousa appeared everywhere in America, from bandstands in amusement parks to big city concert halls.

Sousa had played Atlantic City before, but when Frank Gravatt bought Steel Pier in 1925, he made sure that Sousa's band was a yearly attraction. Unfortunately, that first season brought out the worst in weather. "Out of thirteen possible weekends, it rained eleven. Mr. Sousa referred to himself as the Rain God. I referred to myself as the Sap," Gravatt was quoted afterward.

One of the reasons Sousa returned to Atlantic City regularly was that he was married to Jane Van Middlesworth, an Atlantic City native he met when she was sixteen

At the time they were the hottest band in the country: Paul Whiteman plays for a packed Marine Ballroom, 1928.

When Convention Hall opened on the Boardwalk in 1929 with a show produced by R. H. Burnside titled "Here and Now," the music and lyrics were written by Sousa and Raymond Hubbell.

Sousa's last appearance on Steel Pier was in September 1931. He died not soon after, on May 6, 1932, at age seventy-seven, while preparing for a concert in Reading, Pennsylvania. He was the last link to an era that was bursting with patriotism.

C C C C

The Arthur Pryor Band was probably one of the last of the popular concert bands in this period. When he played the Pier on June 11, 1927, special trains from Philadelphia rolled into Atlantic City to accommodate his many fans.

Concert bands were still heard, but there were also other forms of musical entertainment to enjoy on the Pier. Dance bands began to become the favorite form of popular music by the end of the 1920s. White orchestras, influenced by the jazz of black bands such as Fletcher Henderson and Duke Ellington, were beginning their ascent into the mainstream. In 1928, you could dance to the Ted Weems Band in the Marine Ballroom from 9 P.M. until midnight; you could also listen to the Edwin Franko Goldman Concert Band.

The Pier also had its own group of musicians. The Steel Pier Concert Orchestra, under the direction of Roy Comfort, played from 9 P.M. until 1 A.M. in the Ballroom in 1929.

On several nights in 1934, nine bands played on the Pier simultaneously: Estlow's Steel Pier Orchestra in the Music Hall, Vincent Lopez in the Marine Arcade, Joe Lopaz Imperial Hawaiians on the Circus stage, Aldriche's Hawaiians in the entrance lobby, Elkins Opera Music Company in Little Theater, Ted Fio Rita in the Music Hall lobby, Frank Dailey in the Casino theater, and The Royal Phillipino Orchestra in the Marine Ballroom.

Hawaiian and Phillipino bands, with their exotic music, were especially popular for years on the Pier. "In 1936-1937, before my birth, my father, Carman Grove, had the first band at the front of the Pier, called 'Carman Leland and His Hawaiian Islanders,'" said his daughter, Carol Grove.

Then there were the operas. Steel Pier Opera Company first appeared in 1929 and became nationally known for performances of classic operas that were sung entirely in English. Planned by Milton Aborn and Charles Wagner, the company presented "Romeo and Juliet," "Tales of Hoffman" and "Carmen" that first year. Jules Falk was the company's director, leading an orchestra that included members of the Philadelphia Orchestra. The operas were first held in the Marine Ballroom, then in the Little Theatre until 1939.

Organ recitals were also a popular event, usually in the Pier's lobby. Jean Wiener began her recitals in 1928 and stayed until 1932. They were not featured again until the post-World War II years, when Elsie Gross played the Hammond organ from 1946 through 1955. Harold Ferrin then played the lobby organ in 1963 before this practice was finally discontinued.

Canadian band leader Glen Gray and his Casa Loma Orchestra, one of the first well-known white jazz bands, were drawing poor crowds while on tour of the East Coast in 1931. They decided to play their last engagement at Steel Pier in September, expecting to disband afterward. But they were such a hit that they regrouped, went on the road again, and continued as a big success for many years thereafter.

Sometimes you could find the same band playing the same day at different locations on the Pier. In 1931, the Smith Ballew Orchestra warmed up from 5 to 6 P.M. in the lobby, then set up in the Ballroom for dancing from 9 P.M. to 1 A.M.

As a publicity stunt, Abe Lyman's Band actually played on the Pier in a cage — with Proske's trained tigers — in June 1936.

The famous Guy Lombardo was also booked for engagements. He would arrive in his yacht, which he moored at the back of the Pier.

A storm once arose when Paul Whiteman and his orchestra were playing. The Pier always swayed in a storm and after some pronounced swaying, the portly Whiteman excused himself from the bandstand and ran to the farthest exit. He was hard to convince to come back for his engagement.

There were also permanent bands on the Pier, such as John McConnell's Music Hall Orchestra, used primarily for accompaniment for the singers and vaudeville stars that performed in Music Hall. By 1951, Freddie Bowens, who replaced McConnell, led the pit orchestra, and in 1960 the baton was handed to Jules Levan.

Perhaps the best-known band of all was the Marine Ballroom's house band, led by Alex Bartha. Bartha was a native of Atlantic City and a former bank official who started a dance band for the fun of it. Although the band was not known for many recordings, its popularity won Bartha an engagement on Steel Pier, which in turn led to numerous appearances on the east coast. His band was a regular on the Pier from 1933 through 1946, alternating with the headlined band, and could be seen around Atlantic City into the 1950s.

In the July 1943 issue of the music magazine *Metronome*, editor George Simon said, "There are a couple of below-draft-age lads with Alex Bartha's band at Steel Pier in Atlantic City who deserve ear-lending. One of these is Tommy Kaplan, a seventeen-year-old trumpeter with a lovely warm tone and an ability to play some really good jazz.

"An awful lot of you musicians must know Bartha, for he's been the house band leader at the Pier for years and years, and a nice guy, too."

In the summer of 1936, Benny Goodman was in town listening to Bartha's band and was so impressed with trumpet player Harry Finkleman, he hired him on the spot. Known later by his stage name, Ziggy Elman, the young musician was a Philadelphia native who moved to Atlantic City to showcase his talent. He was playing on the Pier when he was just sixteen, while a student at Atlantic City High School.

Chris Griffin, of the Goodman trumpet section, remembers when his boss discovered Finkleman:

We were going through Steel Pier and Ziggy was with Alex Bartha, the house band there. There was this guy in the band, the first trumpet, jumping down to the second level, playing trombone and then jumping down to play the baritone sax, and back again to trumpet.

Ziggy repeated the performance three or four times and Benny, watching, remarked frequently: "Wow! Great! Look at that!" Obviously, he was saying to himself, "We gotta get this guy!"

Sterling Bose was with us — a great Dixieland player, but not really for our band. Benny replaced him with Ziggy.

Two weeks later, we were playing at the Ritz-Carlton Hotel in Boston. By this time, Zeke Zarchey and I are looking for wind because we're trying to keep up with this guy who's like a bus horn — push a button and whew!

However the thought came up, somebody said to Benny — "We're playing awfully loud for this place." And Benny said: "Yeah, I gotta talk to Ziggy." Benny knew where it was coming from because Ziggy was new with us. So he got Ziggy behind the bandstand and I could hear what was going on. And remember, Benny was the King of Swing by then, the biggest, and Ziggy was like me, a new kid on the block.

Benny said, "Hey Pops, too loud. You gotta stop playin' that loud!" And Ziggy said right then: "Benny, I didn't send for you. You asked ME to join the band. I was very happy down in Atlantic City with Alex Bartha and I'll be very happy to go back."

That was the end of that. And to my knowledge, Benny never bothered Ziggy again. He stayed just as loud. And I even learned to play loud — though it wasn't my style — to keep up.

☾ ☾ ☾ ☾

Easter Sunday, April 16, 1938 marked the very first appearance of the new Gene Krupa Orchestra. After enjoying much success with Benny Goodman, Krupa branched out on his own, picking the Marine Ballroom as the location to introduce his band to the public.

George Simon penned a review for *Metronome*:

About 4,000 neighborhood and visiting cats scratched and clawed for points of vantage in the Marine Ballroom of Atlantic City's Steel Pier … and proceeded to welcome … the first public appearance of drummer man Gene Krupa and his newly-formed jazz band. The way the feline herd received, reacted to and withstood the powerful onslaught of Krupa's loud musical attacks left little doubt that Gene is now entrenched at the helm of a swing outfit that's bound to be recognized shortly as one of the most potent catnip to be fed to the purring public that generally passes as America's swing contingent. Throughout the evening, the kids and kittens shagged, trucked, jumped up and down and down and up, and often yelled and screamed at the series of solid killer-dillers.

When the proceedings started, they were lined up 45 deep around the huge bandstand, and when at 1:30 the band led its limp lips and limbs from the field of battle, at least one-third of that number of rows remained in an up-right position — as thrilling a tribute as any opening a bandleader could possibly hope for.

Krupa explained it this way: "At the beginning, I went a bit overboard playing a drum solo at the drop of a hat. One night, old man Sullivan, who ran the Pier, took me aside. The band couldn't have been too old. 'Gene,' he said, 'you're a good kid and a hard worker and everything, but even the Super Chief stops once in a while. Rest yourself. Don't take too many solos. My ears are hurting.' I kept that in mind. And from that time on, the spotlight was shared."

Later in 1938, Dave Tough replaced Krupa as Benny Goodman's drummer. In *Benny Goodman — On the Record*, Goodman remembered, "On Steel Pier, Dave's solo on 'Don't Be That Way,' much different than Gene's famous break, caused an unfavorable audience reaction. This bothered Dave, so he asked me to play it again. This time, Dave came on with an open two-stroke roll, with the accents precisely where Gene had put them. To the uninitiated, it sounded the same as Gene's solo on the record, and the crowd cheered. But the band, aware that what Dave had done was much less difficult than Krupa's effort, broke up completely — Harry James literally fell off his chair. Tough merely acknowledged the plaudits with his secret little smile."

Benny Goodman, the "King of Swing", played the Pier fourteen times from 1936 to 1946. This was an appearance promoted in August 1939.

Steel Pier always had an edge over Hamid's Million Dollar Pier when it came to the bands, booking through the Music Corporation of America big names such as Goodman, Tommy Dorsey and Sammy Kaye. The bands playing Steel Pier also had more opportunity to be heard nationally. As Sammy Kaye's band played on May 28, 1938, the performance was broadcast live over eighty radio stations.

When George Hamid started leasing Million Dollar Pier in 1938, he had to book bands through General Artist, which specialized in newcomers such as Artie Shaw, Woody Herman and hit-makers like Jimmy Dorsey. Yet some of those second-rate bands soon became first-rate, drawing the envious eye of Frank Gravatt at Steel Pier. At one point, Gravatt managed to steal Shaw from Hamid's contract and book the upcoming star for his own Steel Pier.

The business wranglings between the Atlantic City Boardwalk competitors meant nothing to Shaw.

"Steel Pier was one venue," he recalled in an interview sixty years later. "We played millions of places. It has no meaning for me one way or another.

"Steel Pier, or any other place that I played — it's a gig. I know it was on the ocean, but so was Wildwood (on Hunt's Ocean Pier in

Wildwood, N.J.) and we played there. It didn't mean anything."

❝ ❝ ❝ ❝

Frank Sinatra made his first appearance on the Pier at the end of July 1939 with the Harry James Band, earning a mere $75 a week. James had discovered Sinatra just a few months earlier on a radio remote from the Rustic Cabin, a roadside club in New Jersey. Joining Sinatra was a female vocalist named Connie Haines.

"This was her first real job with Harry James," recalled Basil Woolf, who knew her. "Before he put her name up on the billboard, he wanted her to change her name, which was Yvonne Marie JaMais. This would not fit on the billboard. He said she looked like a 'Connie' and gave her the name of Connie Haines, because Haines rhymed with James. She misunderstood and thought he said Connie *Ames*,

Alex Bartha's band played on the S.S. Steel Pier *in 1932, led the Marine Ballroom house band from 1934 to 1946, and then appeared sporadically until 1956. Trumpeter Ziggy Elman left Batha and found fame with Benny Goodman in 1936.*

because after the show she signed quite a bit of autographs with the name *Ames*."

Rosemary Marrandino's father was there when Sinatra debuted on Steel Pier. "In 1939, my father, Angie Marrandino, played sax and clarinet with Alex Bartha's band in the Ballroom at the same time Sinatra was starting his career with the Harry James band. The two bands alternated performances on the Pier. He later got to play with Sinatra at the 500 Club," she told *The Press* in 1998.

During the third week of August in 1939, Ballroom visitors got the chance to see the debut of the Benny Goodman Sextet, with virtuoso electric guitarist Charlie Christian. Christian, an African-American, had auditioned and joined Goodman's band only the previous week.

On August 26, the entire country heard him for the first time during a Goodman "Camel Caravan" broadcast from the Pier. An influence to countless others who played jazz guitar, Christian met an untimely death in March 1942 due to tuberculosis. He was only twenty-five.

On August 10, 1940, a promotion from Pier owner Frank Gravatt, in the interest of a wholesome good time, announced, "Girls: win a date with the nation's hit tunemaker — Larry Clinton — now appearing at Steel Pier. Winner of contest will be the guest of Clinton afternoon and evening August 15, spending the afternoon on the Pier, dinner at the 'Round the World Room' of President Hotel, then back to dance to Clinton's band and sing with the orchestra onstage. Winner may bring a female chaperone. Rules: write your reasons for wanting to have a date with Clinton; can you sing? Open to every girl over 18. Ten runner-ups will receive a guest ticket to the Pier to dance to the band. After dance, will go to Babette's famed night spot where dining and dancing will be unrestrained."

Legendary orchestra leader Glenn Miller had become close friends with George Hamid. Miller made it a point to always play Hamid's Million Dollar Pier. In 1940, the Miller band, which was paid $2,500 a day, gave Million Dollar Pier what was then its biggest weekend ever.

But in 1941, Gravatt contracted with Miller's agent for a whopping $4,000 a day to play Steel Pier. Miller, who had intended to stay loyal to Hamid, was signing so many contracts at the time that he didn't realize that one of them was for Hamid's biggest rival. The band was booked for the weekend preceding Labor Day, when the first of Miller's "Sunset Serenade" radio programs originated from Steel Pier. The engagement with Steel Pier bewildered Hamid, who had always hired the band regularly, before they made it big.

George Hamid, Jr. gave his version to *Metronome* magazine editor George Simon, for Simon's later book about the Glenn Miller Orchestra:

We were terribly hurt that Glenn had decided to play the bigger Steel Pier. We knew they could pay him more than we could, but we figured he would be loyal to us because we had hired him even before he was well known, and Glenn was always known to be loyal to his friends.

We lived in a house on the side of our (Million Dollar) Pier, and who should show up late in the afternoon of the day Glenn was supposed to play Steel Pier but Glenn himself. He had been at our house before, whenever he played our Pier. He was sleeping in the car, walked in and said "Hello" to us all and sat down. He told us he was terribly tired and just wanted to rest a bit. He had been sleeping, so he didn't even see the billboards coming into Atlantic City. He just told his driver to take him to Million Dollar Pier.

Well, Dad didn't know quite how to take this. Here is Glenn, playing for the opposition, but coming to us first just to rest and relax. Finally, Dad asked him why he had gone over to the other side. Glenn was flabbergasted. He had taken it for granted that he was playing our Pier again and just dropped by, as he always had done, to visit. When he realized that Mike Nidorf had booked him into Steel Pier, he was furious. "How dare you book me away from George Hamid?!"

Of course he had to go through with the date, but to show you the kind of man Glenn was, he told my father, "Look, I'm going to make this up to you. Next year, instead of just one, I'll give you two dates!" And he kept his word, too. In the summer of 1942, the Glenn Miller band played our Pier twice, and I don't think he ever did that for any other promoter. In our books, Glenn Miller was a very decent and honorable man.

It became a real battle. Gravatt tried to fool the public and booked the Glenn Miller movie "Orchestra Wives" on Steel Pier that very same week, and rented every billboard on the approach to Atlantic City with the simple message "Glenn Miller … Steel Pier." Hamid, however, had the real deal.

❧ ❧ ❧ ❧

The bands that went on the air from Steel Pier were treated in the same manner as rock bands of today, with the leaders considered superstars. A dance or concert from these bands resulted in the same critique that a rock band gets today when seen in a major hall. Were they good or not? Sometimes not.

One case in point was critic Barry Ulanov's review, printed in *Metronome*, of Charlie Barnet band's July 20, 1941 performance on Steel Pier, broadcast by WOR in New York. "There's no doubt about it, Charlie has done better," wrote Ulanov. "There were some fine moments on this broadcast, but they were few and far between. Charlie … seemed to have impressed his sax section with some of the cardinal rules of good team work, but the rest of the band suffered from sloppiness and roughness. Maybe it was just that this was an afternoon airing."

Barnet, in his autobiography, *Those Swingin' Years*, remembered a better reception a few years later. "Around 1950, we were playing the ballroom at the end of Steel Pier, a half-mile out to sea, when I saw a sight near closing time. Here was a Chevrolet touring car, with a chauffeur and rear-seat window shades, driving into the room. An elderly gentleman with a straw hat was seated in the back. He turned out to be Nucky Johnson, the famous boss of Atlantic City, and he had just been released from the penitentiary.

"He invited me to go with him on a tour of the night spots. Everywhere we went we were treated like royalty. He was quite a guy and I enjoyed the evening immensely, but why he suddenly decided he wanted my company is still a mystery, for I had played Atlantic City

Kay Kyser and the band are all smiles as thousands of fans fill the Marine Ballroom, 1940.

many times without ever seeing him, let alone being his guest for a night on the town."

Even though black musicians were allowed to play in the bands — Charlie Christian, Teddy Wilson and Lionel Hampton with Benny Goodman, and Roy Eldridge with Gene Krupa — it seemed to strike a different chord when it came to singers. The August 1, 1944 issue of *Down Beat* related, "Bon Bon Tunnel, sepia vocalist, was forced to remain on the sidelines during Johnny Warrington's engagement here

at Steel Pier Marine Ballroom. The one-time singer with Jan Savitt has been with the Warrington Philly studio crew for the past two years. The direct order to keep Bon Bon off the stand came from MCA acting on orders from Steel Pier Management. Steel Pier operators have always maintained a white music policy for its Marine Ballroom. Colored attractions have been used from time to time in the Music Hall, Pier's vaude house."

It's true that only white orchestras could play in the Marine Ball-

An empty Marine Ballroom awaits its dancers, and later (right) the night becomes magical, 1950s.

believe it — the people poured onto the Pier," Hamid recalled for Peter S. Levinson's book, *Trumpet Blues — The Life of Harry James.* "We did 27,000 people — the biggest day we had since the war was over. In those days, the girls wore beautiful pastel hats on Easter Sunday, and they all had high-heeled shoes on. They'd go to the Ballroom to dance and they would come out with their shoes in their hands."

room. Duke Ellington, Count Basie, Chick Webb and Jimmie Lunceford played in theaters or in clubs located on the north side of Atlantic City, the black section. Yet, these bands were known to play at the major "white" Times Square and Philadelphia theaters without any problem.

Tom Allen, an African-American historian who grew up in Atlantic City, believes that in the theaters, patrons sat and watched the show and did not dance, so there wasn't any chance for dancing by mixed couples, as there might have been in Steel Pier's Marine Ballroom. "It had to do with the possibility of dancing together, more than anything else, and that would have caused a problem with the Pier's image for tourists."

"I don't feel that the Hamids were racists," Allen said. "It just was good for business not to rock the boat as far as the image to tourists was concerned."

 When George Hamid bought Steel Pier in 1945, his first show was presented on Easter weekend. World War II was coming to a close in Europe, and the Harry James Band had, by this time, become the nation's top dance band.

"Harry's trumpet playing was crystal clear, and you couldn't

The next year, singer Rosemary Clooney made her big debut as a vocalist for the Tony Pastor Band on July 10, 1946 in the Marine Ballroom, along with her sister Betty. This is how Rosemary remembered the day:

Steel Pier stretched far out from the Boardwalk, suspended over the Atlantic on enormous pilings I didn't quite trust. The main theater was toward the middle of the Pier; we were appearing on the secondary stage at the end, where at regular intervals during the day a trained horse would dive from a forty-foot tower into a tank. As we walked the Pier's length, Betty and I were both sure it was going to collapse under us. And when we were backstage, waiting to go on, a tiny part of me wished it would...

Before I even realized I was moving, I found myself out of the wings and halfway across the stage, shaking in my unaccustomed spike heels, my plaid taffeta dress rustling around my ankles. Out of the corner of my eye I saw Betty moving toward me from the other side of the stage. The lights blinded me so that I couldn't see more than a few feet from the stage, but I sensed the people —3,000 or more on the dance floor, waiting for the music to start.

I looked at Betty, the band struck up "It's a Good Day," and we sang...

And they applauded! Then I knew they were on my side.

Again that night, neither of us could sleep, so we dressed and walked out to the Pier, right back to the end. We stood in the shadow of the empty pavilion carpeted with the litter of a big night, and we looked out over the Atlantic. Now, at dawn, I saw that it stretched beyond imagination, and the forces of the waves as they crashed against the pilings made the Pier tremble. I clutched Betty and we laughed, feeling the Atlantic wind on our faces, just laughed with the thrill of it all.

☾ ☾ ☾ ☾

As is true today, people who were fans of certain bands made a point to see them at any cost. Fan John Wira said this about Tex Beneke:

At 16, my one wish was to see and absorb the sounds of a live big band. It was the summer of 1946, and I casually mentioned to one of my buddies that the newly organized Glenn Miller band led by Tex Beneke was booked in the Marine Ballroom on Steel Pier. We decided to go. Departing the bus in Camden, we boarded a train for the fifty-some-mile ride to Atlantic City.

Although the Band's first set didn't begin until 9 P.M. that Wednesday, we decided to spend the entire day walking the Boardwalk. The last train to leave Atlantic City for home was at 11 P.M. After a lunch of hot dogs and soda, we decided to enter the Pier. As 9 P.M. approached, we and crowds of fans began walking towards the Marine Ballroom, out at the far end of the Pier.

As we entered the Ballroom, the strains of "Moonlight Serenade" filled the air and sent chills up and down my spine. I pushed my way to the edge of the stage, where I remained the entire first set. I watched as Tex picked up his tenor sax and the band broke into "In the Mood." I stood mesmerized as the notes bounced off my body, listening to the very songs I had played over and over in the privacy of my bedroom. After about forty minutes, the set was over. Most everyone gathered onto the deck surrounding the Ballroom.

I noticed some members of the band in conversation off to the side. In the center was Tex himself. As I asked for his autograph, he stopped

talking, looked up, smiled, and signed the piece of paper.

For the balance of the evening, the band was on for forty minutes and off twenty. Around 10:30, my buddy, who had been dancing, suggested we get ready to leave to catch the train, but I wanted to stay until the end. So we missed the train. At midnight, we started walking out of Atlantic City until we got a ride from a bread delivery truck headed to Camden. We didn't get home until sunrise. My mother was worried but she understood that we missed the train. I would do it over again in a minute.

It was also the Ballroom where singer Keely Smith saw Louis Prima perform for the first time. "It was the summer of 1947 when I first heard him at Steel Pier," she remembers. "My brother and I were real jitterbug nuts. We went to Atlantic City with my mother and father and out on the Pier there was this Louis Prima Band, which we had never heard of."

She and her brother went to see the band, and she was mesmerized by Prima and his performance. They later met, and in 1948, she joined his band as a vocalist. Five years later, Smith, age twenty-five, and Prima, forty-three, wed. It was her first marriage, his fourth. Prima and Smith became a top draw in Las Vegas through nmost of the 1950s.

May 13, 1947 was an historic day for black bands in Atlantic City. Lionel Hampton's orchestra appeared and performed at a dance for one night on Million Dollar Pier for Hamid, who was now operating it along with Steel Pier. It was the first black orchestra to headline on a pier since Fletcher Henderson's band appeared on Garden Pier in 1932.

Also in 1947, on the national ABC radio program "So You Want to Lead a Band," Hamid presented bandleader Sammy Kaye with a scroll declaring his band the best musical group appearing on Steel Pier during fifty years of Pier history.

During the post-war years, dancing to a live big band was fairly common. On Steel Pier, searchlights at night took on a new meaning with the slogan "When you see the lights in the sky, it's dance time on Steel Pier."

☾ ☾ ☾ ☾

Philadelphian Ed Davis, who had gone to radio broadcasting school for a year, contacted the Pier and auditioned in October 1946 for the job of disc jockey on WFPG. The station's offices and studios were in back of the Casino building, on the second floor. It was a long studio with about four rooms of office space. Hamid's office was downstairs.

Davis landed the job broadcasting live band remotes only because the other disc jockeys weren't interested. He would work nationally three nights a week, with a matinee on Saturday and Sunday. Usually the broadcasts aired from 10:05 to 10:30 P.M., or 11:30 P.M. to midnight. Some were only fifteen-minute programs sponsored by United States Savings Bonds.

Davis recalled Duke Ellington in a 2001 interview:

He liked to do his own announcing, I remember when they put Louis Armstrong in the Music Hall, and then when he came back, they put him in the Ballroom. That's where he belonged in the first place.

Prior to me working there, I used to go to the Pier and watch the bands, never dreaming that one day I'd be up on the bandstand with them. When I saw the Artie Shaw band, just about every member of the band signed my girlfriend's autograph book, but not Shaw. He was never a people person.

I remember broadcasts when you couldn't see any dancers, just people standing shoulder to shoulder to watch the orchestra. Maybe there was a small space in the center, where perhaps four or five couples were dancing. When Vaughn Monroe played at the height of his career, that Ballroom was packed. Louis Prima was a big draw. He had a following from Philadelphia. Gene Krupa was always a big draw. Autograph seekers were very, very popular then. That was a big deal to get the bandleaders' autographs.

Lawrence Welk never played the Pier but many of his stars did. Everybody would come up to the studio for an interview. WFPG was so close to where the action was. Sammy Kaye would come up and they would come up in their swimming trunks and their sport shirts, completely different of what you'd seen on the stand when you put them on the air.

℃ ℃ ℃ ℃

John Wira of the Vaughn Monroe Appreciation Society, relates this story:

I had just turned eighteen and it was Easter Sunday 1948. My brother and some friends were driving some fifty miles or so to see the Vaughn Monroe band in the Marine Ballroom. He asked me if I'd like to go, so I raced upstairs, jumped into my new tweed suit and off we went. I loved music, but I had never seen any performer in person.

The Boardwalk outside the Pier was jammed with people eager to show their new attire, me included. Looking high up on the front of the Pier were the letters "Appearing, The Vaughn Monroe Band." Eager to catch the matinee show, we entered the Pier and quickly walked to the Ballroom, located one half mile from the shore.

The place was bedlam. One could barely move, let alone dance. I pushed my way through the crowd to the edge of the stage where I remained through the first set. I was mesmerized, watching the band perform songs I had listened to in the privacy of my bedroom. I didn't want to dance, I wanted to watch and listen.

During a break, we enjoyed the salt air and splashing of water against the pilings beneath the deck surrounding the Ballroom. It was one of the most enjoyable days I experienced in my then young life.

Another Vaughn Monroe fan remembers: "I met Vaughn in 1950 in Atlantic City. I had been a devoted fan since the mid-forties as a child. My mother's cousin, John McMahon, was a politician there and I spent summers staying with John's mother. John had me come to his house one evening for supper, and while we were waiting for the meal, up drives Vaughn on a motorcycle. John had told him about me and asked him to supper. I thought I'd died and gone to heaven. The time flew and Vaughn had to leave, but first he invited me to the show that evening on Steel Pier, free ticket and all.

"The band was already playing when I arrived. There wasn't much of a crowd as I recall, probably under fifty persons, most of them dancing. Well, he spots me and asks me up on the stage. I guess John had told him that I did a pretty good imitation of him, so he embarrassed me into singing with the band. I did 'Did You Ever See A Dream Walking,' and I don't know if I did it right or not, I was so nervous. The audience applauded, though! I stayed around the rest of the evening, but no more vocals."

Monroe was popular as a bandleader and a person, so on August 7, 1949 the Pier gave an autographed photo of Vaughn Monroe to every adult entering after 6 P.M. And on July 28, 1951, Monroe and his band were telecast live, coast to coast, on his CBS television "Camel Caravan Show."

Ozzie Nelson, of "Ozzie and Harriet" fame, plays for hundreds of dancers in Art Deco splendor, 1934.

Alex Bartha's band would still play the Ballroom occasionally, such as when the Ray Anthony Band headlined in 1951. Anthony's band would play from 2:30 to 5, and 8:30 to 12:30, while Bartha would play at 5:15 to 8:15.

Woody Herman played the week of August 16, 1951 and the band was aired on live AFRS broadcasts. Tenor sax Dick Hafer recalls, "We played Atlantic City, and trumpeter Doug (Mettome)'s downfall was when we came off the Pier. It was sort of raining that night and Bird (bop saxman Charlie Parker) was there. He was working in Atlantic City, and he called Doug over and I saw them walk off together, and we were concerned about him hanging out with Bird. They had a habit, you know. The next night, we got on the bandstand at Steel Pier, and we played the first set and Woody looked back at Doug and said, 'You just blew the raise, Mettome!'

"So even though Doug hadn't played any mistakes, Woody knew. He could hear something."

Some record albums of the day pictured the Pier on their covers. The Elliott Lawrence Band released a live recording on the Fantasy label in 1952 that was titled "Swinging at Steel Pier" and featured a photograph of the Pier on the cover.

The great jazz trumpeter Louis Armstrong became the Pier's first black musician headliner in August 1953. But it was deemed that he was an entertainer and not a dance band, so therefore he played the Music Hall, not the Marine Ballroom.

On April 15, 1954, seven years after he played the Million Dollar Pier, Lionel Hampton's orchestra became the first black band to finally play the Ballroom. However, it was a benefit for the Elks Charity Fund and not a regular season booking, so in all probability tourists were not a part of the crowd.

Jeannemarie (Volk) McGowan, granddaughter of the Steel Pier publicity director Harry Volk, remembers his particular concerns about huge crowds so far out on the Pier. "My grandfather told me never to go dancing out at the end of the Pier, because there's going to be a terrible fire and the Ballroom is going to be cut off. The thing was a firetrap. It was made of wood and there was no way of getting out of there. You were out there dancing with a million people to a band, and if there was a fire, you're gone!

"However, the Dorseys (Tommy and Jimmy), who didn't speak to each other for years, got back together again and appeared on the Pier in September 1954. And I went. There was no way I'm going to miss this. And I went out there. That Ballroom was so old. The floor was like bowed. If you shot marbles, they would all go to the middle of the floor. It was in real bad shape. If my grandfather knew I was out there, I'd have been in serious trouble. But it was worth going. Where else could you spend a buck and a quarter and get all of that entertainment?"

The book *Tommy Dorsey, Livin' in a Great Big Way* quoted another fan who was on the Pier, teenager Jim Duke: "The band played with little verve — understandable, I suppose, given the size and demeanor of the crowd. As the Dorsey Brothers stood near the edge of the bandstand, some guy, obviously three sheets to the wind, kept asking Tommy, 'Do you remember (trumpeter) Bix (Beiderbecke)?' Needless to say, he was ignored. I also well remember the four-bar trumpet chases between Charlie Shavers and another trumpeter, dueling with their horns partially pointed toward each other on 'Well, Git It!' — and the entire trumpet section playing the Bunny Berigan solo on 'Marie.'"

℄ ℄ ℄ ℄

By the mid-1950s, before the advent of rock and roll, CBS Radio still broadcast from Steel Pier and did so through most of the 1960s. The Billy May Band broadcast 9:30 to 9:55 P.M. on July 8, 1956, and the Sam Donahue outfit broadcast twice on July 27, 1957, initially from 5:30 to 6 P.M. and again 10:05 to 10:30 P.M.

Toni Cummins, in *Atlantic City* magazine, remembered the '50s scene: "The ballroom located out at the end was wall-to-wall young adults and big band enthusiasts of all ages. It definitely was the 'boy meets girl' meeting place. The hoods from South Philly, with their pegged pants and duck-tailed haircuts, were much in demand with the locals."

But times were changing. Teenagers were now gravitating toward the rebellious sounds of rock, and rhythm and blues. Even though the big bands were still booked regularly on the Pier, Ed Davis could see a difference.

"I noticed it probably in the late '50s and into the '60s," he said. "The crowds started thinning out by the late '50s at the afternoon dances, especially on weekends. You could tell the bands were on their way out because they weren't attracting the crowds."

Eventually, only night dances were presented by the big bands.

Future teen-idol Bobby Vinton made his debut on the Pier not as a vocalist, but as a leader of a dance band in 1960. "Nobody really came," Vinton remembered. "I don't know how they booked a kid from Mechanicsburg, Pennsylvania. We didn't have that many people dancing. I do recall one day, we must have seen 500 or 600 people walking into the Ballroom. I said, 'Wow, we're a hit.' They all walked past me to see the horse dive into the water. That's where they went that day, and I haven't been fond of horses since, especially if they're jumping into water."

In July 1964, the Duke Ellington Orchestra became the first black band to play the Marine Ballroom during the summer season. Years later, the *Philadelphia City Paper* reported how that day influenced a future Philadelphia star: "On a mid-July afternoon in 1964, a young man ambled down the Boardwalk in Atlantic City, killing time before a concert on Steel Pier by the Duke Ellington orchestra. By chance, his stroll brought him within hailing distance of the maestro. The young fan tentatively approached his idol and nervously said hello. The eminent composer-bandleader smiled graciously and thanked the young man.

"That may have been the only time Harrison Ridley, Jr. spoke with Duke Ellington, but the maestro has had a long-standing effect on Ridley, who's now one of Philly's most well-respected jazz personalities (and) who owns hundreds of Ellington recordings."

Ed Davis was bewildered why it took Ellington so long to appear on the Pier. "I can't understand it because they really packed them in," he said, when Ellington was booked in 1964.

Two years later, in the midst of the civil rights period, the racial ban had been fully lifted on the Pier. The Ramsey Lewis Trio, Ellington and the Count Basie bands all appeared during the peak summer season in 1966.

☾ ☾ ☾ ☾

Sometimes strollers walking past the Diving Bell would crowd the side doorway of the Ballroom when they heard the applause and cheers during a special moment, such as a drum solo by Gene Krupa. Author Bruce Klauber remembered such a moment, recorded in *Atlantic City* magazine: "I experienced a phenomenon firsthand in the summer of 1967 during an afternoon Ballroom set by the Gene Krupa Quartet. I walked in during the last half of the television taping of Ed Hurst's record hop, and when the cameras went off, the gyrating teenagers began to clear out in large numbers.

"But word began to spread that the great Gene Krupa would be playing his matinee performance in a short while, and little by little, people of every age began to appear out of nowhere and crowded around the ballroom bandstand. By the time Krupa was introduced and began playing 'Flyin' Home,' there had to have been 2,000 people in that room — in the afternoon! They still screamed for Gene, as they had thirty years before."

The Mike Pedicin combo became the house band of the Ballroom in 1968 and 1969. Pedicin, a popular bandleader from Philadelphia, formed his first sixteen-piece band in 1940. Not a stranger to the Jersey Shore, he had played gigs in Seaside Heights, Wildwood, Somers Point and Atlantic City:

I played Steel Pier when I was about 12 or 13. I was on the "Horn & Hardart Children's Hour" on WCAU radio in Philadelphia, and I played my sax then. I wasn't very good.

We had a five-piece band on the Pier with trombone, drums, guitar, bass, piano, and I played alto sax. My group played all kinds of music. There was a lot of competition for us. I had to go on that stage with four guys after these big, beautiful orchestras were playing.

We hung out with them. Most entertainers are pretty nice people. And we, being there all summer, we told them where to go for dinner in Atlantic City, if they weren't familiar with the area. There was Count Basie; Frank Sinatra, Jr. came up with a

Between 1932 and 1939 Rudy Vallee appeared thirteen times.

EASTER APRIL-17-1949
HESS
9002-3

Harry James plays Easter 1949. The large neon American flag above the stage now hangs in Baltimore's Lexington Market.

full band; there was the Glenn Miller Band; and Duke Ellington — a lot of big bands. I had worked with Louis Jordan, the Ink Spots, Red Norvo and the Mills Brothers in Somers Point years before.

We played the Pier from 8 until midnight, because people only danced at night by then. We would play forty minutes, take a ten-minute break, come back for a half-hour and then introduce the big band. The band would do two shows and we would do four. We came after them and played to midnight.

The Diving Horse last dove at 11 or so. They had all kind of lights out there. That was a big thing. I had to wait for that damn horse to hit the water. Once he hit the water, we had to start playing anything loud, so that the people who were coming from that end of the Pier would come through the Ballroom. We wanted them to stop and dance and enjoy themselves, because there wasn't much left after the dancing.

One person I remember working on the Pier when I was in the Ballroom was Tiny Tim. What a mess! They had a lot of good acts, though, and they bought them at a pretty good price, too. Everybody wanted to work Steel Pier. The condition of the Pier was very good. It was still in good shape and everything was up-to-date.

❦ ❦ ❦ ❦

When the Marine Ballroom burned down in December 1969 and was replaced by the gold-colored geodesic Dome, Ed Davis added this opinion: "When they added the Dome after the Ballroom burned, it was never the same. The acoustics in the Ballroom were just about perfect. And the Dome just didn't have it at all."

Nevertheless, the few big bands that remained still toured, including Ted Weems, who returned in 1970. He had first played the Pier back in 1925.

Tenor saxman Dick Hafer, in the book *Woody Herman — Chronicles of the Herds*, relates another last hurrah by one of the classic band leaders on the Pier: "In 1970, I was working the Merv Griffin Show, and I took my wife and kids down to Atlantic City. We were driving along the Expressway and we saw this sign at Steel Pier, 'WOODY HERMAN.' My wife said, 'Oh, no, you're going to be going out with Woody all the time!'

"So we went out on the Pier that night to hear the band, and he was in a strange mood. He really had sort of a rock band by then. To me it was. There were a lot of people there who were bugging him about playing our hits like 'Apple Honey' and all those tunes that they associated with him. He got salty with the audience and said, 'Where were ya when I needed ya?' You know, he always told people off if they got on him about anything."

❦ ❦ ❦ ❦

For the entire 1972 and 1973 seasons, the Pier featured the "World Famous Steel Pier Band," a sixteen-piece orchestra that played the sounds of Goodman, Miller and James, and was led by Frankie Lester. Lester was a vocalist who had sung with Tommy Dorsey, Buddy Morrow and Hal McIntyre, and was acting leader of the Billy May Orchestra from 1958 to 1968. Lester and the band performed a forty-five-minute big band show at 8 every night in the Midway Theater.

When the big bands era had at last passed on, George Hamid, Jr. told *Atlantic City* magazine, "I don't think I'm sentimental when I say that I never met a distempered band leader. Even Artie Shaw, who we had on the Million Dollar Pier, was always on time and always tried to please his audiences.

"We had bands until we closed the Pier. As late as 1970, Louis Armstrong was supposed to play for us and we had his contract, but he died before the date came up. There were some tremendous bands by that late date who were very popular, and we played them all. You have to remember, we had a Ballroom, and we had a lot of mature audiences, and the mature audiences loved their big bands. In the Ballroom, we had far more big bands than we had big acts."

Gene Krupa played the Pier twenty-two times from 1938 to 1967. Sammy Kaye was second in appearances, playing sixteen times. Benny Goodman played fourteen dates over the years.

"Big bands were the thing in those days," said George Hamid, Jr. "Big acts didn't mean much. People wanted the big bands. We set all kinds of records with Glenn Miller and Vaughn Monroe when we had the Million Dollar Pier with GAC (General Artist Corporation) bands. Steel Pier had the MCA (Music Corporation of America) bands, which was Goodman, Tommy Dorsey.

"Steel Pier was the magic name."

STEEL PIER MAGAZINE

Steel Pier High
Diving Horses
One of the
20 WORLD FAMOUS ATTRACTIONS

Chapter Nine

World Famous Diving Horses

It wasn't just an icon of Steel Pier — it was the *premier* icon of Atlantic City: the image of a woman on a horse, bareback ... the horse appearing to fly through the air, its legs stretched out in a downward plunge.

It was one of the longest-running acts in show business history, lasting over eighty years, and it was really quite simple. A horse would be led by a handler up an incline ramp until it reached the top — as high as sixty feet above the Pier for some dives — where a female rider in a bathing suit would be waiting. She would climb on and then the horse, when it was ready, would suddenly "dive" into a large pool of water waiting below. That was it. But it really was much more than just that. People who witnessed it in person have never forgotten it, even to this day.

But how did this incredible act develop? The story begins in the Midwest with a man named William Frank Carver.

According to his biography from the Trapshooting Hall of Fame, Carver was known for making outrageous claims that would shock people — until they saw him live up to them.

Born in Winslow, Ilinois on May 7, 1851, Carver had studied dentistry and so received the nickname "Doc". In his travels he lived with Indians who refered to him as "evil spirit of the plains", and became friends with both Buffalo Bill Cody and Wild Bill Hickock. By 1880, he was a renowned marksman, winning a fortune and setting records in shooting exhibitions in the United States and Europe.

It was during extensive travels around 1881 that Carver found the inspiration for the act that would

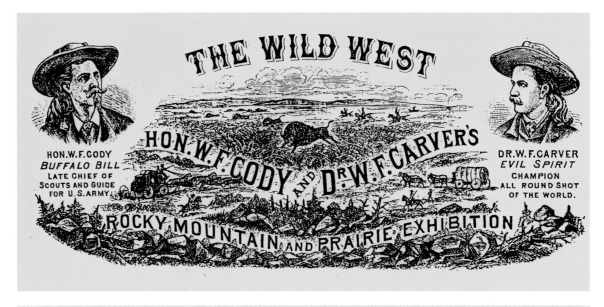

W. F. "Doc" Carver set world records as a skilled marksman and exhibited his talents in the 1880s touring in a Wild West show that he opened with "Buffalo Bill' Cody. When Cody resumed his drinking habit, Carver toured Europe alone with a shooting exhibition.

become his trademark. As the story goes, Carver, on horseback, approached the Platte River in Nebraska, where a storm had badly damaged an old, rickety bridge. As he attempted to cross, the bridge collapsed and his horse was forced to dive into the water approximately forty feet below. The idea for a diving horse act was born. Because shooting exhibitions took up most of his time, Carver didn't have time to perfect his act until about 1905.

An excellent animal trainer, Carver began presenting exhibitions of various animals around 1902 along with his diving horse show (and, remarkably, even a diving elk) at state fairs and carnivals. The diving tower in the early years was a dangerous structure. It was not built of the best materials, and was tall and narrow without much support. In early 1907, "The Great Carver Show" opened the new Electric Park in San Antonio, Texas, charging the public fifty cents to see the five high-diving horses. But on February 17, tragedy struck as eighteen-year-old Oscar Smith was killed during a horse dive into the park's pond. Despite this, the show continued to travel with the diving horses as the main attraction at the Wyoming State Fair in 1910.

Riders came and went. Men and women dove with the horses, but

eventually Carver decided that only young women should become riders for the act. His daughter Lorena was the first female diver and another, Sonora Webster, even became part of the family. Sonora joined the show in Savannah, Georgia in 1924 and her sister, Arnette, became a rider in 1929.

Carver originally thought that Sonora was too small for the task and gave her a job as a stable hand instead. But she persisted and the role of the female rider became a tradition.

ℭ ℭ ℭ ℭ

Sonora Webster was born February 2, 1904 and grew up in Waycross, Georgia. In 1924, when she was twenty, her mother suggested she answer a newspaper advertisement for a woman who could swim and ride horses, and was willing to travel.

"I didn't go at first," she said. "I thought show people wore too much makeup and talked too loudly."

But she finally applied, first diving with a horse from a twelve-foot platform in Durham, North Carolina. Before long, she was diving from sixty feet and touring the country.

"Doc" Carver a few years before his death in 1927, at age seventy-six.

"I was so thrilled afterward of that first dive that instead of being self-conscious, I just threw both arms into the air and gave a big bow and smiled like a Cheshire cat," Sonora explained. "I was so proud of myself!"

"What impressed me was how Dr. Carver cared for the horses," her sister, Arnette (Webster) French, told the *New York Times* years later. "Wherever we went, the ASPCA was always snooping around, trying to find if we were doing anything that was cruel to animals. They never found anything because those horses lived the life of Riley. In all the years of the act, there was never a horse that was injured."

Diving with a horse named John the Baptist, Arnette remembered: "He did a corkscrew dive and would lie in the water — you'd swear he was drowning. Then he'd fly out of the pool! He pulled it on every new rider.

"The challenge of the riders was to remember to keep your head tucked down to one side, so that when the horse raised his head as he jumped up at the bottom of the pool, you wouldn't get smacked in the face."

"Doc" Carver died on August 31, 1927, at age seventy-six. Until then, he managed two shows, one on the east coast with Sonora as the featured diver, and one on the west coast with Arnette. Son Al and then daughter Lorena took over and managed the act.

Sonora and Al married in 1928.

❦ ❦ ❦ ❦

In 1928, Frank Gravatt's Steel Pier didn't advertise the diving horses. Instead, they featured the Hawaiian High Divers and Swimmers, who performed seven times daily at the Pier's ocean end. This was actually the beginning of the Water Circus, though a stage and seating area were yet to be built. Patrons would venture behind the Marine Ballroom, where the Pier ended, to view a 100-foot tower from which the Hawaiians dove.

Sometimes nearby swimmers happened into the Pier area — some more fortunately than others. On August 5, 1928, Helen Kinsella, nineteen, of Wilkes-Barre, Pennsylvania, was swimming around the Pier with another girl when she suddenly threw up her hands and screamed for help. Luckily, John Kanano, a Hawaiian

A rare view of the Water Circus end of the Pier during the period of 1945 through 1953 when the Diving Horse act was not featured.

high diver, was just preparing to plunge into the water as part of the daily exhibitions given on the Pier. Kanano grabbed a nearby rope and dove to the girl, who was by then then being tossed dangerously against the pilings of the Pier. He tied the rope to her and she was pulled up to safety.

The story of how the Diving Horse act became a part of Steel Pier, according to James Hamid, is attributed to his grandfather. Always on the lookout for exotic acts, George Hamid was Gravatt's booking agent at the time he saw the act in the midwest and convinced Gravatt to book it for the Pier.

"An agent by the name of Jacobs sold a Diving Horse act to Steel Pier with the understanding that the horse would dive into the ocean. The act was in California, and when it came to Atlantic City, the owner said it would be necessary to build a tank, as the horse could not dive

into the ocean. So at the expense of $35,000, an addition was added to the ocean end of the Pier so that the horse could dive into the tank and other sensational acts could be put on," the *Atlantic City Press* recounted in a 1941 feature story.

In 1929, the Water Circus area was completed in back of the Ballroom, extending the Pier out a few hundred feet. There was a huge gap from the seating area, which held thousands, to the stage area, allowing patrons an open view to watch the speedboat acts. A large array of lights allowed the area to be illuminated for performances to continue in the evening.

The Steel Pier Water Circus was owned and directed by retired Navy Lt. Commander Frank W. Sterling when the novelty of the Diving Horse first made its appearance in Atlantic City. An advertisement in the June 12, 1929 *Press* set the scene: "See the Greatest Act of its Kind

Ever Presented to the Public — Dr. Carver's Diving Horses. World's only diving horses who leap with a girl rider sixty feet into an eleven-foot tank. A thrilling and daring act you will long remember."

Another ad, from July 15, described it even more colorfully: "The world's only act of its kind — Another great thrilling and daring act — the only act where the life of a human being is left to the intelligence of dumb animals. Three times daily."

Arnette Webster was only sixteen in 1929, the first year she dove on Steel Pier. She would shortly meet Jake French, nicknamed "Frenchy," who was the chief boat and motors maintenance man and driver for the Water Circus, as well as manager of the Pier's boat rental concession. They would marry in 1934.

For the Diving Horse act, Gravatt built the diving platform so the horse would jump facing the audience. Yet it was not an ideal presentation. "We told him that it would be better to have them jump so the audience could see it from the side, in profile," said Arnette. "After the first year, he was convinced we were right, and he tore down the whole ramp and everything to change it around. It might have cost him $25,000 or maybe more, I'm not sure. But he didn't spare any expense. He wanted the best of entertainment — the best he could offer.

"Gravatt also wanted the horse to dive into the open ocean, but we told him it wasn't a good idea. They had been doing that in California, until one horse dove, got confused, and instead of swimming back to the beach, began heading out to sea and drowned. After he heard that story, Gravatt had a diving pool built for the jumps."

Quarter Horses were used because they were smaller than Thoroughbreds. There was a white Arabian, John the Baptist, and a pinto horse named Red Lips, and Scheherazade, who couldn't swim that well. Klatawa, which means "so long" in the Chinook language (Indian), was a show-off who loved big crowds, pawing and tossing his head for them but sulking if it was rainy and the audience was small. He once backed all the way down the ramp when he didn't feel like jumping.

The act wasn't cruel to the horses because most of them liked to jump. You couldn't force them. You had to wait until the horse was ready to jump, Arnette claimed in the *New York Times* in 1997. *"Once you were on the horse, there really wasn't much to do but hold on. The horse was in charge.*

"I remember when people would come to the Pier in fur coats and

Diving Horse. As we took our seats, the horse, with a girl named Arnette Webster (clad in a rubber wetsuit) on its back, was about to jump from a platform roughly forty feet high into a pool. I recall staring at the odd sight of a horse standing as calmly as you please on a platform above a pool just like the kind I swam in [as a kid]. To a recorded drum roll and cymbal crash, Webster urged the horse forward, and the two fell through space, to make the biggest splash I'd ever seen! Wow! And then both the horse and rider surfaced, though for the life of me, I can't recall how they got out of the pool."

The horses, of course, were also afforded celebrity status. Before and after each dive, patrons could visit with the horses in their quarters.

🌙 🌙 🌙

Life was great on Steel Pier for the riders of the Diving Horse act, even though the 1929 stock market crash had thrown the nation into the Depression. Sonora and Arnette had both met their prospective husbands on the Pier, and they fully enjoyed their summer days around the horses and their co-workers. So it was a shock to Sonora Carver when the summer of 1931 turned her life upside-down.

The safety and care for the horses had always been a priority. Yet the girls, in those early years, wore no protective equipment. They

(Opposite) Beginning in 1928, Hawaiian Divers performed their acrobatics from a 100-foot tower located near the end of the Pier. (Above) The Marine Stadium Water Circus grandstand, holding thousands, was built next to the back of the Marine Ballroom and faced out to sea.

stand under umbrellas in the rain and want to see the show. Usually, we did it. It was a lot of fun. It was like getting paid for a vacation. It was a thrill. People would say, 'Oh, there's the girl who rides the Diving Horse.'

"We were the stars of the Boardwalk. Everybody had to see the Diving Horse. That was what everybody remembered. We were a class act."

Customer John B. Abbott was among the thousands who were dazzled: "I remember anxiously getting bleacher seats to see the entered the pool wearing a wetsuit and a bathing cap, but no goggles or helmet. One day, as Sonora rode on the back of Red Lips, the horse entered the water off balance.

Sonora "was fascinated by the horse's shadow and hit the water with her eyes open," Arnette remembered. Sonora emerged from the water and found her vision blurred.

"The doctor said it would clear up in a few days," said Arnette.

But it didn't. The force of the water hitting Sonora's face proved too much and within a period of time, the retinas in both eyes slowly detached. An operation was unsuccessful, and Sonora's loss of sight was irreversible.

"My Aunt Sonora was blinded but it didn't occur entirely immediately, but over a passing of days and weeks," recalled M. F. French, Sonora's nephew.

A large crowd watches the Hawaiian Divers in action. Note the cannon on the left, used in the Human Cannonball act.

By spring 1932, however, Sonora was diving with the horses again as though nothing had ever happened. And as far as the public knew, nothing had happened. The accident had been cloaked in secrecy because that's what Sonora wanted. She didn't want any sympathy because she was blind, and she didn't want anyone worrying about her or the horses. Diving had been her life, and it was going to continue that way.

"I didn't want to make mattresses or cane chairs," she told the Press of Atlantic City years later. "I thought, 'My goodness, I've been diving for eight years. I know every move of the horse.'" As far as she was concerned, "diving blind felt exactly the same as diving with sight." By the sound of the horse's hooves, Sonora knew just where the horse was as it climbed the wooden ramp. When it reached the top, she climbed on. After the dive, she clung to the horse's bridle while they both got out of the pool to the applause of the audience. She would bow, then take the groom's hand as he led her and the horse off the platform.

Eventually her secret came out as she continued to dive in places outside Atlantic City, traveling throughout the states, Cuba and Canada. At one point, she was dubbed the "Blind Venus" by Cuban fans.

Sonora dove with the horses on Steel Pier until 1942, ten of those years blind. She figured she was there by choice and never resented

In 1931 Olympic swimmer and future "Tarzan" Johnny Weismuller (left), along with Stubby Krueger, were early divers at Steel Pier.

summer five of us, calling ourselves The Diving Collegians, joined the famous Steel Pier Water Circus.

My horse, Gordon [Gordonelle], was a real diver and always let me control when to go. How beautiful she looked, running up the long steep ramp with the ocean and sky as a backdrop.

As we entered the water after the dive, I'd duck down and slide along the left side of her sleek neck. ...

There was an underwater ramp at the far end, and with me still on her back, Gordon would climb up and out, sloshing water all over the deck. I would raise my arms and give a big wave to the audience for both of us. It was a golden time, a magical time in my life. You didn't think about it, you just did it, and hoped the horse would cooperate.

❧ ❧ ❧ ❧

Josephine married Martin DeAngelis, a beach lifeguard, and never left Atlantic City. She worked on the Pier with Sonora Carver until 1942.

The *Atlantic City Press* gave its readers some background on the Diving Horse act in June 1936:

Doc Carver's daughter Lorena trains and owns all of the horses. She said that it takes an average of three years required to train a naturally talented horse. Gordonel, however, one of three she now trains, learned so rapidly that he was with a rider after thirty-two days. John the Baptist is 27 years old and is eager as ever for his daily stunts before applauding throngs.

The horses are trained and kept in the winter at Carver's ranch in Quakertown, Pennsylvania, while new horses are raised at her other ranch in California. The present tank is twelve feet deep. She herself made the highest horse-and-rider dive ever recorded, seventy-two feet, to make good a wager her father had contracted with a skeptic."

the Pier for her accident.

After her career, she moved to New Orleans. Having learned to read Braille, she found employment as a transcriptionist for a Louisiana hospital. Fiercely independent, she became active with the Lighthouse for the Blind organization and traveled extensively.

❧ ❧ ❧ ❧

Josephine Knox came to the Pier in 1935 with an impressive diving and swimming resume. She had been training for the 1936 Olympics and had performed in Chicago. She told her story to the *Philadelphia Inquirer* in 1998:

After diving at the Chicago World's Fair in 1934, the following

This view from the crowd, circa 1930, shows the lower training ramp. Interestingly, the riders didn't wear helmets until the 1950s.

In 1936, my sister Grace, who was sixteen at the time, was one of the riders of the high diving horses," Marjorie Otton recalled for The Press *in 1991. "Her big, handsome white horse was named John the Baptist and on July 4, she made her first dive on John's back before a standing-room-only crowd on the Pier. Was I ever proud! I sat in the grandstand with my mother and younger sister, proclaiming, 'That's my sister up there!' But folks didn't believe me.*

𝕮 𝕮 𝕮 𝕮

From 1942 through 1945, most of the Boardwalk hotels were filled with soldiers in training during World War II. Family diversions suffered, as well as attendance at Steel Pier.

"As soon as the war started, the people seemed to vanish," Arnette French explained. "It wasn't like that all the time, but the crowds fell off. You'd get times when you felt Atlantic City had become a ghost town. As the years went on, they had blackouts on the Boardwalk, and you couldn't see much unless there was a full moon. In 1944, there was some serious thinking about packing up the Diving Horse and taking it out of Atlantic City for good. That didn't happen, but that they reached the point that it was an idea suggests how dead things were."

But the reality was that in 1945 the act was closed due to a scarcity of workers. There would be no Diving Horses on Steel Pier for eight years. What had been the biggest act since 1929 was no longer.

When George Hamid bought the Pier in 1945, he had a Water Circus … barely.

"There were no Diving Horses when we bought it," said George Hamid, Jr. Not only that, there wasn't even the end of the Pier where the Water Circus had existed. "We had to put the end back on it."

That was because the Hurricane of Septem-

John the Baptist with Marie taking the plunge.

ber 1944 was the most damaging coastal storm since Steel Pier had existed.

During this period of inactivity, the horses John the Baptist and Gordonelle were retired.

In 1953, Lorena Carver was back and so was the act. After the eight-year drought, a new generation could watch with amazement the sight of a horse in midair. One of the new horses was named Dimah — "Hamid" spelled backward. Diver Marion Hackney began her long career when the act resumed, and she stayed thirteen years, retiring in 1966.

Another rider was Marion Lisehora, who rode from 1953 to 1956. She was hired after graduating from the University of Maryland, as was her husband, a veterinary school student. She remembered her start in a *Pittsburgh Tribune-Review* article... "There'd been a thing in *Life* magazine about the horses that spring, and I read it and thought, 'Ooh.' Then, I was up there working with these people who were actually diving on the horses. One of them left abruptly to get married and they needed another diver. I was the only woman that year in the springboard diving act, and they turned to me and said, 'Would you like to do this?' 'Yeah, I could do that.'"

Lisehora went straight to performing, without a practice run. For her first dive, her husband walked the horse up the ramp to meet her at the top of the platform because the diver who had left to get married had eloped with the trainer.

"My husband said I was as white as a ghost. I'd been told under no circumstances do you let go of the horse. He hit the water and I came off him and I swam out beside him. To the audience it looked fine. That was one of the few times I came off the horse. But I got scared."

But her trepidation soon vanished. Her favorite horse was Dimah.

"I loved him to death," Lisehora said. "He was a beautiful diver and he was by far our favorite."

She still has a small scar on her left thumb due to Dimah entering the water awkwardly and rolling against the pool bottom, scraping her hand.

"But I did the next show," she said. "That was the worst

(Top) Horses and performers pose at the lobby entrance. Steel Pier owner Frank Gravatt is on the far left in the high boots, the rider on the left is Arnette Webster French, and Al Carver is holding the horse on the right. (Bottom) Gravatt greets John Philip Sousa as Marie holds John the Baptist. (Opposite page) The same group posing alongside their reflections in the diving pool.

injury."

She finished that Steel Pier season and four more, and then performed the act in Miami in the summer of 1957.

❧ ❧ ❧ ❧

The ringmaster and master of ceremonies of the Water Circus from 1936 until 1965 was Jack Montez, who fit the role perfectly.

"One cannot recall the Diving Horse and Water Circus without mentioning Jack Montez, the outstanding MC, whose booming voice could sometimes be heard on the Boardwalk, a half-mile away," remembered one patron, Jerry Toplin. "I don't know how many years he held the job, but I remember him from when I was a little kid."

"Jack Montez was the most charismatic showman and host of the Water Sports show," said another from the audience, Henry Weiss. "On more than a few occasions, the reason for our return to the ocean end of the Pier to a show we had seen often and knew by heart, was specifically to watch Montez — in his dapper dress and ever present captain's hat — in action! He wore a navy blue jacket and white trousers."

The view from the top of the diving platform.

Rick Ackerman, a fan, recalled how Montez pumped up the Water Circus' closing act:

The Diving Horse was the finale to the Water Circus. They gave it about a ten-minute build-up. As the horse was ascending the ramp, the announcer would tell you that the horses were trained to do the jump safely, and that once they had reached the top of the tower, they would dive when they were ready. The announcer also said that the horse loved an audience, and suggested the crowd wait till it got out of the tank and back on the deck before applauding. The horse usually looked pretty nervous when they reached the diving platform, but as I understand it, they loved to do the dive and actually had to be restrained for just a moment, so as to let the suspense build.

The announcer, Captain Jack, would say, 'When the horse puts his front hooves over the front edge of the platform, don't take your eyes off him, because that will signal that he's about to dive.' Waiting below, on the wooden platform at the rim of the tank, were his trainers — a

husband and wife team though it was always the woman who stood at the edge during the act. She always wore a raincoat and boots and supposedly had a carrot or two in her pocket.

The horse would then leap into the tank, which was about thirty to forty feet in diameter and maybe twelve to fourteen feet deep. It was an aboveground metal pool. The jump itself was pretty exciting. The horse in mid-air was a thing of beauty, and the splash it made when it hit the water was enormous. Finally, the horse and rider would emerge from the tank via a ramp inside it. They would come up to the deck beside it, dripping wet, and the crowd would go wild.

☾ ☾ ☾ ☾

Another customer remembers the World Famous Diving Horses and the act that followed, the Diving Jackasses, as they were in 1952:

The rest of the day was filled with exciting sideshow acts, such as Mr. Johnson's Boxing Cats, Elsie the Cow and her son Beauregard, and Captain Kelly and his sea lions. Best of all was Dimah the Diving Horse.

The announcer called our attention to the small water tank: "Ladies and gentlemen, Dimah the Wonder Horse is going to dive into this small tank of water. Her rider, Miss Olive Gelnaw, will guide Dimah during her forty-foot drop into the tank. Now we need you to be very quiet. It takes all of her concentration to get it right, or they will miss the tank and fall to their death in the ocean."

The crowd grew silent. Dimah, standing at the bottom of the ramp, was released from her trainer and trotted up the long ramp to the top of the diving platform and her awaiting rider. Miss Gelnaw, standing on a side railing, sprung effortlessly over to the filly's back, landing just behind the harness. She took hold of the leather strap cinched up around Dimah's huge girth before making the big jump.

We held our breath as the filly walked to the edge of the platform and looked out over the crowd. Just then, a sea gull flew by, catching her attention. She lifted her head and sniffed the air, curling her upper lip over her nose. It looked as if she were smiling at us. In a blink of an eye, she slid her two front legs down the ramp and jumped off the platform. Down she came!

Sp-lash! Most of the water in the tank came rushing up in a huge wave, spilling over the sides of the tank, leaving it less than half full. The crowd went wild!

Olympic swimmer Johnny Weismuller helps out a diver in a bit of comic diving in 1929. A few years later, Weismuller would become a star portraying Tarzan in the movies.

The water show ended with the "Diving Jackasses." Two men, dressed in old-fashioned bathing suits, climbed up a ladder to the top of the diving platform and announced that they were going to do a dive better than Dimah. The fat man was going to play the part of Dimah and the skinny fellow was going to be the rider. We all laughed and booed them, saying they couldn't do it. The announcer gave them a count. On the count of three, the fat man dove off the platform, leaving the other man behind. "Hey, dummy, you forgot me!" he hollered to the fat man below in the tank. The fat man climbed back up the ladder complaining all the way, telling the crowd, "And they call ME the Jackass! Why, he can't even count!"

🎵 🎵 🎵 🎵

The clowns in that act were skilled, professional divers who did a number of acrobatic high dives earlier in the show, recalled customer Nancy Molinari.

"During the clowning dives, we would always wait, year after year, for the one clown to jump on the back of the other and dive off the Pier while the MC would announce, 'And there go the diving jackasses.'

Red Lips, Sonora and her seeing-eye dog after the accident.

future wife, Sarah Detwiler, the second summer she was a diver with the horses. During a 2004 interview, she looked back fondly at those times:

My grandparents lived offshore and I was up around Steel Pier, and I made an acquaintance with the groom who took care of the horses. I was very positive on why I would be a good choice to dive. To me, it seemed like a good summer job. So before I left to go back to college in Florida, I sent a note to the groom and he gave it to Lorena Carver ... I had been doing water ballet down at the University, and the horses intrigued me. I finally received a letter from her and told her that I would come up. I looked over the facility and met Lorena Carver and she said, "I know you can do this." No preparation at all. Went right up to the top and wondered if I was going to make it, if I would live. I was a little nervous about it, but I did the dive.

I didn't regret that I was doing it, but it was a little scary at first. I was never afraid or had a fear of horses, heights or diving. This was in the late 1950s and I was only eighteen years old.

There were at least four horses that would dive every day, but Dimah was my favorite. He would hesitate before he dove, and his head would bob up and down.

I can still remember Jack Montez saying, "Ladies and gentlemen, prepare yourselves for the thrill of a lifetime. We present the Carver Steel Pier High Diving Horse!" There was recorded music for all those acts.

I would go up first and the horse followed me. The groom would send the horse up the ramps by itself. The trainer was introduced first,

The show was never complete without that line."

The late Gene Hart, former "Voice of the (Philadelphia) Flyers" hockey team, was very familiar with Steel Pier. His father, Charlie, worked as a talent scout on the Pier, managed the Water Circus and was also a producer in New York. As a roly-poly ten-year-old, Gene became a member of the Diving Hawaiians in the early 1940s. His father then gave him the job of stagehand and comedy diver, where he became well known for his pranks. Hart also filled in as master of ceremonies for Jack Montez at times, gaining experience for his future Philadelphia Flyers Hall of Fame career as a sportscaster. He met his then the rider on the stage, then I'd quickly put the helmet on, got ready and ran right up there as soon as I could. Then the horse was introduced on the stage and he would follow. And I'd be up there ready.

My father-in-law invented an elevator for the horse later on. I had a ladder instead of running up the ramps. There was a little platform there with sides on it and a place for me to sit. Hanging from that was a six-foot incline, sort of like a diving board, and it put the horse on an angle. The horse would slide with his front two legs and then kick off. Because the horse would be on the angle, he would usually do a perfect dive.

They went when they were ready. I can't say the groom would not try to encourage the horse a little bit by gently nudging or pushing, but he wouldn't dare do anything drastic. That would have upset me to no end. I wouldn't want to be on a horse that was agitated. My life depended on that horse doing that in a calm way, so there was no electrical devices or trap doors or anything like that during my time.

Lorga (another diving horse) did take a long time. I remember Lorena Carver saying "Come," with carrots in her hand. But you waited. Sometimes it was five minutes.

I had a horse named Gamal that would run up there and you were lucky you got on the horse. A couple times I was just barely on and I had to really be quick acting to get my position and hold on. We had little side handles and a

In the early '60s a short-lived elevator replaced the ramp; audiences much preferred seeing and hearing the horse clip-clopping up the ramp to the waiting rider.

Dapper Jack Montez was the Water Circus MC from 1936 until 1965.

of the horse like a saddle, but not that far back. I would be seated in back of that roll, which looked like the horse had a collar on. Then it had these two leather horizontal straps large enough for your hands to grab them, so I was holding on to this. Otherwise, it was up to me to use my legs. And the reason for that roll and those handles was so that I wouldn't go over the horse's head.

The horse would hang there for a little while before kicking off. My job was to use my timing correctly and tuck in there real tight by his neck and tuck my chin down, and ride as close as I could to the horse.

And then if the horse would go down in a way maybe a little too steep, that horse would roll, and then I would be under him. That's when you get hurt because there's thrashing legs.

The tank was between ten and fifteen feet deep and about twenty feet across, not really large. It wasn't real deep but was lined with foam rubber with a silver, tough-type of material, so when the horse hits, he hits soft. The water was ample enough to break the speed and the weight. There was a very tough fiber matting for the incline for the horse to walk out of, and water never affected it.

I would ride the horse until he got out of the tank. Lorena Carver would be standing on the stage of the tank and the horse knew to go to her, get his reward, and the blanket was thrown on quickly. That was the end of the act.

You [the customers] could go in the stalls, along the walkway towards the end of the Pier and in front of the Ballroom, and see the horses through glass panels and how they were kept and fed. They were very well kept. They would ride the horses on the beach in the morning and they loved to go in the water and run along the waves.

We didn't keep them if they didn't like the water. I would have noticed if there had been anything unkind because I love animals. They were never in any way hurt or disrespected. In fact, they were taken care of better than the riders were! The ASPCA gave us plaques of approval that were always on the dressing room wall. When Gene was in the show with me he'd bring me a towel, but the horse was the one that got the blanket! The horse was the star.

People were amazed that a horse could dive forty feet and wanted to see it. Sammy Kaye, Frankie Laine, Vic Damone, the Four Seasons and a lot of the bandleaders would come out there to watch.

harness. There was no stirrup; I was bareback. I used my knees to keep my weight back, so when we hung there momentarily, I wouldn't slip over the head. That would have been disastrous. That happened once in training and it was a miracle I didn't get a scratch.

There was a thick roll of some kind of rubber padding that was somehow connected to this leather that was strapped under the belly

Don French has family ties to the Steel Pier Diving Horse act and he shared his story on the *iloveac.com* web site in 2003:

In 1957, at the age of 14, I had the unusual opportunity of living on Steel Pier for the summer. My mother, Arnette French, and her sister, Sonora Carver, were both former diving horse riders in the '20s and '30s. In 1957, the trainer of the horses, Lorena Carver, who was a good friend of my mother's, had a position of groom open, and through my mother, offered it to me. Naturally, I jumped at the chance.

Actually, I knew nothing about horses.

I was soon living in a small room at the end of the stables on the Pier, almost directly across from the Diving Bell. The head groom, whose name escapes me, taught me all I had to know, especially how to avoid being bit or kicked, which happened frequently during the first couple of weeks.

I was soon mucking out stables and grooming three horses. After awhile, I was allowed to walk the horses to the end of the Pier for the show, and boy! Did I like that! I would take the horse to the bottom of the ramp, remove the halter, and the horse did the rest. Dimah was a real ham. He would stand at the top and observe the crowd, paw a little, and pretty much go when he damn well pleased.

I thought that I was going to be a big hit with the girls, but I pretty much smelled like a horse for the entire summer.

Some of the best times were after the Pier closed and everything was dark and quiet. I would stand by the rail and look out over the water and feel as if I was the only person alive in the world.

I could not think of a better place to spend a childhood.

Trained porpoises joined the Water Circus in 1958, adding a bit of aquatic sea life to the comedy divers, Collegiate Divers and high wire acts. In the early 1960s, the Diving Horse took to the road in the fall, headlining at the Trenton State Fair and at sports shows in Washington, D.C. and Wheeling, West Virginia. It wasn't unusual for 60,000 people to attend these events to see the act.

Al Carver, the son of "Doc" Carver, died in 1960. A year later, Doubleday released a memoir by his wife, Sonora, titled *A Girl and Five Brave Horses*. It told her story of the Pier, the horses and her incredible spirit. "It was like flying," she wrote, describing the act. "It was exhila-

rating freedom."

The book and Sonora's story were later the genesis for a well-received 1991 Disney movie titled "Wild Hearts Can't Be Broken," with Gabrielle Anwar portraying Sonora and Cliff Robertson as the crotchety "Doc" Carver.

"The movie made a big deal about having the courage to go on riding after Sonora lost her sight," her sister, Arnette French, told the *New York Times* in 1997. "But the truth was, riding the horse was the most fun you could have and we just loved it so. We didn't want to give it up."

In 1961, Ann Eastham, a twenty-year-old sophomore at Florida State University, rode Dimah and gushed, "He loves jumping!"

"It takes three years to train a horse to dive," Lorena Carver related. "You can make a diver out of only one horse in twenty. It isn't the first plunge that makes a diving horse. It's the second. Lots of horses will jump into water — once. But only a few are eager to try it again.

"First, you have to teach them to walk up a ramp twenty feet high, to get them used to height. Then increase it to forty feet. After that, the dive.

"Dimah was a good pupil. Still, it took plenty of patient training to make him accomplish the feat."

It was actually easier to find horses willing to dive than it was to find girls to ride them.

"You're bound to be a little nervous," said diver Marion Hackney. "Naturally, you depend entirely on your horse, and you must be ready if he does something a bit unexpected."

But if you were the sort who liked to "steal the show," then climbing aboard a diving horse during the heyday of the act was the place for you.

"It was an integral part of Steel Pier operation — probably the most famous part of it," was James Hamid's opinion in a 1980 story in the *Press of Atlantic City*. "Jazz drummer Buddy Rich used to say that he'd have a ballroom full of people watching them set up, the announcement would be made that the horse was about to dive, then they'd be playing before no one."

Michael Brecker, a tenor saxophone player from Philadelphia, noticed the same thing in 1971. "I used to play gigs in Steel Pier, opposite the horse jumping into the water," he told *At the Shore* magazine years later. "We'd have to interrupt the show to watch the horse jump. They would light up a sign announcing when the horse would jump and everyone would go watch.

"One time, with jazz-rock group Dreams [August 1971], I was playing a solo with my eyes closed. And when I opened them, the audience was gone. For an instant, I thought it was my playing. But then I was informed by a band member that they had lit the jumping horse sign."

As for many others, for Steel Pier visitor Gwenn Embury it was the Diving Horse that made the biggest impression:

The High Diving Horses were always my favorite. I must have seen at least six of them over the years. They each had their own style of diving. One would wait a good five minutes before jumping. He would hold his head up and watch the sea gulls fly by. Some dove with their front legs straight out, while others tucked up their legs as if they were going over a jump. One horse would twist in the air and on his side, making it dangerous for his rider.

The riders — all women — would suffer one or two broken bones a year. Most of the injuries came from getting out of the way of paddling hooves. They made it look easy, but it wasn't. Years ago, a rider by the name of Sonora Carver went blind by an impact with the water. The jump was sixty feet at that time, but was then lowered to forty.

Another horse — I think his name was Patches — drew quite an audience. After making so many jumps, he no longer waited for his rider. He would charge up to the tower and take a running jump off the diving board, leaving the rider behind. A couple of the girls tried to leap on him as he flew by, only to be left sailing through the air mount-less. One day, he got up so much speed he almost overshot the pool. Needless to say, they retired him.

             ❦ ❦ ❦ ❦

Not every visitor, though, overflowed with admiration. "I was kind of disappointed the horse didn't jump, but *slid* down a long ramp into the water. But the anticipation was exciting, also the crowds that were there waiting for it to happen." Jackie Palermo told the *Press of Atlantic City* in 1991.

"When I think about seeing the Diving Horse as a little girl of five or six, what I remember most is seeing the horse frantically trying to back up as the front portion of the platform began to drop out beneath him," said spectator Gayle Eaves. "I think I knew, even then, that there was something about this that just wasn't right."

John the Baptist has just pushed off. Notice how tight the rider is holding on and how her head is tucked into the horse's shoulder.

Barbara Gallagher Gose recalls her first dive, which she did on impulse one summer with no training:

My husband was a diver in the water show for 11 years. One day in 1967, he came home and asked if I wanted to dive the horse on the Pier. Of course I said yes.

You had to wear a bathing suit, a bathing cap, and over the bathing cap a football helmet with a chin piece. I was all ready to make my first dive when this girl walked up to me. She had tried out before me and she had done it her own way. She hadn't fastened the helmet the way they told her. And it slipped over her eyes, and she couldn't see and hit her head against the horse. So she walked up to me, just ready to climb the ladder for the first time, and she had two black eyes and a concussion, and she said, "I wish you good luck. I'm the one who did it before you.

I don't think I had time to be scared.

When I first did it, I was excited. And the funny part was, there was no training. They took you to a stable and sat you on a horse, took you to the tower, and said, "Look down. Now do you still want to do it?

Lorena [Carver] didn't want me to do it. She had known me for years, and I had three children at the time, a housewife. But I just knew I wanted to do it. And it was perfect, with the exception of my bathing suit straps falling down from the impact. When I came up, everybody was kissing me and congratulating me. It was great!

I was never really fearful. Maybe if I had done it longer, I might have run into some situations, but I only did it for two summers.

I never did anything like that in my life and it gave me more guts than I thought I had.

Regarding the horses Gamal and Lorga, the latter had a reputation of being the Pier's slowest, sometimes taking as much as twenty-five minutes to make up its mind about diving.

"There was another horse," Gose recalled, "that was just the opposite. It was so anxious to dive, the girl couldn't get on fast enough. One time, she was just starting to get on and it dived off and left her standing there."

Gose's only close call came during her fourth dive. On the third dive, when the horse came up, its knees were bleeding. The other horse, Lorga, was back in the stable because the same thing had happened to it earlier.

The crew decided to clean the tank to see if something was wrong. The tank was built in sections so it could be taken apart to travel with the Hamid circuses during the winter months. It had a plastic lining inside, then a line of gravel bags around the edge to hold the plastic down. One of the gravel bags had opened and spilled, and the horses had been hitting their knees on the gravel.

They cleaned it out, but for the next dive, Lorga seemed to remember the gravel. With Barbara aboard, Lorga dove sideways to avoid hitting it. Gose landed on her side, taking the full impact of the dive. For the next half-hour, she couldn't move or feel anything on her right side.

"Lorena said I didn't have to go again, but I should go right again or I might not ever do it. So I went again, and the next dive was just beautiful."

The only dive she didn't like was the 11:15 P.M. show. "That was the only time I felt uncomfortable. I'd be tired and the tower would be weaving. It would be cold, and the ocean would be pitch black and the people would be looking up at you out of the darkness. That was always the worst one. I would always be up there hoping it would just be over."

☙ ☙ ☙ ☙

As George Hamid Jr.'s management of the Pier was nearing its end in 1974 and 1975, Shae Chandler was the main rider and Bobby Jones had become MC of the Water Circus. Hamid sold the Pier to a group of investors in 1973, who couldn't make a go of it after taking over Pier operations from Hamid in 1976. After three disappointing years, they sold the Pier to Resorts International.

The last Diving Horse rider to take the plunge was Terrie McDevitt. She started diving in 1976 at age seventeen. By 1978, after a concussion, broken toes and various bumps and bruises, she took the last plunge on Labor Day weekend — still loving it. the *Press of Atlantic City* featured her story in September 1988.

"I just wanted an usherette job," she said. But management, with a more important opening to fill, asked her instead to try diving from forty feet on the back of a horse.

That sounded just fine to her.

"I was only in high school and my friends were all working indoors.

I worked in a bathing suit and I had a suntan, and I was making a lot more than they were."

By the summer of 1978, McDevitt was diving five times a day, seven days a week, making $250 a week. Yet even then, that was certainly small compensation for the beating she took in her summer job that year.

"We had a new horse, a mare named Shiloh. She was trying to twist through the air, like she was fighting me. She just threw her head back and hit the top of my helmet with that hard bone of her forehead. I didn't come out of the water for a while. They went looking for me."

That last year of 1978, the Pier was devoid of nearly everything that had made it famous through its glory years. There was no Water Circus, no comic divers, no Russ Dotson and the Diving Collegians — only the horse. And they were asking for donations to keep the act going.

"You never know what the new owners will do," Owen Laurence, an Australian who had tended the horses since the late 1950s, remarked in the *Press*. "Everything changes, I suppose. The Pier has already changed a lot.

They (customers) are not so thrilled by the big-name personalities they bring to the Pier anymore. They see them on television anyway.

But, you know, even after we put a man on the moon, people are still fascinated with something as simple as a horse diving into a pool. They still want to see the Diving Horse when they come to Atlantic City. They come back again and again.

Maybe the horse here is the last big attraction we've got at the Pier. It seems worth staying open just to have it here. Who knows, we could be here next year. It's just hard to imagine the summer without being here at Steel Pier.

There's twice the excitement in this doctored publicity photograph of the diving horse Red Lips.

135

Ed Davis, longtime broadcaster on Steel Pier's WFPG, recalled the last season painfully. "In the last days of the act, it was just pitiful. My gosh, there were just a handful of people there, maybe fifty people. Before, I remember seeing the stands just packed with people, thousands, just standing there waiting. There was always a big fanfare and the MC would introduce the horse and rider by name. You could hear a pin drop. And then he'd dive.

"They were passing around a casino cup for money to buy oats for the horses. Just a smattering of applause. It was the end of an era. It was a news event because it was the last jump. It was sad."

"I saw the Diving Horse act many times," said Bes Hackney-McGee. "But in the '70s, before the demise of the Pier, it was so sad. The only act that appeared in the Water Circus was the Diving Horse. By that time, it was depressing even being near the Pier."

"The equipment was getting pretty shaky and the whole thing was looking very rundown," McDevitt described the scene a decade later for a retrospective story in *Philadelphia* magazine:

The Water Circus, which used to be the biggest thing on the Pier — the one thing you never missed when you

There were smaller crowds in the late '60s.

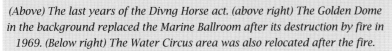

(Above) The last years of the Divng Horse act. (above right) The Golden Dome in the background replaced the Marine Ballroom after its destruction by fire in 1969. (Below right) The Water Circus area was also relocated after the fire.

were a kid — was gone. There weren't any amusements, nothing. It was just me and the horse. About to make our last dive — ever.

We opened a bottle of champagne before the act with the trainer and some people from the Pier. It got kind of sentimental and weepy. For me, it was the end of my childhood, or innocence. Diving with the horse was more than a summer job. When it ended, I was nineteen...

It was a gray day on the end of the Pier. Clouds, no sun, and the ocean was very rough. Only a few people showed up.

I was diving on Powder. There were two other horses, Amir and

Shiloh, but I wanted the last dive to be on Powder-face. He was the best. I hardly ever had a bad dive on Powder. Nine out of ten dives were nice and smooth ...

After a while, you get relaxed with it. You feel like nothing can go wrong, so you start to get loose with the horse. Then, all of a sudden, you'd get a bad dive and it was like landing on cement.

That last day, they announce me and I went out like always, in a damp bikini. I did my bow. Everybody applauded. When they announced it was the last dive — it got real quiet. I went up the ramp. No drumroll, because there wasn't a band. No divers, no clowns, no high-wire acts, no human cannonballs — just me and the horse.

Powder came right up the ramp. When he got to the top, I climbed on. I waited for him to decide when to go, like always. He took his time. He didn't want to go. It was cold up there, and he knew the water in the tank was freezing. He hated cold water and so did I.

Powder finally made up his mind. He put his hooves over the edge and down we went. It was perfect. A nice, smooth dive and a good, soft landing. When we climbed out of the tank there was plenty of applause. Everybody knew it was special. It was the last time anybody would ever see the act.

It was a little sad, you know, but it was a great dive.

🌙 🌙 🌙 🌙

The "New Steel Pier" opened on Memorial Day 1993 and featured a *donkey* — without a rider — plunging thirty feet into a twelve-foot tank of water. The act was an ignoble epilogue to what had once been a magical event, and it was neither novel nor popular. Pier owner Donald Trump, amid public complaints by animal rights activists,

Dimah and an unidentified rider (above); Marion Hackney and Dimah emerge from the water (opposite page).

asked manager Anthony Catanoso and his brothers to cancel the act after one season.

But "the more they picketed, the better the crowds were," said Catanoso. He called accusations of animal cruelty "outlandish" and said the animal was treated well.

❧ ❧ ❧ ❧

Gone are the brave and athletic young women divers. The most famous diver, Sonora Carver, returned from New Orleans to live out her life near Atlantic City and died in Pleasantville, New Jersey on September 20, 2003. She was ninety-nine years old.

"She was a legacy," Carver's nephew, Jerry French, told *The Press* a few days later. "She represented strength, courage, fearlessness, but also the fun of the times. She represented Atlantic City at the height of an era."

The Diving Horses will never return. The public and animal protection agencies would never permit such an act again. It has vanished into the memory of the thousands who were on hand to witness the spectacular World Famous Diving Horses on Steel Pier.

Chapter Ten

Wacky Stunts & Exhibits

S ome of the weirdest and wackiest stunts, objects, exhibits and people made their way through the front doors of Steel Pier throughout its long history. One never knew what to expect. But then, Atlantic City had always been the place to see all things unique and unusual.

In 1921 and for many years thereafter, you could see professional nurses watching over living babies in the Infant Incubators. This popular exhibit was on the Boardwalk opposite Million Dollar Pier, under the slogan "Everybody Loves the Babies."

Dupont, the creators of innovative textiles, and the Crane Company (plumbing fixtures) developed exhibits showcasing their products, and RCA Victor built an exhibit

The General Motors Exhibit faced the Boardwalk and displayed the
newest automobiles and appliances. It was open year round from 1925 to 1933, left, then returned from 1947 through 1968.

house right on the Boardwalk and Park Place in 1933 to show off the latest in phonographs.

The first promotional stunt on Steel Pier was as simple as holy matrimony. Mr. and Mrs. Haywood Bates were married on the Pier on July 4, 1898, only a few weeks after the Pier's grand opening. They received $10 in cash, a suite of furniture then valued at $35, and a set of dishes. Half a century later, George Hamid invited the couple to the Pier's fiftieth anniversary party in 1947, but Mrs. Bates had suffered a hip injury and the couple could not attend.

Because it had the most available space in the city, the Pier was the site of various conventions and meetings in the offseason. The Atlantic City High School Class of 1909 held its graduation ceremony in the Music Hall, which was at that time the name of the Ballroom at the Pier's end. Beginning in 1918, the Kennel Club of Atlantic City held annual dog shows in the Ballroom every April.

New cars line the lobby during the Ford Motor Company Exhibit circa 1936.

In May 1919, the second Pan-American Aeronautic Convention and Exposition rented the Pier. Members spent the month stunt flying and participating in aerial contests from the newly created Atlantic City Municipal Airport.

On November 30, 1922, the U.S. Weather Service opened a station on the Pier with instruments that could measure tide, temperature conditions and wave records. The station remained in use until 1969, when it was destroyed by the Marine Ballroom fire.

General Motors became the first big name to rent exhibit space on the Pier. Opening in 1926 and running until November 1933, GM exhibited its new line of automobiles and other products year-round from

a huge space in the front, overlooking the Boardwalk. Ford replaced General Motors shortly thereafter, showcasing the largest automobile show in the East.

In 1935, over one million people visited Ford in a modern, re-decorated exhibition hall that featured a completely equipped model service station.

There was also a display called "The Car in the Clouds," creating an optical illusion so that a full-sized Ford V-8 and a female model seemed to assume toy-like proportions.

"I was at the Ford Motor Co. Exhibit during the summer of 1936,"

An enormous crowd during Easter, 1933, converges on the beach to check out new General Motors vehicles.

Stanley Slome wrote on *ILoveAC.com* sixty-six years later. "At age 8, I enjoyed going to the Exhibit and getting behind the wheel of the new Lincoln Zephyr, both in the sedan and coupe models. Ford had a promotional movie theater film promoting its models. There were a lot of booklets about Ford models and we kids used to take a few, cut out the pictures of the cars we liked, to paste up in a scrapbook. It was lots of fun for Depression-era kids."

"It was in the mid-'30s and I usually stood in front of the Ford

Pauline Hill and urban redevelopment knocked down all the structures from Virginia Avenue to the Inlet and made what we called 'Pauline's Prairie', they were on the Inlet side of the Pier and all of a sudden, their attendance dropped in half. The result was that they left."

❅ ❅ ❅

Probably the most famous stunt was the appearance of Alvin "Shipwreck" Kelly during the summer of 1930.

Flagpole sitting had become a wacky national fad during the late 1920s, with people all over the country attempting to stay aloft on flagpoles for as long as possible. But no one could top "Shipwreck," who became a national celebrity.

"Employed as a professional stuntman in Hollywood, Kelly decided to attempt to sit on a flagpole in 1924, responding to a dare from a friend," reports the specialty web site *Badfads. com.* "He sat upon the pole for thirteen hours and thirteen minutes, and began a national spectacle and a

Nelson's Boxing Cats were a big attraction in 1934.

Exhibit," Jim Thomas recalled for author Russell LeVan's *Memories of Atlantic City, New Jersey.* "I was engulfed in a veritable sea of Palm Beach suits and Panama hats, and ladies in evening gowns. The grandeur, the finery, the slow strolling pace of the Boardwalkers is indelibly etched in my memory — and all this during the Great Depression."

Ford left during World War II but General Motors returned in 1947 and remained on Steel Pier until 1968. By that time, the GM showroom was the last remaining national exhibit in Atlantic City.

"They didn't renew their lease," explained George Hamid Jr. "When

career for himself."

It was reportedly his experience as a member of the *Titanic* lifeboat crew that earned Kelly the nickname of "Shipwreck." It was also reported that as a professional boxer, the ex-sailor had been decked so often that fans yelled, "Sailor Kelly has been shipwrecked again!"

On June 21, 1930, the thirty-eight-year-old Kelly ascended Steel Pier's 125-foot mast on the front of the Casino building. Seated only on a thirteen-inch padded disc made out of a car brake drum, Kelly would eat, sleep and even take a bath while perched on the pole. Kelly's wife,

Frances, along with three-year-old son Alvin Jr., visited him regularly by being pulled to the top of the mast in a bo'sn's chair.

Then on July 14, Kelly broke his own record of twenty-three days. He felt fine and had no intention of coming down, despite weathering three thunderstorms and a hailstorm. He had been putting on weight and cut out one meal a day. Kelly spent his time reading, writing, sleeping and reading fan mail, about 100 letters a day. He listened to the radio every night and also broadcast his experiences from his perch.

Finally, on August 8, Alvin "Shipwreck" Kelly descended at 4:13 P.M. after an incredible forty-nine days, a world record. In preparation for his descent, a pretty female barber went aloft and for an hour and a half gave him a haircut, manicure, and a liberal application of cologne while family, city officials and 20,000 people waited below on the Boardwalk.

He had some difficulty with the use of his feet when he landed, because he hadn't walked since June 21. Kelly shook hands and received a congratulatory telegram from Captain Jack Evans, a man whose own stunt had been to be buried alive for one week.

Kelly, paid $100 a day for the stunt, told reporters that he came down because "I missed my wife." An *Atlantic City Press* feature story, written a decade after the event, summarized Kelly's 1930 stunt on the Pier for owner Frank Gravatt:

"Shipwreck" Kelly came to the Pier with the idea of an endurance contest atop one of the Pier's poles. The compensation was based on the length of time he remained on the pole. His previous record was twenty-three days at Carlin's Park in Baltimore. It was believed he would stay up only a week, but it turned out he

The 100-foot aerialist stunt pole dwarfs the Diving Horse ramp, 1931.

Flagpole sitter Alvin "Shipwreck" Kelly drew big crowds throughout the United States during the Roaring Twenties. In 1930 he set a world record (forty-nine days) for flagpole sitting on the Steel Pier. He is seen here climbing the guide wires.

Aerialists such as the Wallendas often had to contend with sea breezes that could effect their precise movements; 1933

(Left) Comic acts like Spark Plug were entertainers in a makeshift costume. (Right) On this raised track, a human shares a bicycle ride with a real performing bear.

remained aloft seven weeks. If he had stayed up there many more weeks, his compensation would have been so high he would probably become the owner of the spot where he was working. When he came in to receive his check after this stunt, he asked Gravatt, "Who is crazy now, me or the fellow who made the contract?"

❦ ❦ ❦

Although most stunts were dangerous, they were contracted for the Pier with the assumption that the stunt person knew what he or she was doing. Sometimes, shocking accidents left the crowds aghast. The worst two happened in almost identical fashion, almost exactly a year apart.

On August 2, 1930, within sight of thousands of people on the Boardwalk and Steel Pier, parachute jumper Harry Powers was killed when he fell 1,500 feet from an airplane and slammed into the ocean. His regular 8 P.M. stunt, being shot from a cannon attached to the bottom of an airplane, had been a regular feature, and he had safely made the descent hundreds of times. As he jumped that last time, the crowd waited in vain for the parachute to open.

On July 30, 1931, Roy Forrest, thirty, who had obtained a job as a parachute stunt jumper only a week before, was flown in a plane over the ocean for an 8 P.M.. jump near the end of the Pier. After circling to attract the attention of the crowd for the twice-daily stunt, the plane nosed up and Forrest jumped. But his parachute failed to open and Forrest, plunging in a free fall from about 1,600 feet, was killed instantly, a shocking spectacle witnessed by some 10,000 visitors.

❦ ❦ ❦

When the new Ocean Stadium opened in 1929, George Hamid found acts from around the globe that astounded the audiences of the Steel Pier Water Circus. Among them was the "Human Cannonball," Mademoiselle Alexme, a French girl who was the only woman in America performing this feat. Three or four times daily,

Death-defying acts were performed at the end of the Pier in the Water Circus area. This sixteen-foot globe held a speeding motorcycle ridden by a woman named Cedora, 1931.

she was shot from a giant cannon ninety feet above the water to land in a net suspended from the side of the Pier. However, one day there was too much *oomph* in the mechanism and she soared clear over the net, into the ocean. Mademoiselle Alexme was daring enough to be shot from a cannon, but landing in the ocean was entirely another matter — she couldn't swim. Luckily, an attentive Hawaiian diver saved her.

Along with the Hawaiian divers, the Great Water Sport Carnival presented attractions in the ocean around the outer Pier, employing sea sleds, ski-boards, aqua-skis and aquaplaning riders pulled by motor boats at forty-five mph.

In 1930, thanks to Hamid, more thrilling acts could be seen. There was the man towed through the air by a plane 1,000 feet over the ocean, and the Six Hustreis from Germany, a balancing act on a high wire.

Next year there was a death-defying act that was performed inside a sixteen-foot-wide iron globe. A female motorcyclist, Cedora, doing upside down loops, revved her bike up to seventy-five mph. It was among the most exciting acts the Pier ever presented.

The Water Circus performed seven shows daily from 2:30 to 10:30 P.M.., and there was always a chance for injury. During a night performance on August 12, 1932, as about 2,500 spectators looked on, two young women performing on a trapeze fell seventy-five feet to the floor of the stage. One of the women, hanging by her feet, had slipped, and the second performer fell with her. Thousands of people gathered around as an ambulance took the aerialists from the Pier to the local

In 1929 Mademoiselle Alexme, the "Human Cannonball", was shot out of a cannon four times a day and once flew over the net and into the ocean.

hospital.

Irene Berger, twenty-one, died of a broken neck. The other woman suffered broken legs, a broken back and a punctured lung. Part of what had been billed the "World's Highest Aerial Act," the trapeze artists never used a safety net in this particular show during the years it was performed in the United States and Europe.

Tiny Kline, suspended on a trapeze from a blimp high in the air, performed startling stunts on flying rings in 1933. Her trademark finale was to descend from the blimp, clinging to a strap with her teeth, until she had both feet on the Pier and took her bows.

The years passed, most without a major incident. Yet the risks were always present because many performers used no protective equipment. On June 17, 1955, an acrobat fell fifty-five feet from a swaying, sixty-five-foot pole before 3,000 horrified spectators. Robert Atterbury, thirty-eight, was presenting the first public appearance of a new act. He fell onto a wooden platform on the Pier as the audience shrieked. He broke both feet and his pelvis in the fall.

☾ ☾ ☾ ☾

In 1930, Pier owner Frank Gravatt saw a dead whale on exhibit at a state fair in Toronto. He spoke to the exhibitors and bought the giant carcass, paying $15,000. Gravatt had to hire a flatbed freight car in Toronto to transport the mammal back to New Jersey.

"A seventy-ton whale named Colossus lies on its right side in a specially designed and constructed all-steel railroad car in which it is taking a tour of the country," reported The *Atlantic City Press* on December 1, 1930. "The whale is perfectly preserved with 300 gallons of embalming fluid and shows no signs of the desperate battle that preceded its capture off the California coast."

The whale, at sixty-five feet in length, was the largest ever to be exhibited in the United States. It was shipped and placed on its own elevated, enclosed platform, half a block long on the Pier. But a problem arose, perhaps not totally unexpected. A few months after its arrival at the Pier, there were complaints that the whale was emitting a foul odor. A nearby hotel owner called the mayor, calling the exhibit a nuisance. Gravatt asked for a twenty-four-hour respite to ascertain if this problem really existed. After much experimenting, the whale was deemed safe, and it became, literally, Steel Pier's "biggest" attraction. It remained at the Pier until 1931, exhibited in a box in the water next to the Pier.

Gravatt continually sought new oddities. He was determined to offer so much to see and do that customers would leave knowing they had to come back, simply to get it all in.

On June 4, 1931, William G. Swan, a twenty-nine-year-old local stunt flyer from Atlantic City, piloted from the Bader Field airport, on the bay side of Atlantic City, what was reputed to be the first rocket glider in aviation history. The craft stayed aloft for almost thirty minutes before Swan returned to the airport, executing a perfect landing.

Powerboats and water skiers were always a part of the Water Circus.

The glider, with ten rockets attached (only one was fired for the stunt), was also equipped with pontoons. It made flights several times daily, and later, the machine was retired and showcased as a Pier exhibit.

Corporate sponsors such as Frigidare and Delco exhibited their products, but it was the unexpected that kept customers flocking through the front doors. Throughout the Depression years, Steel Pier staged some of the craziest things anyone could imagine. One was

Professor Nelson's Steel Pier Boxing Cats, "the funniest animal act on the American stage today," punching it out in a small ring four times daily in the main lobby.

Heavyweight boxing champ Primo Carnera showed up only days after he won the title over Jack Sharkey in 1933, and proceeded to get into a bout with Abdy's Boxing Kangaroo.

The Goodyear Rubber Co. had a truck tote a twelve-foot-tall rubber tire around the city before posing in front of the Pier on the Boardwalk.

In 1934, Goliath, billed as the largest sea lion in the world arrived, weighing in at 6,000 pounds. Perhaps most amazing was that he was a finicky eater, turning up his nose at anything except a certain kind of fish shipped from Cincinnati, and if he were not fed that particular fish, he would go on a hunger strike.

❦ ❦ ❦

It was always a wild scene on Steel Pier when animals were

Goodyear displays the world's largest tire in front of the GM exhibit, 1930.

around. One summer day in 1932, a Water Circus diver was bit by a black bear and lost the use of his left hand. While he was resting in a bunk after his act, the bear wandered in and attacked the man before being caught.

On April 6, 1932, the *Atlantic City Press* reported a humorous tale concerning another circus animal:

Cured of a bad case of colic by a pint of whiskey, Zoobu, a 350-pound infant elephant in the animal incubator that was brought to America by explorer Frank Buck, fell and broke his leg.

The baby's bellowing was heard all over the Pier. A hurry call was

sent from the hospital in Atlantic City for X-ray equipment from the Philadelphia Zoological Gardens and the Ringling circus in New York for elephant experts.

The X-ray showed that the leg had been broken between the shoulder and the knee. Zoobu was the first captive elephant to suffer a broken leg.

The leg was set. Shooting her was out of the question, as the baby elephant is valued at $10,000 by Frank Gravatt, owner of the Pier.

With the assistance of twelve men and a block and tackle, the elephant was held in position on her side while the leg was set and

The finicky Goliath weighed in at 6,000 lbs

placed in a plaster cast.

Local veterinarian Dr. Louis Goldberg then put the leg in an iron brace for a month, the first time such a procedure was used for an animal.

❆ ❆ ❆ ❆

The next year, Jesse De Carawin had an act that consisted of a bear cub walking on its hind legs and taking bows. One day the bear bowed too much and stepped right off the stage and into the ocean. There were no railings at the edge because performing divers routinely sprang from the stage. De Carawin ran to the front of the Pier and onto the beach, hailing lifeguards to dispatch a boat to the Pier's end. Meanwhile, the cub was clinging in terror to one of the pilings. De Carawin dove into the water and managed to get the cub into the lifeboat, and it was rowed safely back to the beach.

Some pranks left people scratching their heads in amazement. Bandleader Abe Lyman and five musicians played in a pen with Captain Roman Proske as he danced with a tiger. Monkeys received

haircuts in barber chairs, camels roamed the Pier, and animal celebrities appeared over the years. You could meet MGM's Leo the lion, Borden's Elsie the Cow, Gargantua the gorilla, Pete the "Our Gang" dog with the ring around his eye, the amusing Sharkey the seal, and the aqua-skiing Rex the Wonder Dog.

Arnette Webster French, the long-time Diving Horse rider, remembers when a dog was spotted in nearby Ventnor Bay, playing with kids on a raft. The dog was enjoying the water so much that its antics were described to Frank Gravatt. He decided this dog would add spice to the Water Circus. According to the *Atlantic City Press* in 1934: "Rex, a super-intelligent Belgian Shepherd dog, learned to ride an aquaplane as it bounced over the waves of the open sea behind a speedy motorboat. His performance was so joyous, with such evident pleasure and pride in his accomplishment, that he won even more applause than the husky youths who form human pyramids and do headstands on the leaping boards."

French had retired from the Diving Horse act in 1931 due to rheumatic fever. However, she went to Water Circus owner Frank Sterling and convinced him that she could still perform in the circus. She appeared as a skier, usually towed by a speedboat driven by her husband, Jake. On water skis, French would do backbends, stand on her head, or ride with Rex, who was billed as the "World's Only Aquaplaning Dog."

In 1938, the famous gorilla Gargantua the Great was first presented in the Ringling Brothers' Circus. Years earlier, when he was small and named Buddy, he had been featured on the Pier for two seasons. Gargantua wasn't the largest or most ferocious gorilla in the world, but his features told a different story. During his voyage to the United States in 1931, a sailor had accidentally thrown nitric acid on the gorilla's face, leaving a scar that looked like a hateful sneer. Circus press agent Roland Butler then transformed the live exhibit into Gargantua the Great. The act was undoubtedly boosted by the popularity of the jungle thriller "King Kong," so almost single-

After a Water Circus performance in the 1950s, the large crowd files out next to the Marine Ballroom.

handedly, Gargantua rescued Ringling Brothers from the severe financial bind it found itself in by the end of the Depression years.

❦ ❦ ❦

A unique contest was offered in August 1935. Philadelphia architect William Koelle, who had redesigned Steel Pier and built the General Motors showroom in 1926, designed the Little House, a modernistic home that would cost $5,000 on the open market. At the end of the exhibit, which was sponsored by the Federal Housing Administration, the house would be won by one lucky contestant. The rules stated "in the event the fortunate person lives outside of Atlantic County, $800 in cash will be donated toward the cost of moving the home to any location chosen by the winner. Otherwise, the lot is situated in an ideal location in Absecon (on the mainland outside Atlantic City) and their home will be moved from the Pier and placed ready for the occupant, at the expense of the co-operative contractors and management of Steel Pier."

A rebuilt two-story dwelling called "The Home of 1936," with just about every innovation, plus experimental ones, opened a year later on the Pier. Additions were made in 1937 and it was renamed "The Home of the Century," welcoming 500,000 visitors each summer. The home was built with a Formstone exterior and included a utility room, laundry room, playroom, kitchen, bedroom and Formica bar. It featured a tower staircase and balcony in the living room, and it was equipped and furnished by 130 national manufacturers. The market value was set at $7,500. Moderately priced, quality furniture inside represented the factories of leading American manufacturers. The structure was built so solidly that hurricanes left the house untouched.

It was temporarily called "The Victory Home"

The Home of the Century was built in 1936 and was destroyed in the 1962 storm. (Right The latest furniture and appliances were exhibited in "The Home of the Century.

during World War II. The postwar years presented the first all-gas "Freedom Kitchen," sponsored by the American Gas Association along with the contributions of eighty national manufacturers.

Unfortunately, "The Home of the Century," a favorite for many, was a victim of a runaway barge that cut through the Pier in the March 1962 storm.

❛❛ ❛❛ ❛❛ ❛❛

All through the Depression years, the fun never stopped. On June 30, 1936, Charles Newton, eleven, of Philadelphia, was declared the winner in a freckle contest in connection with "Children's Week in Atlantic City." He had 1,895 freckles, the judges declared.

The next month, Jack "Rich" Allen, an aerial dancer, performed 100 feet above the Boardwalk atop the Pier. He stayed there for 246 hours, breaking all records for such an act.

On May 28, 1938, "Shipwreck" Kelly returned. Standing on his head on a disc, he spun on ball bearings at the top of a 210-foot pole in the stadium.

By this point, owner Frank Gravatt just shrugged his shoulders. He had seen it all during the hard times of the Great Depression, when many came to Steel Pier to try to forget their troubles — and sometimes found they could not.

"People would try to jump from the end to commit suicide," he said. "We'd have lifesaving equipment behind every sign, and the high divers were always on alert just in case."

❛❛ ❛❛ ❛❛ ❛❛

One of the most enduring attractions on Steel Pier was the famous Diving Bell. Built in 1942, the bell held fifteen people and went down thirty feet into the ocean. Designed with twelve portholes that offered unrestricted views of nautical life, the bell was also equipped with safety devices, telephone communications and air-conditioning. It was capable of resurfacing at the touch of a button. The Diving Bell was buoyant and was lowered below the waves through a winch and pulley system, riding straight down on a steel column.

Here is the "modern" living room of 1936.

Large crowds of beach-goers watch as patrons leave the General Motors Exhibit in the early 1930s

An unusual angle of an aerial stunt above the ocean.

(Above) Arnette Webster French waterskiing with Rex the Wonder Dog. The shepherd-mix was a favorite from 1934 to 1942. (Right) Arnette and Rex take a break between shows.

It was designed and built by Californian Edward Martine, with the backing of Frank Gravatt. The steel for the bell was rolled in Youngstown, Ohio. Martine, who was a welder, put it together on the Pier and eventually bought out Gravatt for the rights. The Beck family, which had maintained the bell for Martine since 1947, bought it in 1955 and ran it until the Pier closed in 1978.

"The only way it was profitable was my father (Barton Beck, Sr.) had the engineering experience and the right tools," Barton Beck, Jr. told *The Press of Atlantic City* some years later.

"It was cylindrical, and the top was conical. It was steel, watertight, with a main door sealed against a rubber gasket that was closed hydraulically. And there were twelve-inch portholes," he said.

While the actual descent of the bell was thrilling for the crowds, many people were disappointed with the murky view, marred by clouds of sand and sediment.

"Mostly all you could see were a couple of nearby wooden beams with algae and mussels attached. It was sort of eerie," he said. "Sometimes you could see a sea bass, mullet, dog sharks; every now and then a flounder would be disturbed; stingrays, weakfish, bluefish."

However, the return ride to the surface usually lifted everyone's spirits. "The best part for me then was how fast it came back up to the surface," Beck said.

The Diving Bell's most famous day was on August 22, 1949. Ruth Ehlers, age seventeen, and Louis Villani, twenty-one, both from North

Bergen, New Jersey, were married in the bell, thirty feet below the ocean. The couple first met on the bell in 1948, and on a later return trip, Villani proposed. Ehlers wrote to Pier owner George Hamid: "A fortuneteller told me that good luck would be ours if we wed right in the same spot where we met." Hamid promptly granted the request, knowing good publicity when he saw it.

On the big day, a crowd of 500 gathered to witness the procession and also to hear the ceremony, which was audible on speakers. With the bride in her wedding dress and carrying a bouquet of dahlias and ferns, the wedding party marched onto the Pier to the strains of the "Wedding March," played by the Stagg McMahon harmonica trio.

Villani and Ehlers were both nervous as they entered the bell, accompanied by maid-of-honor Louise Miranda of Union City, best man Phillip Casavino of West New York, seven-year-old flower girl Vicki Gold of Atlantic City, the Reverend J. Ramon Vann of New York City, and two newsmen. That flower girl, daughter of the well-known Atlantic City photographer Al Gold, is now Atlantic City historian and author Vicki Gold Levi.

Though the bell was electrically lit and cooled, the ocean outside appeared dark and menacing, churned up by winds. Fourteen minutes later, Vann pronounced the couple man and wife, and the bell returned to the surface. Villani carried his wife over the "threshold" as they stepped from the bell, pelted with rice and confetti, and hurried to a reception on the Pier.

Gifts poured in from all over. In Atlantic City, the Grossman-Kensington Furniture Co. presented the couple with an expensive bedroom suite, and the Jeweler's Exchange gave the bride

Crowds never got tired of stunts that featured pretty young women, especially when they were hooping it up on a wheel.

In 1938 the Zacchinis were billed as "human projectiles who are shot from a repeating cannon one after the other."

Visitors to the Hawaiian Village, on the right, look up at a high-wire act between the Casino and Music Hall theaters, 1932.

a diamond ring. They planned to spend part of the honeymoon at the Brighton Hotel while mulling over offers to appear on radio and TV.

☾ ☾ ☾ ☾

Some were afraid to ride the bell for fear of being trapped underwater, but many tried it anyway. Through the public address system, customers could talk to their friends waiting above. Speakers were placed on high poles so those on the Pier could hear the voices, and sometimes screams, from below.

"When I was nine, I wanted to go in that big blue-and-white Diving Bell. My mother wouldn't let me go in it, saying, 'It may not come back up!' So I pitched a big fit and cried my eyes out," Anna-Marie Weber told *Atlantic City* magazine twenty years after her visit in 1961. The little girl got her way, and down she went.

"I was scared to death, but I just had to go on it. All we saw was dirty water. I was afraid it would spring a leak, and I just knew that chain was going to break. When we got up, I said I would never go in that damp, dank, icky thing again!"

The horrific March 1962 storm tore away the original bell and a huge portion of the Pier. Later, as the Pier was being rebuilt, the Becks located another Martine bell that was on Catalina Island off the California coast. They bought it and shipped it to Atlantic City, where it was added to the reconstruction of the Pier. Barton Beck, Sr. made improvements on the original design, and the second Diving Bell was open for business by July.

By the time the Pier closed in 1978, admission to the Diving Bell cost a dollar. The bell held ten people, and the ride lasted five minutes. It remained on the Pier long afterward, rusted out and surviving the fire that destroyed the rest of the Pier in 1982.

In the early 1990s, it was saved and restored, and now sits on an outdoor display in the Gardner's Basin section of Atlantic City. To many who see it now, it brings back memories of their first murky glimpse from below the sea.

☾ ☾ ☾ ☾

When George Hamid acquired the Pier in 1945, the strange Pier attractions continued just as they did under Frank Gravatt's management.

The Bikini Atomic Bomb Exhibit filled space in 1946 when Hiroshima and Nagasaki were still fresh in the minds of Americans.

Some of the exhibits in 1947 included the Animated Museum (front lower deck); movie horses Flicka, Thunderhead and Smokey (Marine arcade section); The Lord's Last Supper with figures in wax (main arcade at front); The March of Time in wax (Casino arcade, upper section); a wildlife exhibit (main arcade, center section); and the Navy Artist at War (Casino arcade, center section).

The very popular "Ripley's Believe It or Not Odditorium" opened in 1949 in the front upper arcade. It was moved to the center main floor by 1952, and finally ended up at the Boardwalk and lobby entrance, ten years later.

On July 19, 1952, Steel Pier announced: "See and talk with Ronald Harrison, who is buried alive! He's gone underground to protest against high prices, and doesn't plan on coming up TILL INFLATION HAS BEEN CURBED! While down, he hopes to break the world's record of forty-one days and nights, now held in Paris, France."

Harrison, a fifty-year-old half-Sioux Indian from Florida, was actually buried under six feet of dirt in a coffin with glass sides. He was fed through a tube.

On August 29, he set the record at forty-two days and nights. The "Digging Up" ceremonies began at noon that day. It is unknown whether or not his stunt actually curbed inflation.

A display of water moving in rhythm to music came to the Pier in 1953 via Radio City in New York. Called "The Dancing Waters," it made a big splash with visitors.

Authentic Hopi cliff dwellers of Arizona presented their snake ceremony in 1957, complete with live snakes, along with "other weird and primitive Indian dances," as the program said.

The Little Theatre, originally the location for the kid shows of the 1930s until the 1950s, became an exhibit space, with the Modern Home Exhibit, Tropical Exhibit and Streets of Hong Kong occupying that area into the early 1960s.

A Military Museum Exhibit could be seen on the second floor of the Boardwalk end in 1958. An Armed Services Exhibit was later presented.

A spectacular daredevil, former Olympic diving champion Joe Hackney, at age sixty-five, dove 100-feet into the ocean from the Steel

In 1964, sixty-one-year-old Dixie Blandy became the world champion flagpole sitter as he sat atop the Steel Pier sign for seventy-eight consecutive days.

The Diving Bell submerges and pops to the top after a journey to the bottom of the murky ocean.

Pier helicopter. The stunt took place out near the Marine Ballroom on July 25, 1962 (a previous dive was from a Navy blimp). You could win a free trip to Miami Beach that same year by entering the Lano-Tan Beautiful Tan contest. Final judging was held in September in the Marine Ballroom. And speaking of tans, every year you could meet the current Miss Steel Pier, a lovely representation of Atlantic City's virtues.

Animals still played a large part in the Pier's activities. A porpoise playroom opened in 1961 with a steel tank containing 20,000 gallons of water for the playful mammals. Direct from the Seattle World's Fair, the world's largest stuffed polar bear greeted visitors in the lobby during 1963. A duck played the piano.

No one could resist the fortune-telling parakeets. Perched on a tiny wooden stage, visitors would pay a dime and the parakeet would walk along a tiny ramp, go inside a box fashioned to look like a temple, choose a fortune from a pile of folded papers and hand it to the fascinated patron.

In 1964, flagpole sitter Dixie Blandy set out to break the world's record on the Pier. Born in 1902, the Creole stood five feet four inches and weighed a stocky 150 pounds. His first flagpole sitting was in 1929 in Tampa, Florida, earning him $600. In 1933, he claimed the title "Champ of Flagpole Sitting," with seventy-seven days and nights at the Chicago Exposition, handily beating "Shipwreck" Kelly's Steel Pier record of forty-nine.

On August 25, 1964, the sixty-one-year-old Blandy broke his old record atop Steel Pier, lasting seventy-eight consecutive days.

During his celebrity career, Blandy had six wives, divorcing three and widowed from three. He met his younger wives through telephone conversations with fans who were on the ground. In 1965, he held the pole sitting world title; in Stockholm, he lived on a pole 125 days, sitting on a chair 200 feet high. In 1974, while he was performing in Chicago, his flagpole collapsed and Blandy fell to his death. He was seventy-two.

In the spirit of Houdini, Ron Fable was handcuffed, shackled, locked in a trunk and lowered into the ocean for a twenty-seven-second escape on August 31, 1966. The next year, on August 31, Hamid greeted eighteen Canadian Boy Scouts who had ridden their bicycles from their hometown of L'Assomption, near Montreal. The youths spent most of the day on the Pier.

The actual *Gemini VII* spacecraft, insured for $50,000, was exhibited on the Pier in 1970. In July 1975, for a change of pace, there was the Steel Pier Diaper Derby and Baby Crawling Championship.

Probably the last hurrah was in 1977, when the entire summer on the Pier was devoted to breaking records published in the famous *Guinness Book of World Records*. Every day there were people trying to make a name in the record books while attempting crazy stunts. The nuttier ones included Master Chi, lying on six-inch nails while a car drove over him; there were the World's Fattest Twins, more flagpole sitting, a pinball marathon, and a twist marathon.

Bruce Condella, eighteen, broke the world's pinball record when he played for over ninety-two hours — and almost collapsed afterward.

Atlantic City Mayor Joseph Lazarow established a new record for handshaking after he exchanged greetings with more than 11,000 people in front of the Pier, breaking President Theodore Roosevelt's record. Lazarow nearly broke his hand, and required treatment for a dislocated bone.

When the Pier closed after the 1978 season, only radio station WFPG (1450 AM) remained, broadcasting from the Pier where it began in 1940. Known as WIIN after June 13, 1978, the station moved off the Pier in May 1981.

There was never a dull moment on Steel Pier as long as people were willing to display a gimmick; as long as strange animals fascinated patrons; as long as daredevils paraded their skills; and as long as weird or educational exhibits taught the masses. Today's carnival sideshow pales in comparison to what Steel Pier once offered America.

Chapter Eleven

There She Is, Miss America...

Every year until 2006, millions of television viewers watched the annual Miss America Pageant originating from the Boardwalk's historic Convention Hall. The pageant had become an Atlantic City tradition soon after its inception in 1921. It began as a promotion to extend the summer season past Labor Day so the city could bring in more revenue before winter.

Richard P. Endicott, who later became the general manager of Steel Pier under Frank Gravatt, directed the first pageant. The contest received strong publicity around the nation, even appearing in newsreels.

A petite, smiling Margaret Gorman was crowned the first Miss America on Garden Pier on September 8, 1921, complete with a visit from "King Neptune," ruler of the pageant.

Trophies were presented to the finalists on the stage.

A Governor's Ball was held on Steel Pier the following day, with governors and mayors of various states in attendance as guests of honor.

A year later, a Motion Picture Ball was held for the fifty-seven Miss America entrants (there were more than one from some states). The Universal Film Company shot screen tests of each, promising contracts to those with potential.

Armand T. Nichols, a former mayoral secretary, was named Pageant Director General from 1924 through 1927. In 1926 and 1927, the pageant needed a larger space for its activities and was moved to the ballroom of Million Dollar Pier. Due to negative publicity, coupled with the Depression, the pageant ended from 1928 until 1931. Nichols took the pageant south to the beach town of Wildwood, New Jersey, in 1932. When it did not gain much publicity there, Nichols tried to return Miss America to Atlantic City.

Finally in 1935, Frank Gravatt and associate Eddie Corcoran enlisted help from the Variety Club of Philadelphia. Corcoran hired Lenora Slaughter from the St. Petersburg (Florida) Chamber of Commerce to help. Slaughter stayed on for over thirty years as executive secretary until retiring in 1967.

On September 7, 1935, the Miss America festivities, officially titled "Showman's Variety Jubilee — American Beauty Event," proceeded for the first time on Steel Pier. At 11 A.M. screen tests were scheduled for beauty and talent contestants. That evening at 8 P.M. in the Marine Ballroom, final judging commenced for the crowning of Miss America 1935 by "King Neptune", who earlier had led a Boardwalk parade before 350,000 spectators.

Judges included producer Earl Carroll, illustrator Russel Patterson, and Nils T. Granlund, master of ceremonies of the Paradise Restaurant in New York. In front of an enormous audience of about 15,000 people, girls competed from fifty-three cities. The title was awarded to Henrietta Leaver, nineteen, of Pittsburgh, who sang a popular song and performed a dance for the talent portion, which counted for twenty-five percent of her score. King Neptune, played by Captain Thaddeus Cowden, a ninety-one-year-old fisherman, placed a jeweled crown on her head.

At 10.30 P.M., the American Beauty Ball held forth with members of the Morris Guards acting as escorts for the Inter-City Beauty Contestants. The Ball was held in conjunction with the Pier's regular attractions.

The show was such a success that the Miss America Boardwalk Parade and Pageant returned to Atlantic City in full regalia. A year later, the entire week leading up to the crowning was filled with activities. On September 8, 1936, the selection of Miss Junior America was presented, as well as a Mardi Gras Ball and First Preliminary Talent Contest. The next day, the second Preliminary Talent Contest took place, followed on September 10 with the third Preliminary Talent Contest, an Award of the Official Coiffure of 1936 and the American Beauty Ball. A Championship Ocean Swim, Presentation of the Winners of the National Fashion Show and dancing were the events of September 13, leading up to the big day.

On Saturday, September 14, the Annual Steel Pier six-mile Championship Swim began at 1.30 P.M. Finals in the Talent Contest and selection of Miss America 1936 began at 8.30 P.M. in the Marine Ballroom, hosted by Bob Hall. Of the forty-eight girls initially entered, fifteen finalists vied for the crown, based on musical and dancing talent, and appearances in bathing suit and evening gown.

The winner that night was Rose Coyle of Philadelphia. A committee of magazine illustrators and theater art directors made the selection before 10,000 people in the Marine Ballroom. Miss Coyle received a trophy, a plane trip to Hollywood and a screen test.

New Jersey's own Bette Cooper, seventeen, became Miss America 1937 in the Pier's Marine Ballroom, but the teenager was so shocked and frightened by actually winning that she ran off with her escort that very night and never returned. Newsreel cameramen, reporters, photographers and pageant officials waited in vain for her to appear. George D. Tyson, executive director of the Jubilee, explained that Miss Cooper wasn't feeling well and had been ordered to bed by her physician for a few days' rest.

She was to have appeared in vaudeville on the Pier for five days at a salary reported to be $200 a day. "Bette is not the type of girl to appear in vaudeville," stated her father, LeBrun Cooper. "She isn't robust enough for the professional grind. She just entered on a lark. Her mother and I want her to finish school first to get polished off, then do something that isn't strenuous, like modeling for magazine covers."

Night view touting Miss America, 1937

She became a Miss America only in spirit, as she never really accepted her crown.

An ad from 1938 proclaimed: "Spectacular Fur Fashion Show! $500,000 in mink, sables, ermines — Presented by Bonwit Teller, Philadelphia — Modeled by fifty Pageant Beauties — auspices of Showman's Variety Jubilee, September 11, 1938, 9 P.M., Steel Pier, all seats reserved $1.10." Marilyn Meseke, twenty-one, of Ohio was later crowned 1938's Miss America, selected among forty-four girls representing twenty-two states and twenty-two cities.

Patricia Donnelly, nineteen, of Detroit won the following year,

Standing room only in the Marine Ballroom during the Miss America presentation.

A wide variety of Miss America activities would last for a full week leading up to the final crowning.

selected from a group of forty-three. Some 8,500 people were on hand to witness her crowning.

"The contestants never went anywhere without their chaperones, but my friend Walter Rossi, and I, who were guards to the dressing rooms, managed to get to know some of the contestants during pageant rehearsals," wrote Russell LeVan. "One contestant I will never forget was a nice young woman from the South. She was so proud to be representing her state. Her parents, however, were good Southern Baptists and thought the pageant violated their religious principles. They disowned her right before the pageant, and it nearly broke her heart.

"The new Miss America and the three runners-up performed at the Music Hall for a one-week engagement. From there, they went to New York to begin their national tour."

After 1939's crowning, the Miss America Pageant left Steel Pier during the war years, moving instead to the confines of the massive Warner Theatre on the Boardwalk. But the day after each new Miss America was crowned, the new queen still returned to the Pier for an appearance on the Music Hall stage, a practice that lasted several years. In 1947, the pageant moved to Convention Hall, where it remained until the conclusion of the 2005 pageant.

During its early years, Steel Pier had been used for various convention meetings and special organizational shows year-round. When the Miss America Pageant was considered all but finished in 1934, it was Frank Gravatt and his Pier that came to the rescue. In the five years that the pageant was hosted at Steel Pier, it rose to become the pre-eminent pageant of its kind, bringing national status to Atlantic City.

Advertisement from 1938 promoting the final night of the Miss America pageant in addition to all the other Steel Pier offerings.

GEORGE A. HAMID *Proudly Presents*
STEEL PIER ..
SOUVENIR PROGRAM and GUIDE BOOK
Showplace of the Nation
Where to go, What to see & How to get there
25¢
DAILY TIME SCHEDULES *for all the* MAMMOTH EVENTS

Chapter Twelve

Kids: In the Audience & On Stage

Atlantic City was a resort where the entire family, especially children, could enjoy its beach and Boardwalk. In fact, children's balls and carnivals had been held on Young's Pier even before Steel Pier opened in 1898.

In 1912, a baby show was held in the ocean end Ballroom on Steel Pier, where spectators voted for the prettiest, cutest, fattest, best dressed and favorite twins.

Children's Carnival nights were held in the Ballroom every Tuesday and Thursday evenings during the 1920s.

In 1928, the Bon Air Summer School held classes for children ages five to twelve in the Vanity Concourse, located in the center of the Pier. Under a competent and experienced faculty, the program included creative arts, rhythm tennis, handcrafts, beach games, hiking and swimming. There was special attention paid to "habit training." While parents enjoyed the rest of the Pier's presentations, their little ones would be taught refined behavior.

And then there were the talented children who were making a mark for themselves.

❧ ❧ ❧ ❧

Ever since producer Hal Roach called for kid actors to become the feature part of his "Our Gang-Little Rascal" series in 1922, stage moms from all over the country have been trying to get their "talented" kids into pictures or shows.

Shirley Temple became the darling of Depression-America in 1934 when she was four years old. Milton Berle traveled in vaudeville with his mother for years before he reached puberty. Jackie Coogan starred with Charlie Chaplin before he grew up to be Uncle Fester on "The Addams Family," while Jackie Cooper of "Our Gang" was nominated for an Oscar for his performance with Wallace Beery in 1932's "The Champ."

By the early 1930s, kid shows were common in movie theaters across the country. Each city had talented children who would sing, dance, or play a musical instrument on stage, hoping to gain a ticket to stardom. These talent shows became very popular with kids as well as adults.

Steel Pier decided to go this route and came up with the idea of a children's theater, a space where talented youngsters could perform in front of other children. The venue, the 1,000-seat Little Theatre, opened in 1931, presenting one performance daily, five days a week. It was the only theater of its kind in the United States devoted exclusively to children's talent.

In 1933, the Pier presented special shows for children at noon daily. Marionettes, Punch & Judy puppets, Pete the "Our Gang" dog, and Hardeen — Houdini's magician brother — offered entertainment for the young folks.

Another treat for the kids was to get their voices tested for the radio by "Daddy" Dave Tyson, a former Steel Pier minstrel performer. These auditions were held daily, except Sunday, in the Ocean Hall, and by 1934, the shows for children were an everyday activity. Daddy Dave

was the host and producer of a troupe of eighteen talented boys and girls, with an average age of twelve, who would perform juvenile stage revues such as "A Gypsy Fantasy," complete with music, dance, and song. The children who performed were from Atlantic City, Philadelphia, and other out-of-town locations. Also on hand were Alexander the Magician and the Sue Hastings Marionettes; birthday celebrations were given top priority, as were Disney cartoon shows.

On August 14, 1934, Steel Pier offered an apology to the adults who came the previous morning and might have been "annoyed" by the 7,118 children who were there to see radio stars "The Goldbergs" and other exclusive Steel Pier presentations. "These children had the time of their lives; it was an event to them they'll never forget. It was a special occasion. There'll be more room today," promised an official of the Pier.

Because of the increase in popularity, by 1938 the shows were presented four times daily. Titles such as "Around the Campfire," "Beach Patrol," "On a Bus," and "International Broadcast" were directed and produced by Daddy Dave and his staff, entertaining thousands during the summer.

In 1939, the Children's Theatre opened for its eighth season. It had started in 1931 with one performance a day, five days a week; by 1939, there were four shows daily, seven days a week. Auditions were held every weekday morning, with children coming in from far and near. The children received actual stage experience and training for proper stage entrances and exits, and developed self-assurance and professional polish.

In the post-war years, particularly during the 1950s, innovative promotions were entirely geared to bring more young people onto the Pier. On Friday, June 13, 1958, there was the "Seventh Annual High Schools Nite!," which offered discounted admission to high school students, and was billed as the place to be to "meet and greet your friends!"

From the early 1950s until at least 1971, each Friday morning was "Cowboy Morning." Children could get onto the Pier at half-price between 9:30 and 11 A.M.. for special cowboy movies and could stay all day. Cowboy prizes were given out, as well as a new twenty-six-inch bicycle every week.

In 1971, Elsie Day Fridays added Borden's ice cream to the mix at

Daddy Dave revue from 1941.

half-price until 2 P.M., probably because attendance had been falling by that time. Also that year, T-shirt Day gave the first 1,000 children a free Steel Pier T-shirt.

"During the summer months, we would get 'Elsie Morning' passes to Steel Pier, where they gave away a bike once a week," recalled one regular visitor. "A group of neighborhood kids would get together, with our paper bags of baloney sandwiches, and we would stay all day. What a great time we had! Then we would walk over to the General Motors Exhibit where we would sit in every car."

"When we were nine to twelve years old, we would go to the A&P Supermarket on Pennsylvania and Atlantic Avenues and get coupons that were good on Fridays, which was Cowboy Day," remembered

Kevin McCartney. "It cost us fifty cents. What a deal!"

"We ate our bagged lunch on the picnic deck overlooking the ocean, and sat in 'Tony Grant's Stars of Tomorrow' for hours so we could have front row seats when the show started," Herba Rubinfine told the *Press of Atlantic City* years later.

In 1947, the year that "Daddy" Dave Tyson died, Tony Grant began staging the shows in the Little Theatre. Grant had played vaudeville as a member of the Two Barons, a dance team, and later had a dancing school in Wilkes-Barre, Pennsylvania, before opening a dance school in Atlantic City.

"I'd been bringing acts to Daddy Dave for years. Inwardly, I wanted to do the show, and when Dave died and I was asked to take over the theater, I was ready," Grant said later in a *New York Times* feature story.

In 1949, Grant took over the Children's Theatre, and it became known as "Tony Grant's Stars of Tomorrow." He immediately made his presence known by producing acclaimed shows titled "Minstrel Daze," "Swing School," "Follies of 1950," and "Glorifying the American Child."

Pete, the famous "Our Gang" dog, appeared and posed with kids and grownups alike, sometimes wearing a hat and "smoking" a pipe.

In 1954, the Tony Grant group moved to the center of the Pier to the Ocean Theatre, which had been renamed the Midway. The Little Theatre had become home to exhibitions.

There were forty-five child actors by the late 1950s, and some — including Connie Francis and Frankie Avalon — became big stars.

Grant also had access via TV exposure due to a weekly show he produced in Wilkes-Barre in 1956.

During the week-long shows on the Pier, the cast of Grant's productions often booked rooms together. "The Clarendon was a nice rooming house where many of the Tony Grant performers stayed. I remember stopping by there to see some of the girls," said one Pier regular who claims he and his friends slipped into shows all the time without paying admission. "My cousin was a dancer and actually appeared on the 'Ted Mack Amateur Hour' TV show as a result of their being a part of the 'Stars of Tomorrow.'"

"I remember staying at the Clarendon Hotel on the beach block of Virginia Avenue, where Mr. and Mrs. Martin Casper created the safest haven for all of the performers on the Tony Grant show," said Michael Jones. "I remember my first week there and wandering down one morning only to find the entire hotel checking out! I didn't realize the shows changed every week!"

Bob Green-Orwigsburg was fifteen when he sought his big chance in 1966. "I appeared on Steel Pier with my rock band on the Tony Grant 'Stars of Tomorrow' show. I remember the band having to come down to Atlantic City to audition in February of that year. Two shows a day, for a week. I still remember those microphones that were on pulleys that came up from holes in the stage."

He also recalls "the words from the corny finale song that we all had to learn: *'Thank you, folks, for watching our show. Performing for you is a pleasure, you know!'*"

The audience loved when Earl Nichols, Jr. played his tenor banjo for "Tony Grant Stars of Tomorrow" in 1969. "I played two shows a day, one in the morning and one at night. At one of the shows at night, the audience kept applauding. Tony kept sending me back out (for a bow). Finally he said, 'We have never had an encore, and we are not going to start tonight.'"

John S. Wilson of *The New York Times* came backstage to Grant's productions in 1973 for a feature story:

More than 300 kids come a week in July and August to dance, sing and play instruments in a 1,700-seat theater.

Tony Grant, sixty-six: "Years ago, we presented as many as eight shows a day, but it was too hard on the children. They had come [from] as far as Texas or Canada to spend one week in Atlantic City and they wanted to be on the beach, so we started using two different casts each week. Now we use three casts, and we do only three shows a day."

With twelve acts in each show, Mr. Grant is faced with the task of polishing up a total of thirty-six new acts a week....

"At the auditions, I give each act from one to four stars. I don't really turn an act down. I just say, 'I'll get in touch if I need you.' That way, when I need substitutes, I've got a good bench."

All the children come at their own expense, paying for travel, lodging, food, and costumes. Steel Pier pays them nothing...

"These are not just ordinary children. There has never been an incident with them. Nobody has ever been sent home.

"We have four rules. A performer is not allowed to be on the Pier in costume. A performer is not allowed to sit in the first ten rows of the theater. No chewing gum on stage. And if you're old enough to smoke, you're too old for the Children's Theater."

🎵 🎵 🎵 🎵

During the early 1970s, Andrea McArdle was a part of the troupe not long before she burst into stardom, opening Broadway's "Annie" in the title role.

In 1976, the Tony Grant Show moved to the Casino, the only building with a theater after the renovation that knocked down the Music Hall and Ocean theaters. During more renovations in 1978, Tony Grant's theater moved again. The space was a fraction of its size — a converted paint shop. Still showcasing 150 kids a week, Grant seemed apprehensive. Resorts International was now the city's first gambling casino. It was the dawn of Atlantic City's makeover as the casino capital of the east coast.

"I just hope we can keep 'Stars of Tomorrow' alive once Resorts takes over," Grant said at the time. "This show just wouldn't be the same somewhere else. Where would we go? Where could we take it?"

But time was running out on "Stars" and the Pier. The "Stars of Tomorrow" continued until the Pier closed forever at the end of summer 1978.

After everything else had been and gone, Tony Grant's "Stars of Tomorrow" and the Diving Horse were the last bastions of the classic years of the Pier.

1953: Tony Grant's All Star Show

Chapter Thirteen

Movies & Hollywood Attractions

Motion pictures do not usually come to mind when one is discussing Steel Pier. But since the beginning, movies had always been a major part of the Pier. Short, silent films debuted on the Pier in 1908, shown every evening at 8:30, except Saturday and Sunday. By 1918, motion pictures ran daily at 3:30 and 8 P.M. in the Ballroom.

Although the films were not the blockbusters from Charlie Chaplin or Gloria Swanson, nor major silent-era hits such as "Birth of a Nation" or "What Price Glory," they did feature up-and-coming stars. For instance, Marion Davies in "Enchantment" and cowboy star William S. Hart in "Traveling On" both played the Pier in 1922.

By 1924, films would be shown in either the Ballroom or the Casino Hall at the front of the Pier.

After Frank Gravatt bought the Pier in 1925, the movie policy rapidly changed. During the week of November 5 that year, Steel Pier shared a Paramount Week promotion with downtown Atlantic City theaters Colonial, Liberty, City Square and Central. Paramount movies were shown continuously at the theaters for a full week and on the Pier in the Ballroom.

The following year, movies on the Pier were shown exclusively in the Casino Hall at 4 and 9:30 P.M.

Gravatt's improvements to the Pier culminated in 1929, which is considered the beginning of the Pier's golden years. This was the first year the famous Diving Horses made their appearance, along with many other unique attractions. Actor Ronald Colman's first all-talking picture, "Bulldog Drummond" — the screen version of the hit Broadway play — premiered at a May 29 gala at the new Ocean Hall theater, which was built in the center of the Pier. With the film commanding an admission price of $2 in Times Square, in Atlantic City an astounding $5 was the admission price on the Pier.

At the same time, a silent photoplay of "Plastered in Paris," starring Sammy Cohen, played with no fanfare at all in the Casino Hall.

The public's fascination with movies brought the million-dollar Hollywood Exhibit to the Pier in 1929, featuring props used in the making of well-known films. In 1930, cosmetic artists accommodated women who wanted to be "made up" like a movie star.

A favorite among visitors, the exhibit changed features each year. In 1937, the Hal Roach studios lent displays from its "Topper" picture, RKO-Radio sent costumes worn by Katherine Hepburn and Lily Pons,

In the 1930s, the motion pictures were as popular as other Pier attractions.

Charlie Chaplin's "City Lights" gets a first-class presentation, 1931.

In 1930, Steel Pier remained open year round. Here it is as it appeared during the Christmas season, showing "Morocco".

Hollywood Exhibit display window showcasing famous costumes used in motion pictures, circa 1935.

"That was when they had very strong movies and people couldn't afford to go to places like Florida then," said George Hamid Jr.

"When you had the big movies, they drew people. Atlantic City was a year-round resort then because there were no other places. Piers were able to stay open year-round."

Paramount Pictures signed an exclusive contract with Steel Pier in 1930 and 1931; thus the Paramount name appeared on the front marquee. Jackie Cooper's "Skippy," Adolph Menjou's "The Front Page," and the Marx Brothers' "Monkey Business" were just a few Paramount productions for which Pier owner Frank Gravatt paid as much

and MGM prepared a set of original Chinese props used in "The Good Earth" and props from "Tarzan Escapes."

The brand-new Music Hall theater, located in the center of the Pier, opened May 29, 1930 with "The New Movietown Follies of 1930," starring comedic actor El Brendel and a big stage revue.

The decade of the 1930s was perhaps the most creative on the Pier for motion pictures. With the advent of sound, a Depression-weary public flocked to theaters looking for entertainment that would temporarily let them forget their worries.

Steel Pier remained open throughout the year during this time. Labor Day, usually the official end of the summer season, signaled the closing of most of the exhibits and stage shows until the following spring. However, movies and dances in the Marine Ballroom continued

as $15,000 per picture. "Palmy Days," an Eddie Cantor comedy, had its world premiere on the Pier September 21, 1931.

There were also exhibits featuring famous studio animals like the MGM lion Leo and Pete from "Our Gang/Little Rascals" comedies. Both children and adults lined up to have their picture taken with the famous canine, who was so popular that he wound up staying on the Pier for consecutive summers.

"On a cold Sunday in January, circa 1936, my parents were driving me to Atlantic City and there was thin ice on the roads," remembered visitor Carl Bailey, Jr. "We were heading to Steel Pier to have my picture taken with the dog that played in the movies of 'Our Gang.' I still have that picture today."

Other top movies to play the Pier at this time were "Scarface," with

"Our Gang" dog Pete sings along with famed tenor Morton Downey.

Paul Muni; "Frankenstein," with Boris Karloff; "It Happened One Night," "The Invisible Man," "Cleopatra," "A Star Is Born," "My Man Godfrey," and "Wuthering Heights." Mae West's "Belle of the Nineties" had its world premiere on Steel Pier in 1934.

The three theaters of the Pier, Casino, Music Hall and Ocean, were now showing movies on a continuous basis, from 10:30 A.M. until 2 the following morning. The importance of movies at the Pier was not to be taken lightly and was prominently advertised.

There were also special presentations of films that were not for commercial release. "Dream of My People," the "first singing and talking picture made in the Holy Land," featuring cantor Josef Rosenblatt, was shown in May 1933 in the Ocean theater for a benefit of the Atlantic City Free Hebrew School.

In August 1934, film comedian Harold Lloyd was at the Boardwalk's Apollo Theatre to attend the world premiere of his latest comedy, "The Cat's Paw." He visited Steel Pier and exclaimed to Frank Gravatt, "Never in my wildest imagination could I ... visualize such a remarkable entertainment feast as you offer for one ... admission! Out in Hollywood, we've heard of Steel Pier, but no one believed that it's possible to spend eighteen hours and never see the same show or attraction twice!"

The year-round hours came to an end in 1938, although New Year's showings continued for a few more years. From 1942 into 1943, though, the Pier was open every weekend with dancing, movies and vaudeville for the large number of servicemen and women stationed at Boardwalk hotels during training.

George Hamid purchased the Pier in 1945. "We went from three movies to two, simply because movies were harder to buy. They were expensive," explained George Hamid, Jr. in a 1988 interview.

Besides the main features, there were always newsreels, comedies, cartoons or other short subjects included within the program.

At this time the Pier began booking "B" pictures, such as "Charlie Chan at the Wax Museum," "Model Wife" with Joan Blondell, "Leave It to Blondie," and "Tarzan and the Leopard Woman." While these were first-run pictures, they certainly were not of the same caliber as the films showing at Atlantic City's main theaters.

Yet there were a few highlights during this decade. In August 1941, former Steel Pier minstrels Bud Abbott and Lou Costello, now Hollywood's top comics, returned for an appearance along with their latest picture, "Hold That Ghost."

July of 1946 was an historic month, as Walt Disney's "Make Mine Music" began an exclusive showing on the Pier and was held over for an unprecedented three weeks. Immediately following was Howard Hughes' "The Outlaw," the risqué western that exposed much of Jane Russell's ample bosom. The film's release was held up by censors, and Atlantic City had planned on banning the film due to pressures from

"Cleopatra" with Claudette Colbert received top billing over comedian George Jessel, 1934.

local church groups.

Hamid responded in a statement: "We feel that we are not violating the reputation of Steel Pier for good, clean entertainment now, nor the morals of anyone, and we are presenting 'The Outlaw' starting Sunday." A few days later, city officials were served with a court injunction restraining them from interfering with the showing of the film.

When it was finally released, of course it became a hit because of the publicity; it played three weeks on the Pier. Appearances by Jane Russell during that run helped it tremendously.

"The reason we booked the picture was because United Artists

couldn't sell it anywhere," said George Hamid, Jr. "My father and I looked at the picture to see if it was risqué, and it was nothing but a mediocre western. There were no sexual implications at all. We booked that picture into both the Casino and Ocean theaters to packed crowds.

"Jane played the first two weeks of the three-week run. And since it was a world premiere of a much-discussed 'naughty' picture ... she was the unhappiest, scared person you ever saw in your life. She came out to sing three songs and she couldn't sing a note. She wasn't a singer. But the people loved her. But she got a coach and they taught

In 1964 teenagers couldn't wait for the Beatles' first movie, "A Hard Day's Night". It was the first of many rock films that would play the Pier.

In 1941 Abbott & Costello appeared to promote their movie "Hold That Ghost."

Jersey, and Helen Scharff of Philadelphia.

"The Burglar," a 1957 movie starring Jayne Mansfield and Dan Duryea, was shot in Atlantic City, and the Pier plays prominently in the story. At the end of the film, gangsters are following Mansfield and Duryea. The stars duck into Steel Pier and try to escape by going through the Fun House in the basement.

Though the Pier was closed, it appears in the background in Louis Malle's excellent 1980 film "Atlantic City", with Burt Lancaster and Susan Sarandon, while being discussed during a Boardwalk stroll.

her how to sing and she came back to the Pier and was a damn good attraction."

Steel Pier itself was featured prominently in at least two motion pictures, and was mentioned by name in some others. "Convention Girl," a cheap 1934 production that starred Rose Hobart and featured Shemp Howard of the Three Stooges, was filmed at the resort. A long montage features a group of people walking through the Pier, enjoying the exotic animal exhibits; then they join a large crowd watching the Water Circus and Diving Horse at the end of the Pier.

"Convention Girl" actually played on the Pier in September 1934 in what had to be a surreal moment as patrons watched a Hollywood film that showed scenes of the exact location where they were. Interestingly, the cast included four girls who won parts in a contest held a few months earlier on the Pier: Ethel Powell of Atlantic City, Esther Gallagher of Pittston, Pennsylvania, Martha Fisher of Berlin, New

Other films — such as 1944's "Atlantic City" with Constance Moore and featuring the song "By the Sea," and 1946's "Three Little Girls in Blue" with June Haver and George Montgomery, featuring the tune "On the Boardwalk (in Atlantic City)" — centered on the resort's early years. They were filmed in Hollywood, with stock footage of the Boardwalk spliced in.

The 1944 "Atlantic City" had a big opening on Hamid's Million Dollar Pier on July 29 that year.

"The King of Marvin Gardens," a 1972 film with Jack Nicholson and Bruce Dern, shows the resort in the off-season during its days as a crumbling but fascinating relic before the casinos arrived.

❦ ❦ ❦ ❦

On December 25, 1953, the Hamids opened the newly remodeled

Ocean Theater, equipping it with the most modern amenities, such as CinemaScope and 3-D with stereophonic sound. The theater held 2,300, and the stage was forty feet wide and sixteen feet high. The opening movie was "Here Come the Girls" with Bob Hope.

The theater remained open that winter, harking back to the pre-war days of winter movies. First-run movies such as "The Glenn Miller Story" were shown, but by spring, it was back to the Bowery Boys and "B" westerns. Other features of that decade were Debbie Reynolds' "Tammy and the Bachelor," and "Return of the Fly."

"Not quite B-movies," clarified George Hamid, Jr. in a 1988 interview. "Movies after the war were booked on percentage. The first week you'd pay forty percent, then thirty-five percent and down. It got so that a real big picture could earn $45,000 in Atlantic City. We couldn't afford that. What we did was buy the lesser A-pictures. The studios knew which ones were going to be blockbusters."

The Boardwalk's Stanley, Virginia and Warner theaters, and the downtown Shore, Hollywood and Center theaters were all owned by the Hamids during the 1950s, enabling them to book and control almost all the major motion pictures in Atlantic City. They changed the name of the Warner to the Warren, with hopes that stage shows would bring crowds back. But property taxes proved too expensive, so most of the structure was torn down in 1963 and replaced with a bowling alley. Today, only the façade remains as a part of Bally's Wild West Casino.

Steel Pier's Casino and Music Hall followed the Ocean's lead and were both equipped during the 1950s with stereophonic sound and capabilities for Cinerama, with the addition of larger screens.

By the 1960s, rock and roll had become entrenched in America's culture and on Steel Pier. On July 22, 1962, Frankie Avalon and Annette Funicello's "Beach Party" made its world premiere on the Pier, with Avalon appearing in person.

The Beatles' "A Hard Day's Night" opened on August 5, 1964, and played continuously from 9:30 A.M. each day for two weeks to a mobbed Casino theater full of teenagers. A year later, their second movie, "Help!," also played to large crowds.

Sonny and Cher showed up in their 1967 romp "Good Times," followed by Herman's Hermits in "Mrs. Brown, You've Got a Lovely Daughter," and the Monkees' "Head" in 1969.

Of course, there was other '60s light comedy fare, such as "Yours, Mine, and Ours" with Lucille Ball and Henry Fonda, and "Call Me Bwana" with Bob Hope and Anita Ekberg.

George Hamid, Jr. tried to keep the movies on the Pier up to standard family fare in the early 1970s, even though it seemed that movies were going into a moral decline. The motion picture ratings, which first appeared in 1968, made family-type movies harder to find. Sex and violence had become a staple of most movies.

Most of the Pier's pictures were rated PG, such as John Wayne's "Rio Lobo," Alfred Hitchcock's "Topaz," George C. Scott's "The Hospital," and Frank Sinatra's "Dirty Dingus Magee." Others included "The Andromeda Strain," "Cactus Flower" with Walter Matthau, the Beatles' "Let It Be," and the re-release of "West Side Story." When Hamid left the Pier in 1975, the movie bookings ended.

The famed Music Hall and Ocean/Midway theaters (the Ocean had been renamed the Midway in 1954) were demolished by new owners prior to the 1976 season, leaving just the Casino theater on the Boardwalk front to show movies. Until it closed in 1978, older films with a family theme were brought back, but by that time nobody seemed to care.

The majority of movies shown on Steel Pier weren't considered classics. In fact, most were "B" films that probably played the "grind" theaters of New York's 42nd Street. But you didn't go to Steel Pier for the movies, unless it happened to rain and you wanted to be inside for hours on end. You went primarily for entertainment and dancing. The movies were just part of the admission package, but they were also part of the Pier's charm.

Geo A. Hamid PROUDLY PRESENTS

STEEL PIER

MAGAZINE

THE AMUSEMENT CITY AT SEA

STEEL PIER

THE SHOW PLACE
OF THE NATION

DAILY
TIME SCHEDULE
OF EVENTS

ATLANTIC CITY, NEW JERSEY

25¢

Chapter Fourteen

Easter Sunday on The Pier

Atlantic City's biggest days of the year were Labor Day, Fourth of July, Memorial Day and Easter. Steel Pier would open Memorial Day with name stars, though not the biggest celebrities. The bigger names would come in around the Fourth of July, when the crowds became large, and remain until Labor Day, when lesser-known performers would be booked for the rest of September.

Easter was a different story. Atlantic City had always attracted a tremendous crowd Easter weekend, usually a half million or more. The famous Easter Parade on the packed Boardwalk would last all day. Families would be dressed in their finest, showing off the latest fashions. It was a flurry of furs, bonnets and suits, a blatant statement of prosperity and refinement.

The Boardwalk had become as fashionable

as New York's Fifth Avenue. President Ulysses S. Grant, a guest at the United States Hotel, joined in the parade of 1876, before the Boardwalk piers had been built.

During the twentieth century, there would be a choice of movies and shows to see throughout the city's theaters, in addition to dancing and dining all weekend long. Steel Pier, as well as Young's Million Dollar Pier and Steeplechase Pier, remained open all year until the end of 1938.

Though entertainment drew the crowds to the shore Easter Sunday, the religious aspect remained an essential ingredient, as an estimated crowd of 2,000 to 4,000 gathered on the beach at Maryland Avenue in 1925 for the Easter sunrise service. The service was broadcast over station WPG — a first in those early days of radio.

After Frank Gravatt bought the Pier, efforts were gradually made for the Pier to become a part of the Easter activities. In 1927, there were concerts by Vessella's Band, as well as dancing to the Radiotone Dance Orchestra. Special operatic concerts on Palm Sunday and Easter Sunday were presented, as well as the usual showing of motion pictures.

Alex Bartha's local orchestra filled in nicely from the late 1930s until the early 1950s. Movies were always shown Easter weekend, and most of the Pier operated as if it were a normal summer day.

Sunrise services began around 1936 at the Water Circus area at the Pier's end, and carried on into the 1960s. At 5:45 A.M.., the musical interlude would begin, and at 6 A.M. the services would commence as the sun rose over the ocean. The circus bowl seated roughly 5,000 people, and it was not unusual to have a full house. In 1939, Bishop Edwin Holt Hughes delivered the address, and an organ and a choir of 200 furnished the music.

In 1940, the weather proved too cold, and services were moved indoors to a theater where 3,000 people attended.

In 1933, radio stars Amos 'n' Andy appeared Easter weekend, and two movies were shown. Here's a partial list of who played the Pier on other Easter weekends:

Year	Stars	Bands	Added
1933	Amos 'n' Andy		
1934	Sally Rand		
1935	Rudy Vallee		Movie: "The Little Colonel"
1936	Major Bowes Amateurs	Jan Garber	Movie: "Captain January"
1938	Dixie Dunbar, Belle Baker	Gene Krupa (Sat.)	
		Kay Kyser (Sun.)	
		Alex Bartha (both)	
1939	Joe E. Lewis, Helen Morgan	Harry James (Sat.)	Sunrise Services 6 A.M.
		Benny Goodman (Sun.)	
		Alex Bartha (both)	
1941	John Boles	Tommy Dorsey	
1942	Ink Spots	Jimmy Dorsey	
1946	Vaughn Monroe	Harry James	
1947	Marion Hutton	Frankie Carle	
1950	Five DeMarco Sisters	Jimmy Dorsey	
1953	Four Aces	Vaughn Monroe	
1954	Al Martino	Tony Pastor	
1955	Jaye P. Morgan	Ralph Flanagan	
1958	Four Aces, Denise Lor	Charlie Spivak	Grady-Hurst Record Hop
1959	The Mariners	Al Raymond	Diving Horse
1960	Dion & Belmonts	Buddy Morrow	Grady-Hurst Record Hop
1961	Bobby Rydell	Maynard Ferguson	Hurst Record Hop
1962	Linda Scott	G. Miller/McKinley	Hurst Twist Record Hop
1965	Les Paul	Les & Larry Elgart	
1966	Peter & Gordon, Staff Sgt. Barry Sadler	Al Raymond	
1968	The Happenings	Mike Pedicin Quintet	
1969	1910 Fruitgum Co.	Paul Mann	

Easter sunrise service held in the Water Circus area at the end of the Pier. Note the distance between the clergy, musicians and worshippers.

Billboard advertising Jimmy Dorsey appearing on the Pier Easter 1942.

On a typical Easter weekend, the Pier would open on Saturday from noon until 1 A.M. Sunday hours were from 9:30 A.M. until an hour past midnight. Beginning in 1960, the Pier would open only Easter Sunday, at 10 A.M.. This could have been a response to the decline of both Easter visitors and the city itself.

"I remember going to sunrise services on Steel Pier Easter morning in 1947 and 1948. They were always held at the Water Circus end of the Pier, and when the service was over, they threw flowers into the ocean," recalled visitor Bill Martin.

The service in 1950 began at 6 A.M. with music by the Orpheus Singers. The speaker was the Reverend Joseph Sizoo, president of the Brunswick Theological Seminary.

"Everyone always had a brand-new Easter outfit, complete with a large picture hat bought at Gottlieb's on Atlantic Avenue and a corsage of fresh baby rosebuds to match. After church and the customary walk on the boards with girlfriends, you would head for the biggest show bargain — Steel Pier," remembered Toni Cummins in *Atlantic City* magazine some thirty years later.

For Ron Kane, Easter weekend on the Pier was the biggest date, besides the prom, for him and his friends from the Philadelphia area. "Girls wore wide, felt skirts, a turtleneck sweater and scarf under the neck. Guys wore royal blue pegged pants, box-toed shoes and a gold silk shirt. The biggest thing with the boys was the General Motors exhibit. I think I saw the first Corvette there, about 1954."

On Saturdays, the Pier would have 3,000 people and on Sunday, the crowd would swell to about 30,000. In 1946, a record 35,000 people jammed the Pier that Easter Sunday to dance to Harry James and his band.

By the late 1950s and early 1960s, the Grady-Hurst Record Hops were held on Easter Sundays, beginning at 4:30 P.M. and lasting four hours.

But it became apparent by the end of the 1960s that Easter weekend in Atlantic City had dramatically changed, with crowds greatly diminished. As the Hamids tried to hold the Pier together into the 1970s, they knew that the Easter show could not continue to make a profit. Saturday business had died, and people were coming down not for the weekends, but only for Easter Sunday. Almost a decade before the Pier itself closed, the Easter program had run its course.

In a 1974 Easter week interview with *The New York Times*, George Hamid, Jr. reflected on what once was: "The only Easter parade on the east coast that means anything is in Atlantic City. If we get a pretty Saturday and Sunday, you won't be able to walk on the Boardwalk, and I'll wish I was open."

It was a special time to visit Atlantic City, religiously and socially. But as the city crumbled, so did tradition.

Chapter Fifteen

The Rock 'n' Roll Years

Geo. A. Hamid proudly presents

THE SHOW PLACE OF THE NATION

STEEL PIER

ATLANTIC CITY, NEW JERSEY

AN AMUSEMENT CITY AT SEA

Souvenir Program

DAILY TIME SCHEDULE OF EVENTS

25¢

Most historians pick 1955 as the beginning of rock and roll, though rhythm and blues groups were around since at least 1949, and the jump swing of Louis Jordan even before that. But 1955 is the year that rock and roll came to the masses by way of Bill Haley and the Comets' "Rock Around the Clock," the theme from the movie "The Blackboard Jungle."

With Steel Pier owners George Hamid, Sr. and George Hamid, Jr. so closely attuned to the music trends, it was not surprising that Bill Haley and the Comets became the first rock and roll band booked at Steel Pier. The rising stars came into the Music Hall during the last week of June 1955, along with comic and master of ceremonies Gary Morton (who later became Lucille Ball's husband after she divorced Desi Arnaz). It was only the beginning of the summer season, but the Comets were a major draw. By that time, they were a well-known musical act along the southern Jersey Shore, having already played small clubs in Cape May and Wildwood in previous years.

In August, the Crew Cuts — famous for doing the "white" sanitized version of the Chords' "Sh-Boom" — were the headliners. It was the first taste of what was to become a trend at the Pier.

The following year brought in Pat Boone, who had a number of hits already under his belt and was fast becoming the heartthrob of female teenagers. His squeaky-clean image contrasted with the rhythm and blues songs that he remade into hits.

Now the number one band in the country Bill Haley returned in August 1956 and was an even bigger smash.

By 1957, it became clear that rock and roll was not going away. A disc jockey by the name of Dick Clark had taken over the "American Bandstand" television program in Philadelphia, which was only a little more than an hour away from the shore. Teenagers devoured this music and couldn't wait to do the latest dance steps in their club basement or in front of the television cameras.

George Hamid, never one to back away from a new trend, welcomed the rock and rollers with open arms. It meant big business at the Pier, especially with the teenagers who poured into Atlantic City during the summer.

The Diamonds, featuring their big hit, "Little Darlin'," shared the bill with a young Steve Lawrence in July. Lawrence, a singer on the old Steve Allen "Tonight" show, along with his new wife, Eydie Gorme, had started out as something of a teen idol. With hits such as "Footsteps," his face appeared in teen magazines next to Boone's and Haley's. While the teens were bopping to the Diamonds and Lawrence in the Music Hall, their parents were in the Ballroom out over the ocean, dancing to Woody Herman and his Third Herd Orchestra.

☾ ☾ ☾ ☾

In 1958, the Pier kicked off its usual Easter weekend program. This time, however, two disc jockeys and television personalities from Philadelphia welcomed teens into the Marine Ballroom for a record hop that lasted from 5 until 8:15 P.M. Their names were Joe Grady and Ed

Hurst, and they would remain on the Pier for many years.

At 9 P.M., the Charlie Spivak Orchestra took over. The contrast between the two musical styles was intriguing, considering most venues at that time would never dream of mixing the two under one roof. But on Steel Pier, anything was possible.

An Atlantic City native, Hurst began his radio career in 1944 at WFPG in Atlantic City while only a junior in high school. In 1946, he joined WPEN in Philadelphia, originating "The 950 Club" with Grady as his partner. The show became a top-rated radio program for the next ten years. It was the first teenage dance show, a forerunner to television's "American Bandstand," and it remained on the air until 1955.

"We were offered the 'American Bandstand' show originally, before (original host) Bob Horn on Channel 6 — before anybody," Hurst stated in a 2001 interview. "But we were under contract to Sun Ray Drug, which owned WPEN, and they said, 'Nothin' doin'."

"The Grady & Hurst Show" ran on Philadelphia television throughout most of the 1950s before the DJs staged record hops on Steel Pier. A June 1958 TV program listed the show telecast live in Philadelphia on WVUE every Wednesday, Thursday and Friday, in addition to the regular "Record Hop" in the Marine Ballroom from 4 to 8 P.M. on Saturday. A year later, the show was telecast only on weekends from 1 to 3 P.M. in the Ballroom.

"We used to do the TV shows live Saturdays and Sundays from 1958 to 1960, because there was no tape then," Hurst said. "And we had the highest rating of any local shows during the summers."

By 1961, the program was called "Summertime on the Pier," with Hurst going solo in the weekend time slots. Later syndicated across the country, the show provided millions of teenagers the opportunity to dance at the Pier and also then watch themselves on television.

"The show was syndicated, but each year got worse," explained Hurst. "The town got worse and the Pier was booking terrible attractions. It was not very comfortable. In order to save money, we taped three two-hour shows at each session. We taped from 8 in the morning to 8 at night! The kids brought three changes of clothes, so they were all right. They would stay all afternoon. They loved it! They were the stars!"

Philadelphia teenager Donna Hall was one of them. "When I was on 'Summertime on the Pier,' I was not told we were taping two to

STEEL PIER

SHOW PLACE OF THE NATION

Presents *America's Brightest Stars*

PAT BOONE
AUGUST 20-21

RICKY NELSON JULY 2-3

LENNON SISTERS
JULY 4-10

LOUIS ARMSTRONG
JULY 29-AUGUST 4

FRANKIE AVALON
JULY 16-17

THREE STOOGES
JUNE 26-JULY 2

Along with Louis Armstrong, the Three Stooges, and the Lennon Sisters, teen idols Pat Boone, Frankie Avalon and Ricky Nelson were prominently featured.

three shows. So the next Saturday when the show appeared, I came out with the same clothes on, when everyone else changed theirs. So, I was walking down the streets of Philly one day and this guy yelled out, 'Hey, that's the girl from the Steel Pier show!' And guess what I was wearing? The same black and white striped shirt. I don't think I wore that shirt again, but it was sure nice to be recognized."

"We had a select group of dancers," Hurst said. "When we did it in the Ballroom, we had a lot of room. But when it burned down, we put it in the Casino up front and there was only room for 100 kids. We couldn't use the Golden Dome that replaced the Ballroom because we couldn't light it properly and it had no stage."

After the final year of televising the show solo in 1978, Ed Hurst reunited with Joe Grady on WPEN radio from 1981 to 1987, when Grady finally retired. Hurst continued to host a show in the late 1990s that brought back music from the days on the Pier.

Bill Haley and his group returned again in 1958, as did Danny and the Juniors, the Philly group that popularized "At the Hop." Their second hit, "Rock and Roll Is Here to Stay," became the anthem of young America.

A very young Paul Anka, of "Diana" fame, arrived in July of 1958, as did the "Honeycomb" man, Jimmie Rodgers. For Anka, it was the first of hundreds of performances he would give Atlantic City, including the showrooms of today's casino hotels.

But nobody could have forecast the events of the Labor Day holiday of 1958. As usual, the Hamids at Steel Pier were searching for a blockbuster act. They found Ricky Nelson.

"The only reason that we got Ricky Nelson," recalled George Hamid, Jr., "is that he had never made a personal appearance. I knew from my spies that if he ever did, it was going to be huge." Hamid received a call from an agent that he knew at the MCA agency. Ozzie and Harriet Nelson had played the Pier several years earlier with their orchestra, and because of their association with George Hamid, Sr., they wanted Steel Pier to host their son Ricky in his first public appearance. Ricky had been featured regularly on his parents' weekly TV show, "The Adventures of Ozzie and Harriet", with songs that were hitting the Top 10 charts. Thanks to TV, Ricky was becoming a major rock and roll star.

But George Hamid, Jr. was skeptical. Nelson wanted $10,000 for two days.

Only one year earlier, Hamid's reluctance to take a risk turned out to be a huge blunder. The William Morris Agency was promoting a new singer for the extraordinary fee of $12,500 for three

In 1960, Chubby Checker was the first black solo rock and roll performer to play the Pier.

STEEL PIER in presents the NATION'S TOP STARS of STAGE SCREEN and TV

DION
June 23-28

CHUBBY CHECKER
June 29-July 5

RICKY NELSON
July 6-7

Ricky Nelson looks out at the crowd that began lining up on the Boardwalk before dawn on August 31, 1958. His appearance set the Steel Pier single-day attendance record of 44,221.

days. Hamid's reply was "You're crazy asking that much for a kid who had one hit record! Besides, the country is never going to buy a guy whose first name is Elvis."

Because of Hamid's rare lack of foresight, Elvis Presley never appeared at Steel Pier.

"Turning [the Morris Agency] down was the biggest mistake of my life," George Hamid, Jr. admitted later, "but it didn't seem like a mistake at the time."

With Ricky Nelson, he would be taking a chance on someone who had never performed on stage. Yet he wouldn't forfeit a second big opportunity to get on board with rock and roll.

Hamid called Dick Clark in Philadelphia, who talked him into signing Nelson, lest he make a decision he would regret.

☙ ☙ ☙ ☙

At dawn on August 31, George Hamid, Jr. received word that something big was happening in front of the Pier. When he arrived on the scene, thousands of teenagers were in lines snaking down the Boardwalk.

"Kids were lined up for over a mile, from the box office down to Hackney's Restaurant at 6:30 that morning," he said. Hamid knew they were there for his headliner, but he never imagined that so many kids would be ready to stampede the Pier just to see Ricky Nelson.

"I rushed to the Pier and advanced the opening time from 10 A.M. to 9 A.M. It was the most rewarding and most hectic day of my entire theatrical life," he remembered in a 1986 *Press of Atlantic City* account of Steel Pier's greatest day.

When the Pier opened at 9:30 that morning, the Music Hall's seats were filled within fifteen minutes. The first customers, however, had to sit through a few movies, one being the forgettable "Once Upon a Horse," starring Dan Rowan and Dick Martin, later of TV's "Laugh-In" fame.

At 1 o'clock, the stage show began. After some minor vaudeville acts, comedian Henny Youngman, who probably had no idea what he was getting into, promptly walked out on stage to do his act of one-liners. The teenage crowd screamed and yelled for Nelson, giving Mr. Youngman more than his share of hecklers. He knew he was licked and promptly gave up the stage.

Frankie Avalon and Annette Funicello are welcomed by George Hamid, Jr. at the Diving Bell, 1963.

"A theatrical mismatch if ever there was one," Hamid said. "I did something unusual. I went out and introduced Ricky because I didn't think they were going to stand still if Henny Youngman introduced him. I never saw it before or since — when he walked on that stage. Every kid must have had a flash camera, and for one five-second span, it was daylight. We had maybe 2,500 people in the theater, and it was 1 o'clock, and there were already almost 12,000 people on the Pier. And I thought, 'There's no way we're going to do this!'"

Hamid watched from backstage as bedlam erupted, and knew something had to be done to accommodate the countless teens standing in line on the Boardwalk. They had to be diverted so that Ricky could leave the Music Hall safely and proceed to the much larger Marine Ballroom in the back of the Pier.

After the 1 o'clock show, a young fan in the crowd was picked as a decoy and whisked out the side door into a limousine. Fans, thinking he was Ricky, ran after the vehicle, while the real Ricky, along with bodyguards and policemen, ran to the back of the Pier.

"I waited outside the side entrance with one of my girlfriends and I caught a glimpse of Ricky Nelson in his limo leaving," remembered one fan, Jan Williams. "I got up to the window and pressed my face so close I could actually see in and saw him close up." Whether or not she had been close to the real Ricky was unclear. A year later, the decoy — Fabian Forte of South Philadelphia — also became a teen idol and played the Pier to his own adoring fans.

The remaining shows that day were held in the spacious Marine Ballroom, accommodating up to 10,000 standees. Nelson was the first rock and roll performer to break the Ballroom's orchestra-only policy, and he was the Ballroom's first solo singer since Frank Sinatra on

South Philly's Bobby Rydell was a regular at the Pier, appearing eight times between 1960 and 1974.

Labor Day 1950. Hamid and Nelson had, by purest accident, unknowingly given birth to the modern rock concert.

"By necessity, we presented the remainder of his performances in the Ballroom. And he was a prisoner. There was no way he could get off the Pier," Hamid remembered. "There was no other way we could have played to all the people who were coming on the Pier. We had maybe fifteen police get us out to the Ballroom and back in. And unfortunately, it was the hottest Labor Day that I remember."

"When 10,000 people broke out of the Ballroom, the Pier began to sway!" Ed Hurst recalled. His partner, Joe Grady, a nonswimmer, feared that the Pier would eventually collapse. He called it quits on the Pier after one more year of the record hops.

Ricky Nelson set the all-time Steel Pier record that day as 44,221 people came through the turnstiles from 9 A.M. until midnight, breaking the record of 41,000 set by Frank Sinatra exactly eight years earlier. Bodies were packed so tightly together in the stuffy Ballroom that girls fainting from the excitement and oppressive summer heat had no place to fall. The only unobstructed exit was through the rear door of the stage. Burly security guards collected the swooning females and passed them up onto the stage, right past Ricky Nelson, to get them out to fresh air. And that electrified the audience more.

"Once the kids saw that," Hamid said, "they all started 'fainting,' figuring they were going to get backstage."

It was the wildest day in the Pier's history. Long-time *Press of Atlantic City* reporter Frank Prendergast recalled the day in a 1986 feature story:

They shouted, they screamed, they fainted, and they fell. Not since Frank Sinatra leaned his slight frame into the wind of sighs as he crooned songs of love, has a teenage tempest been seen on the Pier.

The room was so jammed that those who fainted had no room to fall down. Their knees buckled, but the crowd held them up.

It was like stuffing sardines in a can. I think maybe some of the kids were faking the faint ...

Back then, it was amazing to see so many kids get together to see one guy who, as I remember it, really didn't sing that well. That's probably because neither he nor the crowd really had a chance to hear him sing. Nobody listened, so nobody knows if he was even singing. He stood on the stage, strummed his guitar and opened his mouth. But with each number he no more than sounded the opening chords on the guitar when every youngster in the ballroom seemed to know what was coming. Immediately, a mass shriek overwhelmed everything and everybody.

Nelson would play the Pier five more times, including the Pier's second-biggest gate ever: 43,774 in 1961. None of the later appearances, however, were as wild as the first.

"On that particular day, Rick was the hottest attraction in the world," said Hamid.

☾　☾　☾　☾

The 1950s closed out with a return appearance of Nelson, along with teen idols Tommy Sands, Bobby Darin, Frankie Avalon ($4,000 for the week) and Fabian. In fact, for two days, you could have seen both Ricky Nelson and Bobby Darin playing separate shows.

"It was Fabian who really took my eye," fan Bonnie Erwin later told *Atlantic City* magazine. "My boyfriend was old enough to realize that I was just a silly bobby soxer. He was jealous as I screamed my lungs out, but it didn't affect our relationship."

The Easter weekend show of 1960 finally put pop music over the top. Usually that weekend, one of the biggest of the year, was reserved for traditional singers or middle-of-the-road entertainers. That year, Dion and the Belmonts showed up on Easter Sunday, singing their current hit, "Where or When?"

Rock fan Claire Welgus Whitlock had the particular advantage then of being the young daughter of the night doorman at the Traymore Hotel at Illinois Avenue. "My friends and I used to hang out at the Steel Pier stage door. We met most of the singers at the time — Bobby Rydell, Dion, Del Shannon, etc. I gave Ricky Nelson the key to the city. Most were very nice to their fans. I was crazy about Paul Anka, and one summer when I was about thirteen, he stayed at the Traymore. My dad called home from work one night — it had to be after 11 P.M. — and said that Paul had just gone out for dinner and I should take a jitney to the hotel and wait in the lobby to meet him when he got back. All went as planned and Paul couldn't have been nicer."

What is notable during the reign of rock and roll at the Pier, however, is the conspicuous absence of African-American performers. Performers like Louis Armstrong — considered "safe" by the paying adults — were welcome, but rock innovators like Chuck Berry, Little Richard, Bo Diddley, the Flamingos, and the Coasters never played there. Even though Steel Pier was open to rock and roll, it appeared to be open only to certain kinds of rock and roll — namely, unthreatening, white teen-idol types. Then, in 1961, Chubby Checker finally broke the color bar as a headliner with his huge hit, "The Twist."

"The Twist" was the number one hit not once, but twice in successive years — a feat that has never been repeated. Chubby Checker,

Rising pop stars like Brenda Lee were often booked with established stars, such as singer Al Martino.

because of the song's international popularity and his South Philadelphia connection, became the first black solo rock and roll performer to appear on Steel Pier.

That it took six long years after the inception of rock and roll for this event to happen was a reflection of the bias that still permeated most of American society. Although it was the music of African-Americans that influenced many of the nation's youth, it became the white performers who garnered most of the accolades and became stars. Chubby's breakthrough made it possible for other black performers to eventually play the Pier.

George Hamid, Jr., defending his pick of headliners, said "Our goal, always, was to play the hottest attraction."

Tom Allen, an African-American who grew up in Atlantic City, gave his view of the city's racial aspect: "If you look at a map, Atlantic City is below the Mason-Dixon Line, and so you had the practices that mimicked the places that were farther south. Your dividing line in Atlantic City was Atlantic Avenue. To the north was the black community. To the south, going towards the Boardwalk, were the hotels and restaurants, and they were segregated. There was a part of the beach at Missouri Avenue that was reserved for black people, known as 'Chicken Bone Beach.' It goes back to the '20s.

"The kind of entertainment that was at the Pier, we weren't really welcome at those dances. It was cultural differences. It's not likely you're going to go up to Steel Pier to hear Tommy Dorsey when someone like Ella Fitzgerald is at the Club Harlem on Kentucky Avenue. People's ears are tuned culturally."

The early 1960s brought more big-name stars. It was not unusual to visit the Pier during that period and witness performances by Paul Anka ($3,500 for the week), Brenda Lee (who played the Pier seven times), the Everly Brothers, Bobby Rydell, James Darren, Dion, Del Shannon or Jerry Lee Lewis. Frankie Avalon cost Hamid $5,000 for the week, while Fabian cost $2,500.

In 1962 Hamid, Jr. summed up the difference between the rock stars and those who played vaudeville: "It used to take somebody like Sophie Tucker ten years to get her name in lights." He said. "Now you're on the marquee if you cut a single record. I just can't take paying these kids $10,000."

South Philly's Bobby Rydell, who played the Pier eight times,

recorded a 45 RPM record titled *Steel Pier*. But it wasn't nearly as big a hit as *Wildwood Days*, his homage to another Jersey Shore hot spot.

The audiences on the Pier were still predominately white, although more and more blacks were gradually attending the rock and roll shows, especially Dick Clark's, where groups of both races were billed equally.

☾ ☾ ☾ ☾

Clark, who from 1960 through 1964 brought his "Caravan of Stars" revue to the Pier, introduced a slew of young singers and groups to the summer dancing crowd. He featured stars such as Jimmy Clanton, the Crests, Bobby Rydell, Dee Dee Sharp, Jan and Dean, Johnny Tillotson, the Shirelles, Joey Dee, and The Supremes.

Clark commented:

I remember one time we were playing the Pier and we must have appeared after a terrible storm, because we could feel the Pier swaying out at the Marine Ballroom. The pilings under the Pier must have weakened. I even remember seeing the huge Coca-Cola sign swaying a bit, and George Hamid, Jr. came to me in the middle of a show and told me on the side that they would have to shut down for a while to reinforce the pilings.

Well, I said to George that you couldn't do that. You'd have a riot with all of these kids here. What I did was to tell my acts to just dog it — play as terrible a show as you possibly could do. Eventually, the kids slowly left the Ballroom and the area, because they were watching a truly awful show! It was the only way to safely get them out of the area so that the Pier could be repaired.

"It was the summer of '62," explained Hamid, "and we had just finished connecting the main part to the Ballroom. [A barge had cut through the Pier during the March Storm of '62.] When we put the lighting fixtures in, we hung them by chains instead of a rigid thing, and when the breeze came in through the windows, which were open all the time, they would move a little bit, and people got the impression that the Pier was actually swaying. I went out and said to Dick that the only time this illusion occurs is when you break your crowd. You have 6,000 people standing — when you break them, they all go out together. I said, 'Dick, what can you do to let them drift out instead of all together?' He said we'll have an autograph session after the show and they'll *crowd around and drift out slowly."*

((((

It was said of George Hamid, Jr. that he booked acts with an uncanny premonition. He would sign unknowns and see them climb the ladder to success when they played the Pier. One was Neil Sedaka, who performed at Steel Pier at the beginning of his career when he was about nineteen, and did three or four shows each day.

However, teen tastes changed once the Beatles and "The British Invasion" made their mark on American audiences. The Beatles were the biggest musical act since Elvis, and they changed the course of musical history. Overnight, it seemed, teen idols were forgotten and in their place stood four British mop-tops singing their own songs and blasting out chord changes on their guitars. Sappy background strings were gone, replaced by the rebellious rhythm of pounding drums.

On August 5, 1964, "A Hard Day's Night," the Beatles' debut movie, opened exclusively on Steel Pier. Since the Pier was a hotspot for teenagers, it was only logical to open the Beatles film there. It was a smash and stayed at the Pier for many weeks, a rare practice at that time.

"I remember watching 'A Hard Day's Night' at Steel Pier continuously from 10 A.M. to 11 P.M., four times on the first day it came out," one fan recalled.

Hamid booked the Beatles themselves for the Marine Ballroom for August 30, 1964, immediately following the Democratic National Convention, which was headquartered in Atlantic City that year. Hamid realized, however, that the demand for Beatles tickets would exceed the capacity of the Marine Ballroom, so he moved the venue to the vast auditorium of Convention Hall. The Beatles were paid a then-whopping sum of $25,000.

"I couldn't put them on the Pier because it would have fallen into the ocean," Hamid remarked in 1988. "The Beatles would have been impossible. From having experienced the Ricky Nelson situation, we knew it couldn't have worked on Steel Pier.

"We were the only stop on the Beatles tour where they didn't have near riots, because I knew what to do. I had it leaked out that they were going to the Shelburne Hotel — they went to the Lafayette. I leaked out that they were coming down in my limousine — they came in on a helicopter. I had two limos at the airport, and they looked out

from the helicopter and couldn't believe nobody was there."

After a press conference held at Convention Hall, the Beatles quietly checked into the Lafayette Hotel. But it wasn't quiet for long:

"From the moment they arrived, word got out and their hotel was surrounded by thousands of pleading, screaming fans," Hamid said. "Looking at the police barricade and the surging crowds, I could only think of a medieval castle under siege.

"We finally got them out of town by parking a huge bus in front of the hotel and sneaking them out back in a fish truck."

Hamid was responsible for purchasing two pairs of eyeglasses for John Lennon, as well as promoting their next area performance two years later. Tickets to the Beatles show at JFK Stadium in Philadelphia on August 16, 1966 could be purchased in the Steel Pier Music Hall lobby.

((((

Ever-changing music trends delivered a variety of performers during the rest of the 1960s. Hot British groups like Peter and Gordon, Herman's Hermits, Freddie and the Dreamers, and the Dave Clark Five appeared. Hamid found success with most, except for one band named the Animals. "Trying to deal and communicate with them — their backstage manner was terrible, their performance was not exciting, and it didn't turn the kids on at all," he said.

The New York Times covered Herman's Hermits on the Pier in August 1965:

An estimated throng of 10,000 persons jammed the entrance to Steel Pier tonight to attend a performance of Herman's Hermits, a British rock n' roll group.

About thirty off-duty policemen were hired to protect the five young singers from the howling mob.

During an afternoon performance, more than 8,000 youngsters crammed into Steel Pier's Ballroom to hear the group. At least thirty persons in the audience were treated for heat exhaustion, and five policemen were stationed on the stage to protect the group from the crush.

The singers had to duck under the barrage of love notes and stuffed animals that were hurled at them.

"I saw Herman's Hermits performing at the Pier in 1965 and stay-

Dick Clark brought his Caravan of Stars to the Pier from 1960 through 1964. This advertises the 1963 edition.

Teenagers line the stairs in the back of a packed Marine Ballroom to see "Philly's own", the host of American Bandstand, Dick Clark.

Segregation in Atlantic City was evident in living quarters and on the beach. Next to Million Dollar Pier was "Chicken Bone Beach", where entertainers like Sammy Davis, Jr. and Nat "King" Cole could relax without harassment.

ing across the way at the Terrace Hotel-Motel. Fans were singing 'Henry the VIII' to them outside the hotel," remembered one fan, Kenneth Knops.

The same grueling show schedule of earlier vaudeville stars also pertained to most rock acts. They had to perform for a full week, playing four shows a day and five on weekends. Frankie Valli of the Four Seasons remembered it in a 2002 interview:

In those days, it was exciting to play Steel Pier, but it was tough work. You did your first show at 11:30 in the morning, and I think you finished about 11 o'clock at night. The show was about forty-five minutes or so and then they showed a movie, and then you came back and did another show. And when it rained, they did as many shows as they wanted — they didn't show the movie.

I think we did do one of the last shots at the Pier in 1975.

The one important thing in those days was if you played Steel Pier,

you got to play to audiences from so many different parts of the United States. Everybody came down to Atlantic City from Ohio, Pennsylvania, etc.

It was pretty old, but in those old theaters there was magic. We did a show in the Music Hall and we also did shows in the Casino. You had to do those things in those days. Four and five shows a day, all over. You did multiple shows everywhere then when you toured ... with Dick Clark, the Brooklyn Fox ...It may have been hard work, but in order to be successful, you had to do it.

⚊ ⚊ ⚊ ⚊

The late 1960s were a defining period for the Pier. It was perhaps its last hurrah. Rock music had become the nation's primary outlet for protest; the Civil Rights movement caused racial strife and animosity as minorities became more vocal and visible.

And so, along with the British bands, Motown invaded the Pier with its infectious pop rhythm and blues. Smokey Robinson and the Miracles, the Four Tops, Diana Ross and the Supremes, and the Temptations all appeared during this time. A strange pairing in 1967 had Frank Sinatra, Jr. along with Stevie Wonder. Dionne Warwick, Ray Charles, and the Fifth Dimension also appeared before the crowds.

"As I got older, six friends would drive to Atlantic City every weekend from May to October," a female fan remembers. "With six girls splitting the bill, we most of the time spent as little as $20 [each] for the entire weekend. This included our room, gas, and meals. We saw Fabian, Frankie Avalon, Bobby Rydell, Four Seasons, The Supremes, Dwayne Eddy, The Temptations, Chubby Checker ... and the Dick Clark shows just literally rocked the Pier."

Paul Steinberg ran a concession stand on the Pier. "I remember Diana Ross stopped by and asked me where the Dick Clark show was," he told the *Press of Atlantic City* for a 1985 story. "We used to get 20,000 people before 6 A.M. on a rainy day. We used to outdraw the Phillies. We'd get a million people in a summer. The Phillies would get 800,000 in those days."

Dave Sheets was a trumpet player in the pit band when Diana Ross performed. "We did nine shows in one day. We played in the theater, ran to the Ballroom, and did another show. Then ran back. We were fighting crowds to get back and forth. They went crazy for them," he related in a 2001 *Philadelphia Inquirer* feature. The Supremes played the Pier six times.

John Schofield played trombone in the house band for ten years. "We played with Lou Rawls, the Supremes, and Glen Campbell. The opening acts were juggling acts, spinning plates. We would work seven days a week, four shows a day."

Though black stars were now headliners, most blacks in Atlantic City didn't consider Steel Pier the only venue in town, according to city native Tom Allen:

One of the hottest entertainment districts on the east coast is what is known here as K.Y. and the Curb — that's Kentucky and Arctic Avenue. If you were there, you might go across the street from Club Harlem to where the Wonder Gardens was and see Stevie Wonder. Aretha Franklin might be at the Club Harlem. And then there were a lot of other clubs all around and they had great entertainment.

So there really wasn't any point to go to the Boardwalk in the season when all the clubs were jumping — unless you were going for a swim. But if you were looking for entertainment, why go over there?

People would go to the Motown shows. Groups like that weren't up there that often, anyway. I never picked up any racism from the Pier. I think there's a mixed bag of response in the black community about Steel Pier. I mean, I went on the Diving Bell. But from the North Side, I don't think you're going to find many people coming to see Ricky Nelson. But then there were a lot of whites that were into black music — soul music.

You would have something at the Club Harlem called the Breakfast Show, and the Club was a half block down Kentucky, off of Atlantic. The crowds would go all the way up Kentucky Avenue, corner of Atlantic. And a lot of the people in those crowds would be white.

I think that the dancing was off the table because they believed it was going to have an impact on the bottom line. And also there's an undercurrent of violence if you had racial dancing and mixing.

That defacto separation may also explain why other rhythm and blues singers like Otis Redding and James Brown never appeared. Or it could have been that both never had any mainstream hits at that point. Motown was middle-of-the-road and more commercially accepted.

☾ ☾ ☾ ☾

On July 1, 1966, Mick Jagger and the Rolling Stones performed in concert in the Marine Ballroom. They were popular but not quite as big as the Beatles; nonetheless, it was a landmark day. George Hamid, Jr. remembers them as gentlemen. He picked them up at the airport and drove them to the Pier in his convertible. Jagger, he said, was "the sweetest young man you'd want to meet, very respectful." There was no drama, only the usual screaming teenage girls in attendance.

Opening acts for the Stones were American groups the McCoys, the Standells, and the Tradewinds. That night, the Stan Kenton Orchestra played in the same arena where just hours before stood thousands of teens.

"The Rolling Stones were nothing at all like the Beatles," said Hamid. "The fans of the Beatles were crazy ... [Jagger] wasn't somebody that people would go out of their way to go crazy over, like they did over the Beatles.

"They were paid $10,000 for one day ... They were only available for that one day. We might have only had 3,000 people on a July 3. That day we had about 8,000. It wasn't sensational, but it paid for the act.

"They were back in the Ballroom and they didn't have time between shows to go out, so I got hot dogs and sodas for them. And they couldn't thank me enough."

A fan named Doug from Philadelphia remembers that day vividly, for it was his first rock concert and it began a lifelong obsession with the Rolling Stones:

My father had done some business with George Hamid, so I was given a season pass for the Pier and we got into the show for free. There were two shows that day.

I was able to get to the front. There was no security and you could stand right at the stage. I was about eight rows back.

The Tradewinds came out first. Their one hit was "New York's A Lonely Town." Next came the Standells with their hit, "Muddy Water," and then the McCoys of "Hang On, Sloopy" fame.

I remember all the screaming when the Stones came out. Mick Jagger was wearing an aqua sports jacket and Brian Jones had on a blue suit with large red and white stripes.

Back then, people had to use an individual flashbulb for each pic-

The rest of the day I was in a daze, don't remember the bus ride home to Philly —just the fact that I had seen the greatest rock and roll band in the world and had gotten to grab Brian's hand.

Doug has pictures from behind the Marine Ballroom as the Stones were running down to their van.

A few weeks after that, I also saw Herman's Hermits at the Pier. At that show, everyone was buying little stuffed bears and Herman (Peter Noone) was reaching down and taking them from all the girls that were trying to give them to him.

After the first show, the girl I was with convinced me to buy one of them to give to him. During the second show, he walked over by us but didn't take the bear. She got mad and threw it at him.

☾ ☾ ☾

The view from back stage at a Rolling Stones appearance, July 1, 1966. The crowd could stand right next to the stage without much security keeping fans from the band members.

ture they took, and I remember everyone throwing them on stage. After one of the songs, there was an announcement that the band would stop playing if people didn't stop throwing the bulbs.

As the band ran off the stage, I went outside on the Pier because I figured they would come by. As their van came by, suddenly a window opened and Brian leaned his hand on it. I reached out and grabbed his hand and was trying to climb into the van until he scowled at me and I jumped back. I also remember thinking I should pull off one of the buttons of his coat as a souvenir, but didn't.

Some of the one-hit wonders — booked at their peak of popularity — were the Cyrkle, Dino, Desi and Billy, O.C. Smith, the New Vaudeville Band, the Happenings, American Breed, Tiny Tim, 1910 Fruitgum Co., and Jay and the Techniques.

More well-known American bands — Paul Revere and the Raiders, the Beach Boys, the Four Seasons, Gary Lewis and the Playboys, the Byrds, Tommy James and the Shondells, and the Cowsills — also arrived at this time. In July 1969, Barbara Cowsill was hospitalized with exhaustion after appearing in the Music Hall on Steel Pier. She stayed in the Atlantic City hospital for five days, the teen magazine *16* reported later that year.

Peter and Gordon; 1965.

Joe Grady and Ed Hurst hosted teen hops as well as television shows, featuring many of the teen idols appearing on the Pier.

"Help!," the Beatles' second movie, was also successful on the Pier, but the Monkees' "Head" did not make the same impact.

Michelle Solomon, at *WSBTV.COM*, was a very young fan of the Monkees:

I'm probably showing my age here, but I remember when I was five years old and I stood outside the stage door. I was waiting for Davy Jones of the Monkees. I had ripped his photo out of Tiger Beat *magazine and was hoping for an autograph.*

My mom waited patiently with me and when he walked out of the door forty-five minutes later, he breezed by and flipped his mop-top head. I didn't get the autograph and ended up not liking Jones or the Monkees ever again. I didn't even watch the episode of "The Brady Bunch" when Jones guest-starred, although I did wonder if he gave Marcia an autograph.

☾ ☾ ☾ ☾

By the 1970s, the flavor of the Pier — and the mood of the entire nation, for that matter — grew entirely different. The war in Vietnam had taken its toll, and America's youth were no longer innocent; they had grown and become liberated. The hippie movement and sexual revolution had toppled every principle their parents had lived by. Baby boomers set out to change the way Americans lived.

"These kids, who are repulsive to ninety-five percent of the respectable people, will be coming in without leaving twenty cents behind, unless of course, they buy a hot dog and some pot," George Hamid, Sr. said with a scowl in 1969. The elder Hamid promised there would be no seedy rock groups on Steel Pier. Only clean, wholesome entertainment would be welcome.

George Hamid, Jr., who took over operation of the Pier after his father's death in 1971, could see the signs of decline in Atlantic City's future. Families were beginning to go elsewhere on vacations, attendance had fallen, and the quality of entertainment on the Pier was becoming more and more mediocre. Yet he embarked on a personal quest to uphold the tradition of Steel Pier as never before. He knew he had to bring in acts that represented the pulse of America, yet balanced a fine line between family entertainment, good taste, and rock and roll. And he did.

By the 1960s, crowds attending rock shows in the Marine Ballroom eventually became integrated.

"Steel Pier has survived all the onslaughts of theatrical change, but of course, we change with it. The Supremes, the Beach Boys — when you have acts like that, you're staying right up with the times," he remarked at the time.

From 1970 until he relinquished his management of the pier in 1975, Hamid brought in rock acts such as Chicago, the Allman Brothers, Kenny Rogers and the First Edition, Canned Heat, B.J. Thomas, Badfinger, the Grass Roots, David Cassidy, the Bee Gees, Delaney, Bonnie and Friends, the Ides of March, Dr. Hook, and in a crazy 1973 pairing, Curtis Mayfield with Blood, Sweat and Tears.

"I saw Delaney, Bonnie and Friends back in about 1970 or 1971 at the old Steel Pier in Atlantic City," fan Dennis Brutosky recalled some thirty years later. "At the time, I was about eleven or twelve years old. They really jammed, and you knew they were all having a great time, and they wanted you to know you were more than welcome. I especially remember when they did 'Soul Shake,' because I really love that song. And, of course, 'Never Ending Song of Love.'

"My sister noticed one of the guys in the band was playing a briefcase and we all just thought that was so crazy and fun. And the stage was filled with friends singing and dancing. After the concert, everyone was totally approachable. It was like a big party, or better yet, a big revival meeting. A real blast. We had a great time."

Lee Loughnane, trumpet player for Chicago, remembered one of their earliest gigs: "I remember we did a show at Steel Pier (September 1970). First it was the monkey act, then the Diving Horse, then us," he told the *ITG Journal* of the International Trumpet Guild.

In 1971, the Nitty Gritty Dirt Band played, with member Jackson Browne. At one point, they sat in the audience in the Music Hall, heckling the movie and the other acts before they went on.

Thrown into the mix were old favorites Frankie Avalon, Bobby Rydell, Frankie Valli and the Four Seasons, Pat Boone, and Brenda Lee. In an ironic note, Chuck Berry finally played the Pier in 1971 as part of an "oldies" package that featured the Duprees and the Dovells. Valli and the Four Seasons played the Pier eight times, more than any other rock group in Pier history.

Teen idol David Cassidy from TV's "The Partridge Family" played the Pier on August 28, 1971.

As noted in his autobiography, *David Cassidy: Could It Be Forever? My Story*, his time spent on the Pier was not fondly remembered.

I broke the attendance record at the Steel Pier, doing three shows in one very long day. It was old and very obviously unprepared for a show like mine and the crowds.

From the time I arrived in town, there were 50,000 kids absolutely jamming this pier waiting for me. There was only one way on and one way off…and security was almost non-existent. They had two guys at the artists' entrance at the stage. It was a joke.

For the first show, at around midday, I arrived and left via an ambulance. That sort of worked. … But some fans guessed I was inside. My cover was blown and I got grabbed a few times getting from the ambulance to the backstage entrance.

For the second show, we needed to be more creative. I walked the entire length of the pier, right through the crowd, disguised as a woman…

By the third show, in the evening, I hid my hair under a hat which I pulled down over my face, put on a pair of shades and raised the collar of my windbreaker up as high as possible. I walked with one of my publicists, a girl named Bryna, as if we were a couple. … Finally, when I was just a few steps away from the stage door, somebody spotted me and grabbed my hat. My hair came tumbling down and everybody could see it was me. Instant insanity! Chaos. Screaming. I managed to make it inside the building, slam the door shut and yell for security….

☾ ☾ ☾ ☾

"I remember being taken to see both David Cassidy and Pat Boone (separate gigs) one summer when I was about three," said Joanne Crumpet. "My dad worked there, so we got free tickets, and my mother was a huge Pat Boone fan! I remember him walking through the audience and my mother screeching, 'Pat! Pat!' and shoving me into his arms! Quite bizarre."

The next year, Rick Hoffman went to a somewhat dismal Badfinger concert on Sunday, July 23, 1972:

My wife at the time and I were weekending in Atlantic City at a hotel from our home in Philadelphia. We knew Badfinger was playing, so we planned to see the show. I had been to Steel Pier when I was about five and was shocked at how decrepit it had become.

There were several venues, and I was shocked to find that Badfinger was going to be playing outside in a small, chain-linked fenced-in area facing the beach with a few rows of bleachers. If you came in through the main Steel Pier entrance into the building, this was on the right side of the main building — it was not on the main outdoor stage, which was over the water and where the horses jumped. I would say this was a jury-rigged area, of sorts, and perhaps short-lived.

We were the only contemporary fans in the audience of less than fifty! I believe they played at least twice that day.

Most people at Steel Pier were tourists. They bought tickets for the day and followed the schedule from feature to feature. I believe the movie was the big event, but there may have been some other, more mainstream, performances inside as well. I was twenty-three at the time and it was all families in the audience with us there to gawk. At that time, I had never been to a show that wasn't all young freaks — hippies, as we called ourselves at the time.

Meanwhile, the time had come and the band wasn't there. In short order, I noticed a couple of young guys in cut-off jeans running from the beach, soaking wet. I forget if they climbed the fence or came through a door. It wasn't much of a fence … and it was the band! Wet hair, no shoes, a quick towel dry and on to the show. It wasn't much. It was a short, well-played set and that was it.

☾ ☾ ☾ ☾

Another fan, Frank Gibson, remembered the band more favorably: "I must admit that seeing Badfinger was the best concert I ever saw at Steel Pier, and I had seen the Stones, the Shondells, the Four Seasons and many other groups over the years there. It was a small area, about 3,000 people. My mom even got to meet some of the members. I know they had a hit or two out at the time. Tickets were $1.50."

Nicky Bell, a Badfinger "roadie," complained of what was a common occurrence: "There was a horse on the Pier. The band would play for a while and then they'd announce this horse was going to jump into the water. Everyone would run over to see it. After he jumped in, everybody would run back to the band. This went on three or four times a day."

Chubby Checker and the Dovells returned to the Music Hall in 1973, playing three shows daily. Singer Ernie Terrell played in the Golden Dome four times daily. George Hamid, Jr. had a business interest in Ernie, who was the late Tammi Terrell's brother.

On August 25, 1974, the Golden Dome was cleared out during the day, then reopened to present a concert that evening by the New Riders of the Purple Sage and David Bromberg.

With new ownership for the first time in thirty years and a diminishing customer base, 1976 proved to be a testing ground for the Pier. Popular acts were aggressively booked. The Stylistics, Melba Moore, the Bay City Rollers, Harold Melvin and the Blue Notes, the Four Seasons, and Isaac Hayes all appeared.

"It was the Bay City Rollers' first American concert performance and the scene in the Hall was wonderfully nostalgically reminiscent of rock and roll it its golden youth," observed *The New York Times* in June 1976. "The girls would scream in ear-splitting unison at the slightest provocation. A soundman later reported that the Rollers mustered 105 decibels of sound, but the girls managed 110.

"The band played for less than an hour, interrupted for five minutes when too many fans crowded on the stage and insisted on kissing the players. There was no opening act, yet nobody complained about the shortness of the show.

"Afterwards, in the dressing room, the band was unhappy about the security and the sound system. In truth, all one could hear through the screams was the vocal, the crunching drums and a little bass."

The next two years saw a different approach. Gone were most of the top headliners and in their place stood mostly "oldies" acts, probably because the Pier had lost money that first year of the new format and switched to a more budget-oriented lineup. Groups and singers such as the Skyliners and the Belmonts, B.T. Express, Ray Charles, Danny and the Juniors, the Spiral Staircase, and Connie Francis made up the list.

By the time the Pier closed in 1978, after mounting losses, big-name acts had already flown to arenas holding 10,000 or more people. The days of a top rock act playing a ballroom were over. Even if the Pier had remained open twenty more years, it would not have been able to compete with the bigger arenas. The business of rock and roll had changed forever.

Geo A. Hamid PROUDLY PRESENTS

THE AMUSEMENT CITY AT SEA

STEEL PIER

MAGAZINE

SCENE OF THE FABULOUS GOLDEN DOME

DAILY TIME SCHEDULE OF EVENTS

ATLANTIC CITY, NEW JERSEY

THE SHOW PLACE OF THE NATION

Chapter Sixteen

Inside a Landmark Resort

During its eighty-one-year existence, Steel Pier naturally changed over time in appearance. After Frank Gravatt bought the Pier in 1925, he steadily added onto the original design, constructing signage that covered both beach sides of the front Casino building as well as the Boardwalk front. He extended the back end with the Water Circus, and continually made improvements within the structure itself.

However, when the Pier first opened, it was an "ornate yet simple structure," explained a local reporter in the June 18, 1898 edition of the *Atlantic City Press*:

"There are three buildings on the structure, one facing the esplanade — the Casino, the dance hall located about midway, and the sun parlor, 350 feet from the end. There's another small circular building between the sun parlor and dancing hall in which there is a huge tank for aquarium porpoises."

Steel Pier was built in the grand Victorian manner. A colonnade of white pillars lined the Boardwalk entrance of the Pier and supported the second level, the two flanks of which extended forward and upward in squat towers, topped with cupolas. Most of the structure, though, was simply a two-story pavilion that was open to the elements. It extended across the beach and out over the ocean — a place to sit, relax and watch people. On both sides of the main entrance it was much like a veranda with rocking chairs, where ladies and gentlemen sat to watch the passing parade.

By 1910, the first exterior sign facing the beach appeared above the open arcade, announcing "Vessella's Italian Band — Martini's Symphony Orchestra." On top of the middle building, it announced "Motion Pictures" and "Cakewalk." Large letters at the end, above the Ballroom, were illuminated at night with the words "Steel Pier."

Due to the weather, structural damage was a constant problem. In 1915, the Ballroom's midsection collapsed. New pilings were put underneath to replace those that had deteriorated.

In an August 1916 letter to his mother, one visitor, S.B. Butler, explained in detail what the average visitor saw:

The structure at the entrance has only seats for people who want to sit down and watch the crowd go by, but there is a hall above

The first large signs were constructed on the Pier's south side in 1930.

which I believe is a Woman's Suffrage Headquarters. Beyond the seats at the entrance is a long seating place called the Arcade, with a raised platform in the center, where an Italian band (known as Vessella's band) holds forth twice a day. The place will seat hundreds and hundreds of people.

Beyond this place is a moving picture theater, and then quite a stretch of pier, and finally out at the end a large hall called the Casino, where a musical organization called Martini's orchestra gives two concerts a day and where they have dancing every evening.

In addition to these things there are, I believe, one or two minstrel shows on the pier every day, and one or two other features of which I can't remember the exact details. To none of these things is there any admission fee. At the entrance to the pier you are charged ten cents thru the day, fifteen cents at night, and this entitles you to the run of the pier. There are countless numbers of people going in all the time, and as they continue to run, I imagine there's no money lost in the scheme, but you certainly get a great deal for your money. I heard several selections by the band and watched the dancing out at the Casino. This pier is particularly beautiful at night, the way it is lighted up.

The front of the Pier circa 1927 showing minimal signage.

℃ ℃ ℃ ℃

A new, flat sign above the entrance to the Pier appeared about 1920, with a simple "Murphy's Minstrels" and "McFadden Health Talks" facing the south side of the front building, overlooking the beach. The Casino building had been extended and built up with additions, and the once-open arcade pavilion was now enclosed, allowing patrons to enjoy the breeze through an open window.

By the early 1920s, Atlantic City's boardwalk and several piers were displaying giant electric advertising designs and billboards that were creative and eye-catching, due to the talents of the R. C. Maxwell Company. Beginning in 1894, R. C. Maxwell was responsible for many of the electric signs in Asbury Park, Philadelphia and other areas, as well as Atlantic City. When the company was sold in 2000, it was one of the oldest surviving outdoor sign firms in the United States.

In 1920, the Maxwell Company established an "electric sign manufacturing plant" in Atlantic City. For over fifty years, it supplied

216

By 1934, the front Casino building was elongated and even more signs were added, such as the Spanish Galleon over the entrance, which was illuminated by colored light bulbs well into the 1970s.

Steel Pier with the classic signs that touted movie stars, rock bands, and the Diving Horse. They were also responsible for erecting the famous Chesterfield sign on Steeplechase Pier in 1927. Possibly one of the largest and most creative displays of all time, the Chesterfield sign boasted 27,000 electric bulbs on two displays, back to back, 215 feet long and fifty-five feet high. It took seventy-five seconds to complete the full circle of animated lighting effects. Alas, it came crashing down during the fire that destroyed Steeplechase in February 1932.

On November 17, 1924, a large fire broke out near the kitchen of a Virginia Avenue hotel on Novermber 17, 1924 and destroyed both the Bothwell and Wiltshire hotels on that street. Flames spread to the roof of the Casino portion of Steel Pier, destroying much of the Minstrel Hall and front entrance, both of which were replaced. The open-ended arcade midway on the Pier that had presented band concerts was also enclosed about this time, providing new space for exhibitors such as the Atlantic City Motor Trades Association.

Before Frank Gravatt bought the Pier the following year, the auditorium and entrance were replaced at a cost of $150,000. Gravatt then made extensive renovations on the Boardwalk front, opening 20,000 square feet of space for the General Motors Exhibit in 1926.

Gravatt spent a small fortune hiring architect William S.B. Kolle to transform the moribund Pier into a spectacular structure, adding new buildings and remodeling and redesigning others. Kolle later went on to build the Home of the Century exhibit on the Pier in the 1930s. Casino Hall was increased from 800 to 1,400 seats, and then increased again in 1927 to hold 2,000 patrons. The atmosphere of Steel Pier changed almost instantly, bringing a new level of excitement.

Radio was coming of age, and Atlantic City's own WPG broadcast station was housed in its separate Marine Studio, out near the Music Hall Ballroom. It later became WFPG, which became an affiliate of ABC in 1945 and was eventually relocated to the north side of the Pier by the 1960s.

A classic postcard of 1929 shows Steel Pier in what would become its familiar look for forty-five years. A decorative Spanish galleon appears above the entrance on the Boardwalk, outlined and illuminated

The construction of the larger signs began in 1934 when the emphasis was to promote the General Motors Exhibit.

Before owner Frank Gravatt expanded much of the Pier, the arcade was still primarily an open area where people could relax and listen to concert bands. Compare this to an earlier view on page 43.

at night with colored light bulbs. The entrance is designed with a starburst sun motif under a semi-circular, laced overhang. White letters on the overhang say "Dancing — Photoplays — Children's Carnival." On the south side of the front Casino building, a horizontal sign announces, "Exhibit of General Motors," along with the "Goldman Band." Under the General Motors signage was an electronic crawl, similar to the one seen on the *Times* building in New York's Times Square.

Gravatt spent lavishly in 1929 as he turned Steel Pier into a vast entertainment complex. He built the large Water Circus area directly in back of the Ballroom for the Diving Horse act, complete with a seating area for thousands. Previously, the Hawaiian High Divers performed from a tower next to the Ballroom, which was where the Pier ended. Now there was ample space for them and many other exciting acts brought in by booking agent and future Pier owner George Hamid, who first worked with Gravatt around 1930.

The Pier, more than 1,600 feet without the circus area, was now eighty feet longer and newly titled "Showplace of Atlantic City."

Gravatt replaced the old solarium in the middle of the Pier with the new Ocean Theatre, designed with the latest innovations for quality motion picture viewing. It was wired for the new sound pictures that were regularly premiered on the Pier.

Texaco became a sponsor, with large illuminated lettering atop the Ballroom, and the signs on the south beach side of the Casino announced in large, lit letters the entertainment stars appearing on the Pier.

In 1930 the Music

Gravatt led a major expansion project during 1929-1930, reinventing the Pier as a serious contender in the entertainment world.

Hall — two years before Radio City in New York opened with that same title — was rebuilt and enlarged, this time with a sprinkler system incorporating the latest safety features. Two side balconies were removed and the décor was distinctly Art Deco. The open arcade between the Music Hall and the Ocean Theatre was enclosed and devoted to exhibit space, and the structure at the ocean end was enlarged, completely remodeled and renamed the Marine Ballroom. The original

arcade roof remained as part of the interior structure of the new Music Hall.

A diorama house display was also built on both sides of the Casino building, and picnic and steamer decks now extended outward from both beach sides. A vertical "Steel Pier" sign was erected on the Spanish galleon, and the Little Theatre was built behind the GM Exhibit for use to present the Steel Pier Opera Company.

The Pier was filled with crowds day and night in 1930.

were reinforced in 1932 for use by the Steel Pier ocean cruise boat that ferried patrons a few miles out to sea for an evening of dance and fun.

In 1934, the large and familiar "Steel Pier" lettering appeared on the south side above the electronic ribbon for the first time. General Motors left the front exhibition hall in November 1933, only to be replaced with new automobiles from the rival Ford Motor Company the following year. In fact, for the Ford Motor Company Exhibit of 1936, the exhibition hall was completely redecorated by Walter Dorwin Teague, a nationally known commercial designer and decorator. White was the predominate color, with blue and red blending along with modern lighting. New, brilliant, electric signs adorned the exterior, and attractive windows faced the Boardwalk. The exhibit contained displays of motors and a revolving V-8 chassis, a regular feature on the Pier until about 1942.

By the 1930s, with all the additions and rebuilding, it was said that the Pier extended almost one-half mile from the Boardwalk — 2,000 or 1,780 feet into the ocean, according to various sources. The country was mired in the worst depression in history, but you wouldn't have known it by watching the crowds of visitors streaming in to see the latest magic Frank Gravatt had to offer.

Throughout the decade, more changes took place. On February 20, 1931, a pot of tar used by roofers flared up and caused a fire that damaged part of the Music Hall housing a Hollywood exhibit. Pilings

In 1937 and 1938, Gravatt spent $275,000 in improvements by adding new marquee signs and had three artesian wells drilled. The Marine Ballroom now held approximately 4,000 people. The theaters ranged in capacity from 1,000 to 2,250, while the Water Stadium area held 5,000 seats.

Full-time cleanup crews worked day and night to keep the Pier spotless. In 1941, the Ballroom was renovated, and a special "cushion" dance floor was installed. The top surface of one-and-a-half-inch maple had a special spring base laid down underneath, designed to prevent leg fatigue even after hours of dancing.

In that same year, a new neon sign, fifty feet high and 120 feet long, made of stainless steel and spelling out *STEEL PIER,* was erected on the roof of the Marine Ballroom. There were five animated-letter signs on the Pier, more than any other single spot in the world.

The wrap-around marquee on the Pier was the largest in the world, measuring 400 feet long and costing $60,000. Gravatt used three twenty-four-foot signs to advertise the appearance of Abbott and Costello in 1941.

The September 1944 Hurricane destroyed the Water Circus, but by that time storm damage was a common occurrence and considered another cost of doing business on the ocean. It was rebuilt in a different shape each time — angular, circular, and square — to see if any of the

Visitors lined corridors, fascinated by the exhibits and exotic animals.

design changes could better withstand the pressures from a northeast storm. A November 1953 storm destroyed the Circus stadium again, and again it was rebuilt, this time with the performance center closer to the audience seating.

There were no diving horses from 1945 to 1952, so the familiar ladder and tank were not seen with the Water Circus during this time.

When George Hamid bought the Pier in 1945, he adopted Gravatt's business sense, continuously improving and renovating. As the Pier celebrated its fiftieth year, it contained 280,000 square feet, with 150,000 square feet enclosed. It was the largest structure of its kind in the world, with 17,800 square feet of exhibition space. The Marine Ballroom was 24,000 square feet, one of the country's largest. There were five large fun houses located on the lower level under the front Casino building, ten feet below the surface of the ocean at high tide. The Casino held 2,000 people; the Little Theatre, 1,000; the Music Hall, 2,250; the Ocean Theatre, 1,400; the Marine Ballroom, up to 4,000; and the outdoor stadium, 5,000. More than 20,000 people could be entertained at the same time, without crowding.

Frank Gravatt ran a tight ship while he was the Pier's owner. Between the Casino and Music Hall was a decorative fountain — a favorite spot for taking pictures.

A rare photograph from the oceanside shows the back of the Marine Ballroom before construction of the Water Circus, 1928.

By 1947, millions more had been spent on remodeling and construction, now with the latest in air-cooling equipment, toilet facilities, safety devices and fire prevention. Among the modern improvements, fire equipment cost $200,000; air-conditioning and septic tanks, $100,000; exhibit room remodeling, $225,000; construction and improvements on radio station WFPG, $200,000; and extension of the outdoor stadium, $200,000.

The Marine Ballroom was redecorated again and repainted with a series of murals depicting tropical and seashore themes. On July 6, 1948, a fire in the Ballroom broke out as the last dancers were leaving the floor, causing $50,000 in damage.

The General Motors Exhibit returned in 1947, paying $200,000 a year rent in the 17,800-square-foot Exhibition Hall. In 1950, brand-new sanitary and modern refreshment stands and equipment were installed at a cost of $200,000.

In 1952, there was another $250,000 in renovations for the Music Hall, including air-conditioning, indirect soft lighting, improved acoustics, and new stage equipment. With a new interior and an entirely new auditorium, designed by Polish architect Tadeusz Glogowski, the Music Hall added 1,000 more seats, with a balcony constructed on both side walls.

The Music Hall interior seemed to have changed in appearance more than any other building on the Pier. When it was enlarged and rebuilt in 1926, utilizing the roof of the former open arcade, the Music

Hall had two balconies, lining each wall of the theater. By the early 1930s, the hall had become entirely redesigned with a modern Art Deco look, complete with large decorative arches that lined both walls. The balconies had been removed, allowing the space to become more open.

But when it was redisigned again in 1952, balconies were built along both sides once more. There is no apparent reason why the balconies were torn out only to reappear some twenty years later.

A new marquee, along with a fireproof, red-and-white-stripe motif that covered the original Boardwalk front façade and added for safety reasons, marked the Pier's appearance in 1953. On Christmas Day of that same year, the "new" $150,000 reconditioned Ocean Theatre, designed by Glogowski, opened. Formerly the Casino, the remodeled theater included a giant thirty-five-by-fifteen-foot, curved Astrolite screen for Cinerama and 3-D projection. It was also equipped for stereophonic sound, and now seated 2,300.

With the Casino renamed the Ocean, the middle Ocean Theatre was renamed the Midway. The Water Circus had a new stage for 1954, along with new and stronger decking, and a new tower and tank for the resumed feature act of the Diving Horse.

On July 30, 1954 a three-alarm fire, fanned by a stiff, fifteen-mph breeze, destroyed the entrance and front portion of the Pier while scorching the front of the GM Exhibit. The blaze, possibly caused by a discarded cigarette or a short circuit, broke out at 5:41 P.M. under the Boardwalk at the Planters nuts store. Five hundred people, mostly children, were evacuated from the Ocean Theatre in the front of the Pier, while another 5,000 attending shows and in exhibit areas on the ocean end remained where they were, or were led to the beach and Boardwalk by side exits. The fire, which caused a reported $400,000 in damage, was under control in an hour. By 8 P.M., thousands were streaming in for uninterrupted evening performances.

Acting as a fire break when flames attacked the front of the Pier was a water curtain set off from the Pier's sprinkler system, confining the blaze to the front and protecting the ocean end of the Pier. Hamid estimated it would cost roughly $200,000 to replace the red-and-white-striped front, which had stopped the fire from spreading. He said the marquee alone had cost $100,000 to erect in 1953. In addition there was damage to the theater, and the entire

(Right) Bandleader Paul Whiteman is surrounded by thousands of fans in the Music Hall, 1928.

This scene from 1936 shows the simplicity of the main marquees and signs; things were a bit different in 1954 (see facing page).

150-foot front of the Pier was a blackened ruin, leading to another remodeling of the marquee.

In 1955, the front building became the Casino once more, the middle building the Music Hall and the back theater the Midway. The Ocean Theatre ceased to exist and the Midway became the permanent home of Tony Grant's "Stars of Tomorrow."

The Pier was using a staff of over 200 highly trained guards and ushers to keep traffic continually flowing. Nurses and attendants staffed strategically placed first aid rooms. Sprinkler systems were located at three-foot intervals for optimum safety.

By 1958, both the Music Hall and Casino were equipped for stereophonic and Cinerama features. William Morgan, a district manager

An almost identical scene from 1954 shows the expansion of the main south sign, giving ample space to promote the General Motors Exhibit. The front boardwalk façade has been covered over with red and white stripes and the twin cupolas have been removed.

for Hamid-owned Warner Bros. Theatres in Atlantic City, became the Pier's General Manager. A Mystery Ride was built, and the Little Theatre presented the Modern Home Exhibit. The Marine Ballroom was touted as now holding 10,000 people, a figure that seemed to change every couple of years. The large "STEEL PIER" lettering above the main signage was replaced in 1960 with a western-style letter motif, echoing newspaper ads that had been featuring that motif since about 1949. A Porpoise Playroom, consisting of a modern 20,000-gallon steel tank, appeared in 1961 in the Music Hall lobby.

In March 1962, a catastrophic, three-day storm took the East

Coast by surprise. Atlantic City measured tides six feet above normal high tide, with waves twenty-five feet high, powered by winds gusting to eighty-four mph. The ocean end of the Pier crumbled under the unprecedented assault, and the Water Circus stage area was swept away. The tank for the Diving Horse washed ashore on the beach in Ventnor, four miles south.

To the north, storm waves ripped a 100-foot barge from its anchorage in the Inlet. Grazing the outer portion of Garden Pier, it hurtled south, straight toward Steel Pier's midsection, and forcibly barreled right through it. Not a sound was heard above the roaring tides and screaming, blizzard-force winds as the barge destroyed almost a third of the Pier and kept on traveling.

Ed Davis of WFPG was manning the studio around 11 o'clock the first night of the storm when he felt the structure shudder from the impact. To his dismay, he discovered he was marooned on the outer section. Returning to the broadcast studio, he spent two harrowing days on the Pier delivering accounts of the storm until the transmitter shorted out.

George Hamid, Jr., was in the Delmonico Hotel in New York and was called and given the news about the Pier. The worst of the three-day storm was over, but calculating the terrific cost was just beginning. The Great March Storm of '62 jumped to the top of the list of natural disasters during the Pier's existence, exceeding damage from the 1953 northeaster and even the September Hurricane of 1944. He discussed that day in an interview forty-one years later:

It was rainy and windy in New York. I had meetings, but got another call saying that we had probably lost the end of the Pier as well. So I flew down to Atlantic City. As we came down the coast, I asked the stewardess if we could fly around the end of the Pier so I could see if we had an end left. I could see that we still had the stadium but not the stage. It was not as sturdy as the Ballroom or stadium itself. We lost that stage about four or five times and had to rebuild it.

We had tried different configurations, but nothing worked when it came to a bad storm. It was on good concrete and steel pilings, but nothing could survive that storm.

☾ ☾ ☾ ☾

The *Atlantic City Press* carried this account in its March 8, 1962

edition: "A group of men marched toward the ocean end of Steel Pier Thursday morning. Expressionless faces searched a section of the funway in front of Tony Grant's theatre. George Hamid Jr., glancing at the wreckage, litter, torn planking and 350 feet of open space between the group and the battered Marine Ballroom, said, 'We're all dazed. The basement with seven funhouses and two bathhouses is gone. The diving bell is gone. The circus stadium is gone. A two-story, seven-room Model House of the Century, erected in 1936, is gone. Water, power and sprinkler lines to the end of the Pier have disappeared. We've lost at least $2 million to the storm. The million-dollar Marine Ballroom, one-half mile at sea, has damage to it, but we can't get out there to find out how badly it was hit.'"

Undaunted, Hamid promised, "By Easter the Pier will be open, and when the summer season arrives, the old attractions will be back," the newspaper reported.

With astonishing speed, the damaged section of the Pier was completely rebuilt, from pilings to decking to roof, by June 17. It replaced the more than 400 feet that was knocked out by the runaway barge and carried away by the March storm.

The Little Theatre was split in half, with one side as a workshop, the other a winter ballroom and also housing the Streets of Hong Kong Exhibit.

A large, neon American flag hung above the Marine Ballroom stage from World War II until the March 1962 storm. Bob Graziosa, a lifelong Atlantic City visitor from Baltimore, later found it in the Pier's basement storage area and asked Hamid if he could have it. Hamid agreed to it, and Graziosa hauled the signage home and restored it, but realized it was too big to display in his home. He loaned it to the Baltimore Civic Center, where it hung for a few years. It was then moved to downtown Baltimore's historic Lexington Market, where it is hung and displayed, fully lit. The neon flag and the Diving Bell in Gardner's Basin are the only two artifacts that have survived the Pier.

☾ ☾ ☾ ☾

From 1968 to 1972, the Pier was dominated on its front end by its first true ride: the Giant Sky Wheel, a Ferris wheel that Hamid obtained by outbidding other amusement operators.

"That ride was very unusual," he recalled in 2003. "We got it from

The north façade of the Casino building featured signage of what the Pier had to offer, 1933. Note the sand sculpture in the center of the photograph.

the New York World's Fair. It was the forerunner of all the giant wheels there are today. And since it was the only one of its kind, we figured we'd put it on the Pier."

At the time, it was the largest Ferris wheel in the United States. The 100-foot high, 100-ton Giant Sky Wheel cost $300,000. It was built by the U.S. Rubber Company for use at the 1964-1965 World's Fair and had twenty-four enclosed gondolas, holding four people each. An average 15,000 people a week could ride it. The wheel itself was so well balanced that in case of a power outage, it could be turned by hand. Safety inspections were conducted daily.

The Pier suffered its biggest physical change on a cold December 27, 1969 when forty-mph winds fanned a huge fire at the outer end, destroying the famous 24,000-square-foot Marine Ballroom and the 5,000-seat Water Circus area, along with the U.S. Weather Station.

The fire, perhaps caused by a short-circuited electric sign, consumed a third of the Pier. A policeman walking the Boardwalk beat reported a "red glow" at the end of the Pier around 6 P.M. Thankfully, the animals that had been housed near the end of the Pier had been

The sleek lobby and box office, 1933. (Bottom) The Casino theater held approximately 2000 people and featured a Art Moderne ceiling. (Opposite page) A huge crowd in 1934 waiting to get into the Casino theater.

The area that was once an open-air arcade was enclosed by Frank Gravatt and became an area where exhibits and theaters intertwined, 1936.

The Music Hall was remodeled during the 1930s with Art Deco embellishments and could hold over 2000 people. Compare this with the photograph on page 227.

with the punches before and we'll do it again," Hamid said at the time.

With almost $2 million in damage, Hamid was faced with the biggest off-season rebuilding job in the Pier's history. The fire destroyed twenty percent of the Pier, an area 400 feet in length and 140 feet wide.

It was decided a large, golden geodesic dome, designed by Buckminster Fuller, would become the new Ballroom, one that was fire-resistant and also the safest structure that could be built. It cost $1.4 million, including new pilings along with a specially designed acoustical system. Anodized aluminum seating was installed, and lighting was beamed from a master console that could bathe the performers or dancers in waves of color. The gold anodized dome was visible at night fifteen miles offshore when lit. It held between 5,000 and 6,000 people, much less than the original Ballroom.

moved when the Pier closed in September. Two hundred firemen finally brought the blaze under control by 9:30 P.M.

"I happened to be standing in front of my house in Margate and I saw flames up there," remembered George Hamid, Jr. "I said, 'Oh, my God!' and I immediately called the police in Atlantic City and they said, 'Yes, it is the Steel Pier.' It was awful."

He surveyed the fire damage and announced rebuilding would be started immediately. "The losses are a major blow, but we've rolled

On June 18, 1970, it was hoisted onto its supports at the end of the Pier.

"We had two large cranes working out there. Every step of the way had to be planned in advance. Even so, we almost lost one crane when it started to slide toward the ocean one day," said Hamid. "With the Golden Dome, Oceanworld and other renovations, Steel Pier is entering an era of elegance.

By 1941 neon and lots of signs had been added to the north.

"If Glenn Miller were only here. Before the war, he drew the biggest crowds. During the '50s, it was Ricky Nelson and a 100,000-gallon, glass-walled tank. In the '60s it was Herman's Hermits. But this is the ballroom of another age, the ballroom of tomorrow."

After General Motors relinquished its exhibition space at the front of the Pier for its second and final time, George Hamid, Jr. spent $2 million to convert that same space for a new aquatic presentation, moving his Aquarama operation from Philadelphia. In June 1970, Ocean World, the first indoor aquatic theater in the United States, opened in GM's old space. Open year-round initially and seating 600, Ocean World presented performing porpoises in a 100,000-gallon, glass-walled tank along with trained sea lions, electric eels, sharks, alligators and exotic fish from around the world. Live penguins could now be spotted in the front Boardwalk windows where automobiles and appliances once were exhibited.

"Our sea theatre is the first of its kind anywhere. Our dolphins and sea lions are all young, fresh and intelligent and full of precocious playfulness," boasted Steel Pier's show program.

The Pier measured 150 feet wide and 2,200 feet long, nearly 800 feet longer than its original length. Yet despite the showy, new attractions, it became apparent that the structure, especially its signage, was rapidly deteriorating. The famed Spanish galleon and beach signs, standing since 1929, appeared rusted and worn. Even the western motif letters that spelled out *STEEL PIER* on top of the beach signs had to come down in 1973.

The last big change to the Pier came in 1976, when new owners decided to knock down the Music Hall and

1932: (Top) A well-dressed crowd waits to see a midnight movie in the Ocean Thearter. (Bottom) A full house awaits the start of a movie.

The great storm of March 1962 left the Marine Ballroom cut off from the rest of the Pier as a result of a wayward barge cutting through.

Aerials after the 1962 storm show (left) the new construction of the Water Circus and the walkway connecting the Marine Ballroom with the rest of the Pier. Note the 1950s expansion of the right side of the Ballroom. (Below) The aftermath of the barge cutting through the Pier resulted in a narrower covered walkway.

Midway theaters to erect rides, leaving only the original Casino building standing. That left a tremendous gap in the middle of the Pier, giving it an unbalanced look.

A wet slide was erected where the Skywheel had stood just a few years earlier. Without the middle buildings, however, the Pier looked empty and sparse. The old signage and the Galleon at last were taken down, while the front Casino building was spruced up with a remodeling and repainted entirely white except for its green roof. It was the last original building to remain from 1898, and it looked almost identical to its opening-day appearance.

The lack of signage at the renamed "New Steel Pier" first appeared shocking, as it had been a familiar sight

(Left) The post-1962 walkway. Notice that the formally ornate front of the Marine Ballroom is covered up due to the storm damage. (Above and opposite page) Hurriedly constructed for the 1970 season, the geodesic Golden Dome replaced the destroyed Marine Ballroom. It would never have the same feeling or ambiance as its predecessor. (Facing page) In 1972 the Sky Wheel dominated the Pier; the Golden Dome occupied the ocean end.

for over forty-five years. The Casino, although remodeled, looked bland and unexciting, which reflected on the Pier itself.

The Golden Dome Ballroom became a disco, enhanced by lasers, in 1978, yet that short-lived fad only hastened the Pier's demise.

This was the last image of Steel Pier before fire destroyed most of it in December 1982. When it closed for business for the final time in 1978, the buildings, sans the water slide, were left to deteriorate while ideas for its future were discussed but, ultimately, unfulfilled.

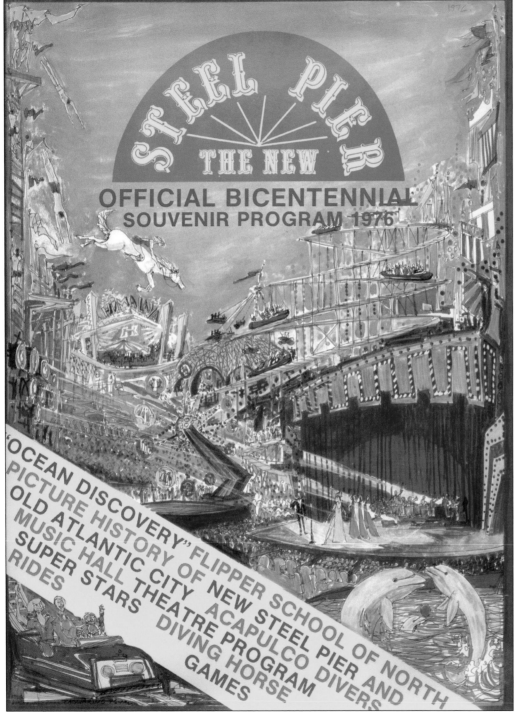

Chapter Seventeen

The End of An Era and An Icon

Steel Pier's demise did not come quickly. It took a few long, tortuous years before it was apparent that its best years were over. Atlantic City's were, too, for that matter.

Although the Pier had booked the hottest acts in the country during the 1960s, the next decade proved to be difficult. In August 1964, the Democratic Convention swept into Atlantic City. For many members of the national media, it was the first time they had been in Atlantic City for many years. What awaited them was a city that was fast deteriorating, complete with old, rundown hotels and a growing minority population besieged with poverty and unemployment. The entire country now saw what had become of "America's Playground," and it wasn't pretty.

On the Pier that week were Milton Berle and dancer John Bubbles, along with the Glenn Miller

Orchestra led by Ray McKinley. The city may have been sinking, but the Pier was still afloat.

Segregation, which had been strictly enforced in Atlantic City for years, had come to an end. No longer was the African-American community contained to the North Side with their own nightclubs, restaurants and hotels. The civil rights movement tore down those barriers, but not without combative results. By 1967, racial tensions were high everywhere in the United States, including on the Pier. That autumn, a dance on the Pier nearly turned ugly before tempers were quelled.

The Giant Sky Wheel, erected on the south side of the Pier in 1968 near the Casino theater, remained an attraction until 1972.

General Motors, a perennial feature on the exhibit floor since 1947, broke its lease and left in 1968, sensing that Atlantic City was not the image GM wanted. That didn't do the city or the Pier any good. Owner George Hamid, Jr. utilized the large former GM showroom as Animal World the following year, and then as Ocean Wonderworld in 1970. Live penguins graced the front window on the Boardwalk, and porpoises, sea lions, sharks, alligators and stingrays were also presented.

Hamid, who had operated Aquarama in Philadelphia since 1965, was well versed with the presentation of aquatic shows. In the former GM space, a 100,000-gallon, glass-walled tank was built for the porpoise shows that faced a 600-seat area.

"It was 1969 when I first realized that there had been a change," he recalled in a 1988 interview with the author. "I had all the theaters in Atlantic City and I could see they weren't grossing what they should. I knew what the Steel Pier gross was, and when I saw that 1969 was substantially lower than 1968, I couldn't believe it. Then in '70 and '71, they stopped going down. That's when I figured that maybe in '72 it was going to be like it used to. Entertainment had nothing to do with the deterioration of Atlantic City."

But on December 27, 1969, a fire destroyed the entire back end of the Pier containing the Marine Ballroom and the Water Circus. Discovered by Patrolman Charles Hudson at 6:06 P.M., the blaze became so great that Ed Davis of the Pier's WFPG radio station saw it from his home in Pleasantville on the mainland.

"I knew the minute I saw the red glow that it was the Pier. I just knew," remembered Davis, the radio announcer who from 1947 to 1968 had introduced the Pier's big bands from the Ballroom as they were carried on national radio. "So I quick got into my car and drove over. The fire could be seen from all over, that's how great a blaze it was. But that was the end of the beautiful Marine Ballroom ... all the memories of who I saw play there. It went very fast. I just cried — I couldn't help it. My God, when I think of all the people that played out there! And it all went up in smoke. Such devastation."

Indeed, the memories that went up in smoke that night could symbolize the end of the 1960s and the end of the Pier, for it was never to be the same again. George Hamid, Sr. was enroute to Florida by car and didn't hear of the tragedy immediately.

"I haven't heard from him and I haven't been able to reach him," George Hamid, Jr. said at the time. "I have telephone calls from booking agencies as far away as Los Angeles ... but I haven't heard from him. When he goes on a vacation, he goes to forget everything. With him, it's no radio, no television, no business. He's off to relax. He has got to be unaware of what happened."

The large electrical sign atop the Ballroom was initially thought to have started the fire, but it had not been lit. However, it was still thought to be an electrical fire from an unknown source.

George Hamid, Jr. discussed with his architect, A. Richard Saseen, plans to build a modern and fully equipped fishing pier as part of the reconstruction. The fishing pier would include a fisherman's rest lounge, snack bar, fish cleaning room, a storeroom for fishing gear and equipment, bait room, and a fishing diagram to aid fishermen.

The new Marine Ballroom was to be engineered so that those who wanted to hear the full blare of music could do so, while other portions would resound with rock and roll sounds that would be controlled to a desirable decibel. None of this came to fruition, however.

Work started immediately. The Hamids wanted something modern, as the Marine Ballroom was very old and was a constant problem to keep cool in the summer. Famed geodesic dome architect Buckminster Fuller was commissioned to design a geodesic structure with a diameter of 110 feet to replace the Ballroom.

By June 1970, the circular building was hoisted onto supports on the back end of the Pier. It was a magnificent gold-anodized structure that was visible fifty miles at sea when lit at night. A specially designed acoustical system was installed, along with anodized aluminum seating.

In 1976 the Music Hall is gone from the Pier. Looking down Virginia Avenue, once lively with hotels and boarding houses, bare lots from "Pauline's Prairie" abound. The Boardwalk's Virginia movie theatre, to the right of the Pier, stands alone.

The Water Circus area, also destroyed in the fire, was rebuilt and reconfigured. Instead of the stadium seating situated directly behind the Ballroom facing out to sea, it was moved to the southern side of the end of the Pier, looking north. The Diving Horse ramp and platform also changed position, for the first time in forty years, and now hugged the Golden Dome along the end of the north side of the Pier.

"If there's ever a hurricane passing this way, this is where I want to be," William F. Morgan, the Pier's manager, told reporters. "The pilings and beams supporting the Golden Dome Ballroom are strong enough to hold the Empire State Building."

"We're using every penny of insurance money, as well as everything else we have," added George Hamid, Jr. in the *Atlantic City Press.* "We're tapped out. We won't have a penny left, but we'll have a beautiful new Pier. We had our choice between re-building the number one entertainment place in the world or building a shorter pier. Building a shorter pier is not our style."

Years later, Hamid reflected on the decision.

"We never thought Steel Pier was going to go downhill any further than what it went in 1969. We thought it was going to bounce back. We could see that you didn't need a 10,000-square-foot ballroom anymore when 5,000 square feet would do.

"I didn't miss the Ballroom. Well, maybe I did. There were a lot of problems with that Ballroom that nobody knows. We busted our ass on those pilings there for years. To air-condition it, or even get cool air in it, was brutal. The decks — it was a very expensive structure because of the way it was constructed. It was a huge ballroom and it was old."

The new Golden Dome Ballroom was dedicated on July 3, 1970, featuring pop singer Oliver and the orchestra of Ted Weems. It was a success, but many would say that it just didn't have the same ambiance as the old Marine Ballroom. Of course not — one was built in a palatial design from the turn of the century, and this was very modern and stark.

Interesting attractions, such as the *Gemini VII* space capsule flown by astronauts James Lovell and Frank Borman, were exhibited, the capsule costing Hamid $50,000 to insure. But the mounting cost of big name talent was making it unattainable. Hamid tried everything to keep the Pier going, yet the handwriting was on the wall. He had been in the business too long not to see what was happening.

☾ ☾ ☾ ☾

By the 1970s, the once-glamorous hotels of Atlantic City had lost their luster. Some, like the Traymore and the Marlborough-Blenheim, were imploded in a public spectacle. Atlantic Avenue, the city's main commercial artery, hosted more vacancies than shops. Movie theaters closed one by one. Prostitutes patrolled the streets. Houses and stores, especially in the Inlet area close to the Pier, were dilapidated and becoming a slum akin to the South Bronx.

The perception was that Atlantic City had become dangerous, with gangs roaming the Boardwalk and main streets, mugging visitors. After 10 P.M., the Boardwalk was deserted and Boardwalk hotels kept their doors locked after dark. There were many senior citizens, residents of Atlantic City, who felt trapped in their rooms and afraid to venture out. The minority black population was growing into the majority.

During the decade of the 1960s, over 10,000 people left Atlantic City, 80 percent of them white. From a population of 59,544 in 1960, that number dwindled to 46,192 by 1973. In 1971, Atlantic City was 43 percent African-American and 30 percent elderly. Unemployment was reported at 6.7 percent, yet the welfare rate encompassed a third of the population. The typical Atlantic City tourist or shopper was poor, African-American or elderly — or all three. Most of the fashionable stores had pulled out of the downtown area, the old nightclubs had turned to go-go dancers as a means to make a profit, and the remaining movie theaters were offering X-rated films.

Joe Latrello was the Pier general manager from 1971 to 1975. He recalled a better time in the Pier's history:

"I remember times when there were so many people on the Pier, it would take forty minutes to walk from the Water Circus to the Boardwalk. It was exciting," he told the *Press of Atlantic City* in 1988. "The Pier suffered from drops in attendance, and when all those rooming houses were torn down, that was just another thing that led to our decline in volume. From 1968 on, everything went downhill. It would've been nice to keep it going. In the whole United States, there was nothing else like it."

Atlantic City Housing Commissioner Pauline Hill's urban renewal plan of the late 1960s made the area near Virginia Avenue and the Pier an eighty-acre urban wasteland, with no housing or buildings. Entire neighborhoods were demolished to the east side of the Pier, and suddenly, instead of sitting at the center of the Boardwalk, Steel Pier languished at its end. Streets that were once full of rooming houses bustling with vacationers, who were Steel Pier customers, were the addresses of vacant lots overgrown with weeds and broken liquor bottles. The area became known bitterly as "Pauline's Prairie," and the economy of the area was hurt badly. Past Virginia Avenue, the Boardwalk was bare, and the stores and hotels that once stretched as far as the Inlet were demolished. Through most of the 1970s, the urban renewal plan was a complete failure.

Artist Bob Johnson analyzed these times in a 1981 *Atlantic City* magazine article:

The mid-sixties period was the last breath for the Steel Pier as a drawing card for Atlantic City. The Pier itself was decadent, it was falling down. You could hear it creaking as you walked along some of it. Paint was peeling and plaster was hanging down in the theater. It was an era gone by. But entertainers were still coming there because it was still the place to go. It packed them in.

But Steel Pier was dying then, making it on sheer momentum. The way I remember the Pier is like an old lady, or like a beautiful ocean liner that had seen its day and was tied up at the shore. There was no reason for it to exist, and it was just going away; I mean, you knew it was going away while you were there. You were going to the "old Steel Pier." You could tell it was just a skeleton of what it was before. It was dingy, and the people with the concessions had been there for years.

☾ ☾ ☾ ☾

The *New York Times* reported on May 28, 1972 that Hamid voiced great optimism in the future of Atlantic City. He related that admissions at the Pier were running at an average of 1.5 million a year. Three hundred workers were employed during the season, and fifty worked through the winter to make repairs, paint and maintain the 200 rows of steel pilings from which the Pier got its name.

Bob Schoelkopf handled the dolphin and sea lion shows in late 1960s and eventually became one of the Pier's assistant managers. "There was some deterioration, but it was an echo of the whole deterioration of a city," he remarked in a *Press* story in 1988. "No matter what you did, the era was fading. People didn't want to come to Atlantic City for one pier, and the other piers were even worse. And people were afraid to walk the streets here."

Dolphin show managers weren't always reputable. "The dolphins weren't mistreated, but they could have had better care," said Schoelkopf, who later went on to found the Marine Mammal Stranding Center in nearby Brigantine. "There were times medical care was given, but it wasn't followed through with because of costs. The absentee owners didn't care for them.

"One sea lion died of a combination of malnutrition and poor care. When I first started, there were twelve sea lion shows a day, and one sea lion was required to do most of the shows. These animals are under more stress than in the wild. This sea lion ended up dying of a bleeding ulcer."

After the General Motors Exhibit vacated the front space in 1968, the Hamid-produced Ocean Wonderworld took over. Note the Art Deco ceiling designs still in place.

In the view of a growing political action group, legalized gambling was the only hope to save Atlantic City. As the campaign took on steam during the mid-1970s, George Hamid, Jr. added a lukewarm endorsement. "I'd like to see it come to Atlantic City, but I don't want it on our Steel Pier. We have too wholesome an image, having built our reputation on offering something for everyone in the family — strictly family entertainment. That doesn't include gambling."

He also vowed that his two cinemas on the Pier would never show anything but G-rated pictures (although some were PG), nor would he permit acid rock to be played or marijuana to be smoked on the premises. "We're not purists by any measure, but we don't allow profanity of even the mildest sort," he said at the time.

On April 27, 1972, the gigantic Traymore Hotel was the first of the Atlantic City Boardwalk landmarks to be imploded. Within minutes, the giant structure that once defined the past elegance of the resort

was gone, signaling an official and tangible end to the Atlantic City that once was. Other hotels — including the Ambassador, the Marlborough-Blenheim, the Senator, the Chelsea — would soon be gone too.

Even with a $3 admission, Steel Pier lost money in 1972 and had basically degenerated into a cheap, tacky, honky-tonk amusement center. Second-tier stars replaced the bigger names that were now unaffordable.

On January 16, 1973, ownership by the Hamid family came to an end. George Hamid, Jr. sold the Pier for about $2 million to Maxwell Goldberg and Milton Neustadter, who owned the Howard Johnson's

By the 1970s, not many people were jumping for joy over dirty and dilapidated Atlantic City.

motor hotel on the Boardwalk; and to Albert Gardner, an accountant. All three also had owned Million Dollar Pier since 1969.

"Atlantic City was in terrible shape before the casinos," related Al Gardner in 2008. "We thought that with our experience with Million Dollar Pier, we could revive Steel Pier and bring the crowds back to Atlantic City."

Neustadter had a different idea than Hamid about the prospect of the tremendous potential of gambling. "We didn't buy the Steel Pier with gambling in mind," he told reporters at the time, "but I would have to answer a big 'yes' to the question of whether we would have gambling. We would love to have a gambling casino on the end of the Pier."

Hamid then leased back the Pier and directed the entertainment through 1975, when he left the Pier for good, as it was getting harder and harder for him to book strong acts and keep the public interested. The biggest headliners Hamid could book that last year were singers Al Martino, Buddy Greco, and Frankie Valli and the Four Seasons.

The last day of Hamid's Steel Pier was September 1, 1975. Featured in the Golden Dome were the rock band Sons of Robin Stone, hardly a household name. Also included were the Thrill Circus and Water Show with the Diving Horse; the Sea Theatre starring high-jumping dolphins; Tony Grant's children's theater; and two motion pictures: "The Poseidon Adventure," already two years old, and "The Mad Adventures of Rabbi Jacob." Admission was just ninety-nine cents for the day. A newspaper ad carried the text "Steel Pier says *Thank You*," a simple personal message from Hamid for thirty amazing years.

"When I left, there were no tears, believe me," he told the *Philadelphia Inquirer* in 2004. "It was gone. Just like the end of tomato season, they're gone."

New owners Goldberg and Neustadter knew little about entertainment, but boasted they had learned the hotel business and could learn show business as well. They promised "major changes."

"For some reason, the new owners didn't want to be associated with us," said Hamid. "Everything had to be *new*."

By the beginning of December, the demolition machines had arrived on the Pier. Goldberg and Neustadter had a strategic plan and would totally reinvent Steel Pier for the 1970s. Gone would be the excess, with only the Pier's strong points remaining. In retrospect, these "new" ideas contributed to the Pier's demise more quickly than anyone could imagine.

The famed Music Hall theater in the center of the Pier, along with the Ocean/Midway theater, was torn down, leaving a tremendous open space that left the Pier looking unbalanced. An "International Rides" area replaced the buildings, bringing in amusements by German, French and Italian companies — including a two-story carousel from Italy — on a "showcase basis."

Years later, in a 2008 interview, Milton Neustadter explained their

Million Dollar Pier, which had lost much of its ocean end to storms, is at the top of the picture. Next is Central Pier, then Steeplechase Pier. Steel Pier, with the Sky Wheel, is at the bottom of this circa 1970 aerial.

motive. "We wanted to change the style and we wanted to base it like our Million Dollar Pier, which was successful with rides. But on Steel Pier, we wanted to bring in more sophisticated rides."

"That was the biggest mistake they could make, because that was the home of the stars from the first World War until then," Hamid observed later. "But nothing could have saved it. They were caught between a rock and a hard place. Business had gone down so drastically in Atlantic City that it was almost a ghost town at that point."

A glimpse of this new mentality was in view when Lawrence Alper, hired as Steel Pier's new general manager, had demolished the old but famous Hippodrome building on Million Dollar Pier a few years earlier, in 1970. Alper had been vice-president and general manager of Million Dollar Pier from 1968 through 1975.

Alper, who also became an operating partner of Steel Pier along with Al Gardner, was responsible for the presentations.

For the first time since before Frank Gravatt had bought the Pier, one could see the entire front Casino building without any distractions. The famous, large presentation boards on both sides were gone, as was the Spanish Galleon decoration that had hung above the entrance since the late 1920s. In fact, the Casino, whose siding was now blandly painted entirely white, looked almost like it did when it was built in 1898, albeit without the decorative work and cupolas.

It was now called "The New Steel Pier," which was probably a death knell, because anything renamed *new* historically means "trying not to be the original." In a bizarre move, the Casino theater was renamed the Music Hall. The *New York Times* observed in May 1976:

Ralph A. Alswang of the Theater Planning Association of New York remodeled the concert theater and redesigned the façade, lobby and entrance. He said he had consolidated three badly rundown halls into a Victorian-type, 2,000-seat modern theater.

Alswang said, "At the beginning, it was a horrible dump. We had to get rid of seventy-five truckloads of trash to get back to the theater's original form. The whole place looked like a coalmine at the height of our excavation. We had to haul out a half century of foolish incrustation."

They also removed the charm.

The designers said the Casino's new lighting and sound systems had cost the new owners almost $200,000.

"Alswang designed probably the plushest dressing room ever built. The room includes thick carpeting, sectional sofas, a bar, kitchenette and other conveniences found in luxury apartments," Billie Fields, the entertainment director, remarked to *The Times* at the end of May 1976.

The New Steel Pier opened on June 19, 1976, completely refurbished and rehabilitated at a cost of $2.5 million. Eartha Kitt was the first headliner. Alper termed the investment "a gamble that had to be taken. We want to get the families back."

"What we've done is create a theme park," he told *The Times*. "We've made a one-stop, one-price center for diversion and amusement. Combined with the Boardwalk, we have everything you could ask for the family."

Ocean Discovery was the new name for Ocean Wonderworld, still presenting the Flipper dolphin show in the Oceanarium and operated in conjunction with the mid-Atlantic region of the nonprofit Oceanic Society of San Francisco and Stamford, Connecticut. However, Flipper's Sea School of Miami was not an act. "It is not a series of tricks, with the porpoises leaping and us giving them fish. It isn't a circus," said one handler. "It will be a real training show."

Basically, it was a "school" for two younger dolphins, Captain Gray and Delphi, who were learning to perform as the summer went on.

The Water Circus and Diving Horse remained, as did Tony Grant's Children's Theater, plus an aggressive line-up of stars to play the revamped Casino, now Music Hall. Names such as Jerry Lewis, Ella Fitzgerald, Count Basie, Frankie Valli and the Four Seasons, Al Green, Melba Moore, Tony Bennett, the Bay City Rollers, Isaac Hayes, the Stylistics, and Harold Melvin and the Blue Notes were touted.

In the Golden Dome were rock concerts starring unknown bands, continuous disco dancing, and karate demonstrations. The Pier initially charged $4 for everything, $5 after July 2, and an extra charge of $2.50 for a reserved seat at a Music Hall show. There was also an exhibit of the world's largest model train set, which had been part of the Lionel train exhibit at the 1939 New York World's Fair.

"I knew the guys who bought the Pier and I told them that I'd help them book the Pier: 'I wouldn't charge you anything,'" recalled Ed Hurst, who had hosted the hugely popular record hops of the 1960s. "But they didn't listen and it was a disaster."

On November 3, 1976, the second time the referendum was held, New Jersey voters approved legalized casino gambling for Atlantic City. The old era of clean family fun was over, giving way to a new era filled with glamour and money. But with the dying, decaying city on the brink of being deserted, it is clear that casino gambling gave it new life. Unfortunately, it could not save the increasingly honky-tonk Boardwalk or the legacy of Steel Pier.

In 1977, the Pier based its theme on the *Guinness Book of World Re-*cords. During the entire summer, different feats were tried in order to get a mention in the renowned book of useless records. For instance, one day a man would lie on six-inch nails while a car drove on top of him. Another day the world's fattest twins would show up. A flagpole sitter brought back memories of "Shipwreck" Kelly from 1930. Atlantic City Mayor Joseph Lazarow even shook the hands of 12,000 people in front of the Pier, hoping to break a record set by Teddy Roosevelt. Instead, he dislocated a bone in his hand. And the Casino/Music Hall

was again renamed, this time as the *Guinness Book of World Records* Theater Musical Show.

The Hanneford Family Circus entertained on the open air site of the original Music Hall. The Water Circus continued with Acapulco Divers and the Diving Horse. Tony Grant's "Stars of Tomorrow" show still held on, and the Sea Theatre presented an underwater ballet. The Pier was open daily, 11 A.M. to 11 P.M.. The days of late-night dancing and movies were long since over.

After only one year, the big names were also gone, probably due to diminished profits. Ray Charles' one-day appearance in August was an exception. Old-hack rock bands like the Skyliners, Spiral Staircase, the Belmonts, and Danny and the Juniors took their place. Big-name acts

were not going to play twenty-six shows a week, as was the custom, when they could play two a night at a nearby casino hotel.

"You have to remember, nobody wanted to work three or four shows a day. The rock acts do one show, draw 15,000 people. Why would they want to do four shows a day?" said Hurst.

The Golden Dome had now been converted into Thrilsphere, an eighty-degree "sight and sound" show featuring a wraparound movie screen. Gone were the days of live music out over the ocean.

Hurricane Belle had severely damaged the Pier in August 1976, and despite a $2.5 million investment to restore it, the Pier continued to lose money. It had been for sale since the Casino Gambling referendum was passed in New Jersey in November 1976, but a sale to new investors was never completed.

Co-owner Al Gardner remembered that the hurricane destroyed the center of the pier and most of the remodeling that had just been completed. "Some rides even fell into the ocean", he said.

It could be argued that the rare August storm was the real death knell for the pier. "After that, we were discouraged. We rebuilt, but it took something out of us," Gardner concluded. With the paint barely dry, the new owners took an unexpected financial hit.

On May 26, 1978, the former Haddon Hall Hotel on the Boardwalk gave way to its new name: Resorts International Hotel Casino. The casino era had begun. This wasn't the Casino of Steel Pier, which meant lounging, stage shows and variety entertainment. This was slot machines, cocktail waitresses, blackjack and roulette. Big-name stars were returning to Atlantic City — Steve Lawrence, Eydie Gorme, Paul Anka, Diana Ross and Frank Sinatra — to the modern theaters in the gaming halls, while a mere 200 yards away, the Pier that they had once played as youngsters was in a sad state, its owners fighting desperately to get their finger back on the pulse of America.

In its last season, the New Steel Pier's attractions included the Diving Horse, Tony Grant, the Cox Family Puppets, Wet Banana water slide, Fun House, Monkey Jungle, Diving Bell, Aquarium, rides, and in the Golden Dome, a Laser Disco and the Thrilsphere movie. The Pier's all-inclusive admission ended. Everything was now a separate price.

But the ownership of the New Steel Pier finally gave in. Their experiment had failed. As much as they had tried, the Pier had fallen too far. It became apparent that they had no focus or direction for their property.

Milton Neustadter summed it up in 2008: "We weren't making money", he explained. "We drew crowds only on the weekends. You can't survive on that."

"No one could have done anything to the Steel Pier," George Hamid, Jr. said afterward. "It was too gone. There was no way it could have come back."

Singer Eddie Fisher and comic London Lee appeared together at the Music Hall on Memorial Day weekend 1978, and singer Ray Charles appeared again that summer. But it was too late. In June, it was announced that WFPG, the radio station that had been on the Pier since its inception in 1940, would be changing its call letters and would soon

move (although that would take another three years).

On July 18, Resorts International bought Steel Pier for a $3.8 million stock-cash deal. By then, admission to the Pier was free, and Resorts didn't spell out any plans for the future. "It was just a good deal on prime Boardwalk acreage. We bought the Pier quite simply as acreage," remarked Resorts senior vice-president Raymond Gore.

The end was near. In late August, the *Press* had this report:

After only a two-week run in July, the variety show Magic, Magic closed. Nobody came. Producer Don Slone added, "We were expecting to go at least five weeks. This was a disaster. We didn't have a fighting chance." The show lost $75,000, Slone's life savings.

Jack Durant, a comic who had played the Pier many times through the years, was Magic, Magic's director. "It was a good show," Durant said. "It had a lot of vaudeville in it. They just couldn't get the people in the theater. I thought it stood a good chance because it was playing the Pier. It was always a special place for that kind of entertainment.

"Maybe there's no place for that anymore. If it can't play the Pier, it can't play anywhere. It's sad to see."

After Labor Day 1978, the New Steel Pier was finished.

"Well, they had their shot. I don't begrudge anyone that," George Hamid, Jr. said at the time. "But when you create a new beast, you have to hope people will accept the new beast. You never know what's going to happen when you start making changes.

"I don't know what Resorts will do with it. But I'll say this: If I had the Pier again, I'd go back to the single admission, 'spend the day' policy. I'd go back to tradition. That's what made it great in the past and I think it could be great again."

"The Steel Pier didn't die all at once," *Press* reporter Laura Italiano wrote ten years later. "It went dark slowly throughout the late 1960s and 1970s, as a marquee can die slowly, bulb by bulb."

☾ ☾ ☾ ☾

Resorts opened the Steel Pier's Casino building in 1979 and presented a few boxing matches, but the facilities were shabby, unpainted, and in disrepair. Later it was primarily used for storage, containing property from the Resorts hotel. Only a portion of the front lobby was open as an amusement arcade, yet radio station WFPG still had its studios on the Pier until May 1, 1981.

In 1979, the last of the rides were removed. Fifty miles away, in Monroeville, New Jersey, signs, character pieces from fun houses and loudspeakers from the Water Circus were auctioned off.

In September of that year, twenty of the world's top weightlifters competed in the Casino, at a charge of $7.50 for adults and $3.50 for children.

And then it languished, a deteriorated derelict shell of what it was, while Resorts tried to figure out what to do with it. Shops, a hotel, a casino and a completely new pier were discussed but nothing materialized. It went from the Queen of Piers to a relic in less than a decade.

Over Memorial Day 1981, boxer Mike Rossman was training for a nationally televised fight against Dwight Braxton, sharing a dusty, cluttered, make-shift gym on Steel Pier with lions and tigers.

"Baseball players have nice clean showers. They don't have to share their training headquarters with lions and tigers. Look at this place. It's filthy, but I've been in some of the worst gyms in Philadelphia," Rossman grumbled to *The New York Times*. The lions and tigers were caged there between appearances for a stage revue at Resorts.

Nature helped Resorts make a decision on December 10, 1982. A pre-dawn fire of suspicious origin destroyed the main Casino building on the Boardwalk and burned out of control for hours. About seventy-five firefighters battled the blaze, which started at 3:20 A.M. and continued until 11 A.M. Arson was suspected, and police held a suspect who was spotted running from the Pier.

Thick, black smoke was visible from ten miles away. The building was equipped with a sprinkler system, but it was ineffective because the fire worked its way into the walls above the sprinkler lines. Luckily, the wind was blowing seaward, saving Boardwalk buildings from being destroyed.

By 9 A.M., portions of the walls around the front of the Pier began crumbling. The awning at the entrance that proclaimed, "The New Steel Pier Presents" just melted away, as did much of the Pier.

Damage was estimated at $1 million. Resorts reported that two

A postcard from the "new" Steel Pier, 2007.

replica cable cars and eight tramcars inside were also destroyed.

The only portion of Steel Pier that had seen its entire history was now gone. The 1898 Casino building, albeit without its cupolas, which had already disappeared during the many renovations, was the last vestige of the original Pier. Only the abandoned Golden Dome and the Water Circus that lay out in the ocean, past the smoldering, skeletal pieces, remained as a reminder that Steel Pier ever existed.

"There is a song that goes 'there is a time to be born and a time to die,'" George Hamid, Jr. told *The Press.* "Steel Pier served Atlantic City and the whole nation beautifully for many decades, and the last three or four years it just stood there, decaying and unused. That hurt me a whole heck of a lot more than it did to hear about the Pier burning. I'd rather live with a ghost than a corpse. I think it's better off being a beautiful memory than an ugly milestone."

Epilogue

Buckminster Fuller's 1970 geodesic Golden Dome of the former Steel Pier lay over the ocean for years, condemned and stranded from the rest of civilization after the 1982 fire. The pilings, decks and remains of the Diving Horse act could still be seen as some sort of macabre monument.

In July 1985, Resorts International, still owners of the property, began to demolish the old pilings, with plans to reconstruct the Pier. George Hamid, Jr. expressed surprise when told the pilings under the Golden Dome had to be removed.

"They're going to be monsters to take out," he explained. "The pilings were installed with the original Ballroom. The Ballroom had a midsection collapse in 1915. They then put in some new pilings in the center. We rebuilt pilings huskily in 1969, and those pilings are big round babies. The pilings that they were putting in were double strength of the pilings of the Chesapeake Bay Bridge. I saw these things — sixty-five feet in length! — to make it 1,100 feet long."

Resorts had begun removing the old pilings to prepare for a $10 million project to rebuild the Pier with a 37,000-square-foot ballroom, aquarium, swimming pool, roller skating rink, restaurant, meeting rooms, lounge, and fishing pier. It was to extend 2,800 feet over the ocean, far longer than the original Pier.

Hamid was glad something was being done. "I hated to see a wreck sitting out there," he told *The Press of Atlantic City.*

Milton Neustadter, one of the Pier's former owners who was now an executive at Caesar's casino, was delighted by the news. "Fantastic!" he exclaimed. "The fact that it would be rebuilt would be further proof that the town is going to improve, and that major money is going into investments other than casinos. Even though this is owned by Resorts, it will be an attraction catering to everybody, especially families."

It never materialized, and the ruins of Steel Pier languished another three years.

Meanwhile, developer Donald Trump acquired the remains of the Pier when he struck a deal with then-Resorts owner Merv Griffin. Trump decided a new pier would rise and become connected with his gigantic Taj Mahal casino hotel that was under construction. In December 1988, exactly six years after the fire, the Golden Dome and the remains of Steel Pier were finally demolished. There was talk that Trump was considering naming the rebuilt structure Trump Pier.

That was fine with Hamid. "He owns it and he's more than entitled to call it Trump Pier," George Hamid, Jr. said at the time. "I remember when my father purchased Young's Million Dollar Pier in 1937; he renamed it 'Hamid's Million Dollar Pier.' A year later, he dropped the 'Million Dollar' part and just called it 'Hamid's Pier.' That's after it had been called 'Young's' for many, many years.

"I don't believe anyone today or in the future will ever re-create what we had on Steel Pier all those years — such as headline artists doing seven shows a day — but I'm very interested in Donald Trump's planned concept."

The Diving Bell today, on display at Gardner's Basin.

Barton Beck, Jr. was the last operator of the Diving Bell, which in 1986 was just a hulk of its former self, rusting away at the end of the Pier near the Golden Dome.

"It was synonymous with the old Pier — the Diving Horses and the Diving Bell," he told the *Press* in February of that year. "I'd like to have people remember it and the Pier the way they were, not the way they ended up. It would be nice to save it. I have a lot of sentimental feelings about her."

In 1988, the deteriorated bell was saved. It was refurbished and is now permanently exhibited at Gardner's Basin, a little more than a mile from where it had brought countless thousands of customers down to the sandy ocean floor beneath the Pier. It is the only relic of the original Steel Pier displayed anywhere, besides the Marine Ballroom's neon American flag that hangs in Baltimore's Lexington Market.

Trump's Steel Pier opened on June 15, 1992 at the same location as the original Steel Pier. It was first used as a helicopter landing pad, bringing in high rollers to the Taj Mahal. Instead of the theaters, vaudeville, and swing music of the days of the the original Pier, Trump's featured only rides such as Tilt-A-Whirl, a Ferris wheel, a carousel and a bungee jump.

Built on thick, concrete pilings, the new pier was also much shorter than the original, reaching out only 1,000 feet. Anthony Catanoso and his three brothers, along with partners Ed Orwell and Taft Johnson, leased it from Trump to operate it under the corporate name of Atlantic Pier Amusements, Inc.

A small diving horse act returned in May 1993. "We're trying to include something for everyone at the pier," said Orwell. The horse didn't have a rider, and it dove from a thirty-foot tower into a twelve-foot tank of water. Animal rights groups protested, arguing that the animal had to endure cruelty in order to perform.

"The more they picketed, the better the crowds were," Anthony Catanoso was quoted at the time. "The accusations of animal cruelty are outlandish. The pony is treated well."

Yet soon the promotion ended, and the Diving Horse act in Atlantic City disappeared again.

Catanoso started out with twelve amusement rides and twelve skill games in 1993. By 2005, Trump's Steel Pier offered more than twenty-five rides and a great reputation for consistency and fun for families visiting the resort. Roller coasters, helicopter rides, a new Ferris wheel and a motorcycle high-wire act that performed four times a day harked back to the "old" Steel Pier, where death-defying acts were commonplace.

Looking for a nostalgia angle, a Broadway musical about the life of Steel Pier during the 1930s was developed and written. Titled "Steel Pier," it opened at the Richard Rodgers Theatre in New York on April 24, 1997. The show starred Karen Ziemba, Gregory Harrison, and newcomer Kristen Chenoweth. Music and lyrics were by John Kander and Fred Ebb; choreography was by Susan Stroman. But even with a group of proven stars in control, it was a flop. It closed on June 28, 1997, a scant two months later.

For historians, the central idea of the show was a total farce, based on a 1933 dance marathon that was never even held on Steel Pier. The dance marathons in Atlantic City during the early 1930s were held on Million Dollar Pier.

❦   ❦   ❦

On June 18, 1998, there was a big party on Trump's Steel Pier to celebrate the 100th birthday of the original Pier. Special guests were invited. Philadelphia Flyers broadcaster Gene Hart, a former announcer for the Diving Horse act, was there. So was Philly radio star Ed Hurst, former Steel Pier WFPG-FM announcer Ed Davis, and former Pier owner George Hamid, Jr. Former Diving Horse performers Sarah Detweiler Hart, Josephine Knox and Arnette French attended. Live music, a large

PLAYBILL

RICHARD RODGERS THEATRE

STEEL PIER

birthday cake and fireworks were part of the festivities.

"People always talk about how it's not what it used to be, but the old Pier wouldn't have been able to survive. It couldn't compete in Atlantic City today," Anthony Catanoso told the *Press of Atlantic City*. "We brought it back to a certain extent, but it will never be the way it was. It was really the landmark in Atlantic City, the icon of the city. Nothing will compete with the casinos now. Everything has moved across the Boardwalk.

"You have 37 million people a year on that Boardwalk, and not all 37 million of them are of gambling age. Atlantic City will always need a place that offers full-sized, first-class family entertainment. You can never tell what the future will be, but you know that the need will always be there."

Steel Pier attracts up to 500,000 visitors a year, just about half of what the original Steel Pier drew in its heyday.

C   C   C

Steel Pier lives on in the minds of many people. Once in a while, original memorabilia is found — usually a sign promoting an act, or an old program. And there are thousands of old postcards that depict the Pier from its beginning to end, photographed from all angles.

On the Internet, there are countless sites that depict the old Pier with nostalgic remarks from people all over the country who remember the "old" Atlantic City of their youth. At *www.Iloveac.com*, a link to "Memory Lane" contains over 3,000 entries. Another great site with pictures and memories is *www.steel-pier.com*.

Steel Pier is at Virginia Avenue and the Boardwalk, where the original stood for nearly a century. On August 3, 2011, the Catanoso family and partners bought Steel Pier from Trump Entertainment for $4.25 million. After leasing the Pier for 20 years, Tony Catanoso stated that the opportunity to own the Pier will enable his company to develop portions of the property, add new attractions and possibly build wind turbines to generate electricity.

There will never be another Steel Pier; that existed in a simple time in American history when the music, movies and entertainment eschewed class — before the late 1960s, when mediocrity prevailed and the Pier's downward spiral began.

As the country changed with protest, so did Atlantic City.

There was a time when people wore hats, ties, and dresses on the Boardwalk, and went to nightclubs or danced to orchestras in the ballrooms of Boardwalk hotels. It was a world without television, and people watched movies in the magical atmosphere of large theaters with balconies. One could only see the President and world events by watching newsreels. Only Steel Pier could combine opera with circus acts, kid shows with Borden's Elsie the Cow. There was once a great audience for unusual presentations and exhibits on the Boardwalk, interesting products from Dupont, Ford Motor Company, or Crane Plumbing — simply because no one could experience these unusual displays anywhere else. One could walk south from the Inlet for miles down the Boardwalk, never spending a penny, yet enjoying the potpourri of fascinating curios, shops, amusements and crowds of people that included millionaires, salesmen, entertainers and auto mechanics.

That world disintegrated into one of boarded-up stores, demolished hotels, residents who were afraid to venture out of their homes, and casual Boardwalk strollers wearing T-shirts, sandals, and baseball hats, to go along with dollar stores and cheap, all-you-can-eat buffets.

As the "nightclub era" died around 1970, television stars became the new entertainers, but without the talent, quality, and experience of the old vaudevillians. Two world wars couldn't stop Steel Pier from offering escapism at its highest level. It took a deteriorating and poverty-stricken Atlantic City to produce a disinterested public that no longer cared about a horse that dove from forty feet into a giant tub of water, and thus to end the era of Steel Pier.

Steel Pier died because people stopped caring about it, and the crowds stopped coming. By the time the casino hotels were built, visitors to Atlantic City wanted to stay inside and play blackjack, slots or craps — not visit a pier. But the casinos didn't kill Steel Pier. It had already begun its slow decline long before they arrived.

In its time, Steel Pier was the greatest entertainment complex to ever exist in the world. There was nothing else like it. Looking back now, it's amazing how much of it was taken for granted, as if it would always be there every summer, offering a different show, lasting an eternity.

Steel Pier Timeline

1898 - Steel Pier opens on June 18 with Minstrels, Grand Cakewalks, Children's Novelty Balls, Promenade Concerts & Dances and Grand Sacred Concerts.

1908 - Motion pictures are first shown.

1920 - An Aero Exhibit in the Arcade and Ballroom present the Wireless Phone.

1922 - World-famous tenor Cantor Josef Rosenblatt performs in the Pier's Convention Hall for the benefit of the Hebrew National Orphan Home of New York.

1925 - Businessman Frank Gravatt buys the Pier and begins its transformation into an entertainment complex. He expands the existing buildings and builds space for attractions such as the General Motors Exhibit.

1926 - Ted Weems' Orchestra is the first name band to play in the Marine Ballroom, WPG radio becomes the only station on an ocean pier. Gertrude Ederle, the first woman to swim the English Channel, becomes the first "big" name to draw a crowd. Famed Irish tenor John McCormack performs, tickets are $2.50 per seat.

1927 - Marion Talley, a star with the Metropolitan Opera, performs in May. John Philip Sousa, America's "March King," makes his Pier debut under Gravatt with two afternoon and two evening concerts.

1928 - "Nowhere else can you see so much for so little money," say the ads. Hawaiian hula singers and dancers, surfboard riders, divers and swimmers perform as a nucleus for the Water Circus. Captain Wilkins, the famous aviator who flew over the North Pole, lectures alongside his plane.

1929 - The Diving Horse makes its Steel Pier debut — along with another first, the human cannonball — advertised on a new sign boasting the Pier as "The Showplace of the Nation." Both feature female performers. Independence Day weekend features "Dutchy" Wilde, "the world's greatest daredevil," leaping into the ocean from a low-flying airplane – without a parachute. Lt. Cmdr. John Philip Sousa returns to the Music Hall to lead four concerts by his famous march band. "Television – the latest wonder invention of the electrical world," is introduced.

1930 - "The World's Mightiest Show –16 hours of continuous amusement starting at 10 AM every day – 20 world famous attractions for one admission." George Jessel becomes the first vaudeville star to headline the Pier in the Music Hall, with Eddie Cantor following. A dead 70-ton whale is exhibited. The ocean end of Steel Pier features yacht races. The Pier remains open year round.

1931 - Exciting attractions are added including boxing cats, parachute jumping, an Autogiro plane and a rocket-powered glider. Ce-Dora defies death on a speeding motorcycle in a 16-foot globe, while six daredevil aerial acrobats perform 100 feet in the air. John Philip Sousa appears for the last time.

1932 - The steamship S.S. Steel Pier offers daily excursions from the end of the Pier. Pete, the "Our Gang" dog, begins an annual summer stay on the Pier, posing for pictures. Rudy Vallee makes his first of many appearances, bringing in record crowds along with Boris Karloff's "Frankenstein" motion picture.

1933 - The Pier proclaims "It's a Big Vacation in Itself." The world's largest captive sea elephant is exhibited. Top radio stars Amos 'N Andy appear on Easter and perform countless times between two theaters to accommodate enormous crowds. George Burns and Gracie Allen appear, as does new heavyweight champion Primo Carnera, who boxes with a kangaroo. A young Milton Berle also appears.

1934 - Broadcaster Lowell Thomas goes national from the Music Hall. "Belle of the Nineties," a Mae West picture, makes its world premiere. On Labor Day, the Pier proclaims, "66 hours of consecutive entertainment – this morning at 8 AM we will be open.... until Tuesday, September 4 at 2 AM." Attractions include the radio cast of "The Goldbergs," the opera "Carmen" sung in English, and Ozzie Nelson's Orchestra with Harriett Hilliard.

1935 - Daddy Dave's Kiddie Revue begins its regular run. "The Little House" exhibits the most modern appliances. Bob Hope, with wife Dolores Reade, appears in May, Guy Lombardo brings his orchestra in August. Miss America is crowned on Steel Pier, which hosts the pageant four more years. Major Bowes' Amateur Hour is broadcast nationally from the Casino lobby in December.

1936 - Ford opens an exhibit in the front of the Pier. The comedy team of Bud Abbott and Lou Costello joins the minstrel troupe. Rex joins the Water Circus as the world's only aquaplane-riding dog. Benny Goodman and Tommy Dorsey bring their famous big bands. The Three Stooges also first appear.

1937 - Rising comics Red Skelton and Henny Youngman make their Pier debuts. Child prodigy Bobby Short appears in a vaudeville Christmas program.

1938 - The Kennel Club of Atlantic City holds its 19th Annual Dog Show, with 600 dogs and 80 breeds present. Drummer Gene Krupa debuts his orchestra in the Marine Ballroom to a packed crowd of screaming fans. Benny Goodman broadcasts his "Camel Caravan" show nationwide from the Ballroom in August.

1939 - The Harry James Band plays for the Easter crowd, and an unknown singer named Frank Sinatra makes his Steel Pier debut with the band. The Four Ink Spots become the first African-American headliners, and the Andrews Sisters first appear.

1940 - Legendary bandleader Glenn Miller appears in August.

1941 - Elsie, the famous Borden cow, is exhibited in her own boudoir. Future "Honeymooners" star Art Carney is an unknown in a July vaudeville program. Abbott and Costello, now stars, return as their film "Hold That Ghost" plays in the movie theater. Rising singer Dinah Shore appears, as does the Artie Shaw Band.

1942 - First season for a trip to the ocean bottom in the Diving Bell. Admission for servicemen is 30 cents at all times, plus they can also send a record back home to their loved ones for free. Wild man Louis Prima and his band perform.

1943 - The minstrels hang it up due to indifference and the loss of many entertainers to wartime. Jimmy Durante is one of the few big names to appear this summer.

1944 - New heartthrob singer Perry Como is featured in August. September hurricane causes havoc in Atlantic City and destroys the Water Circus.

1945 - George Hamid buys the Pier from Gravatt, continuing "all for one admission." The Exhibit of Bombs - "See close up the kind of bombs our planes are dropping on the Japs." Rising comedian Jackie Gleason hits the Music Hall stage.

1946 - The Harry James Band draws 27,000 people on Easter. "The Outlaw," a risqué Western produced by Howard Hughes, receives major publicity and an appearance by star Jane Russell. Rosemary Clooney makes her debut with Tony Pastor's Band.

1947 - The General Motors Exhibit returns to the front of the Pier.

1948 - Television is featured on a giant screen in the Ocean theater. Peggy Lee sings in the Music Hall with husband Dave Barbour and his trio.

1949 - Tony Grant takes over the Kiddie Revue and stays until the Pier's final days.

1950 - All-around entertainer Danny Kaye arrives in July. Frank Sinatra's non-stop Labor Day performances for record crowds cause him to temporarily lose his voice.

1951 - Billy Eckstine becomes the first solo African-American singer to headline on the Pier. He is supported by new comedian Alan King.

1952 - The Steel Pier radio show broadcasts live from the Lobby almost daily from 11:35 p.m. to 5 a.m. with guest stars and promotions. Guitarist Les Paul appears with wife Mary Ford. Gary Cooper's "High Noon" keeps moviegoers captivated.

1953 - The famed Diving Horses return. Young comic Joey Bishop is part of the bill with singer Fran Warren. New singers Tony Bennett and Eddie Fisher appear. Louis Armstrong is the first African-American musician to headline, but plays the Music Hall, not the Ballroom. The Casino is remodeled and renamed the Ocean Theater.

1954 - Former bandleader Paul Whiteman begins a weekly ABC television series, "On the Boardwalk," broadcasting every Sunday from the Midway theater. Popular music is changed forever as Bill Haley and the Comets rock the Music Hall.

1956 - Teen idol Pat Boone stars in July, jazz-stylist Sarah Vaughan in August.

1957 - An eclectic bill in July presents singers The Diamonds, pop singer Steve Lawrence, and the orchestra of Woody Herman.

1958 - Philadelphia radio disc jockeys Joe Grady and Ed Hurst begin record hops, some televised from the Pier. Danny and the Juniors, Connie Francis and Paul Anka are booked. The Pier's wildest day ever is September 1, when over 44,000 pay to witness Ricky Nelson's first public appearance.

1959 - Teen idols Fabian, Bobby Darin and Frankie Avalon appear.

1960 - Bobby Vinton and Johnny Cash arrive, as does Dick Clark's "Cavalcade of Stars," featuring Bobby Rydell, the Crew Cuts and more.

1961 - Chubby Checker becomes the first black rock 'n' roll headliner.

1962 - A monster storm in March pushes a barge through the Pier, destroying the Home of the Century and leaving the Marine Ballroom cut off.

1964 - Duke Ellington is the first African-American band leader to play the Marine Ballroom. The Beatles' movie "A Hard Day's Night" plays the Pier.

1965 - The Supremes, Gary Lewis and the Playboys, Herman's Hermits, Peter and Gordon, and Sam the Sham and the Pharaohs all headline. Future Vegas star Wayne Newton also makes an appearance.

1966 - The Rolling Stones appear July 1 for two shows, along with the McCoys and the Standells. Stan Kenton and his band play in the Ballroom that day. Others this summer are Stevie Wonder, Frank Sinatra Jr. and the Count Basie Band.

1967 - Ray Charles performs during the Independence Day holiday.

1968 - The Giant Skywheel, a ride directly from the New York World's Fair, opens on the Pier. Top acts include the Beach Boys and the Box Tops.

1969 - Tiny Tim proclaims his love for Miss Vicki on the Music Hall stage. The Marine Ballroom, Water Circus and a portion of the Pier is destroyed by fire.

1970 - A geodesic Gold Dome replaces the Ballroom on the Pier's outer end. The Ocean World Theatre of the Sea opens in the vacated General Motors space.

1971 - George Hamid dies May 28 at age 75. The Allman Brothers and the Cowsills are featured in July. Cab Calloway and Chuck Berry appear.

1973 - George Hamid Jr. sells the Pier to a group of businessmen on January 16, but will lease it for two more years. The "Brady Bunch" Kids appear on May 25.

1974 - More TV stars appear, including Danny Bonaduce of "The Partridge Family" and Barry Williams of "The Brady Bunch."

1976 - The new owners remodel the entire Pier, discard all of the classic signs and tear down the Music Hall and Midway theaters. The Bay City Rollers perform to a frenzied crowd. Woody Herman leads the last big band to play Steel Pier.

1978 - The Pier closes for the last time in September, effectively signaling an end to the Diving Horse act and Tony Grant's "Stars of Tomorrow."

1979 - Frank Gravatt dies on January 28 at age 89. The Casino building is used sporadically for boxing and wrestling events.

1982 - Primarily used for storage, most of Steel Pier burns to the ground in a December arson.

1988 - The dilapidated Gold Dome, Water Circus area and Diving Bell are finally torn down as a New Steel Pier arises.

2011 - On August 3, after leasing the Pier for 20 years, the Catanoso family and partners bought Steel Pier from Trump Entertainment for $4.25 million.

Atlantic City Boardwalk Piers

West Jersey Pier	1880-1881	500 ft.	opened July 16, 1880
Howard's Pier	1882	650 ft.	opened July 12, 1882
	1883-1889	856 ft.	
Applegate's Pier	1884-1891	625 ft.	opened June 1, 1884
Young & McShea's Pier	1891-1897	1,400 ft. (1894)	
Young's Ocean Pier	1897-1912	2,000 ft. (1906)	
Central Pier	1922-present	250 ft. (1938)	
		800 ft. (1954)	
Iron Pier	1886-1898	1,003 ft.	opened April 25, 1886
Heinz Pier	1898-1944	650 ft. (shortened in 1913)	
Steel Pier	1898-1978	1,600 ft. (1908)	
		1,780 ft. (1954)	opened June 18,1898
Auditorium Pier	1899-1904	1,000 ft.	opened August 25, 1899
Steeplechase Pier	1904-1988	1,025 ft. (1908)	
		700 ft. (1924)	
		525 ft. (1938)	
		800 ft. (1954)	
		432 ft. (1967)	
Million Dollar Pier	1906-1981	1,775 ft. (1908)	opened July 26, 1906
		1,575 ft. (1938)	
		1,600 ft. (1954)	
Garden Pier	1913-1944	725 ft. (1914)	opened July 19, 1913
	1954-present	675 ft.	

Acknowledgments

This book was a labor of love and it took many years to fully research the story of Steel Pier, the icon of Atlantic City, New Jersey. There are numerous people I must thank for sharing their time and knowledge with me during the course of writing this book.

I owe an immeasurable debt of gratitude to Allen "Boo" Pergament for dozens of hours of help in shepherding this book to completion. I had originally asked Boo for permission to reproduce images from his vast collection of Atlantic City pictures and memorabilia. Not only did he provide at least half the images in this book (Boo, my publisher, and I spent days culling his files), he was invaluable in that most difficult editing task — deciding what NOT to include! (That was a nearly impossible task considering how many wonderful old photos were available.) Further, Boo took a passionate interest in seeing that the book was accurate and complete. He went above and beyond what any author could expect as a courtesy, and he proofed the manuscript and galleys, provided fact-checking, assisted with captions, and personally worked with the designer and publisher in fine-tuning the details.

Robert Ruffolo, another iconic historian and collector of Atlantic City memorabilia, was the other pillar on which this book stands. Bob nurtured the seed of this book in my mind, and encouraged me. Bob owns Princeton Antiques in Atlantic City, an amazing treasure trove of old books, pictures, and any Atlantic City collectibles imaginable. Images from his incredible collection make up the other half of this book, and helped form the foundation of it.

When Atlantic City historian Vicki Gold Levi's book "Atlantic City: 125 Years of Ocean Madness" was published in 1979, I immediately bought it. Vicki had included a fantastic picture of the Steel Pier lobby in all of its 1936 Art Deco-glory. Until then, I had always seen pictures that presented the entire pier but never the interior. Thank you, Vicki. If not for that one picture to whet my appetite, I doubt this book would exist.

In 1984, I found microfilms of the Atlantic City newspapers in the Atlantic City Public Library. It took years of laboriously examining almost every reel from 1898 to 1978 to understand the history of Steel Pier and meticulously write down the exact dates of what celebrity, band and movies played there. A big thanks to the staff of the ACPL; they had been a great help to me in addition to allowing me access to the historic artifacts of their Heston Collection.

I owe a gigantic thank you to ex-Steel Pier owner George Hamid, Jr., who gave me invaluable information that could not have been possibly found elsewhere. I had first traveled to Trenton back in 1988 to meet and interview Mr. Hamid. Since then, we have talked about a dozen times through the years, discussing a specific nuance of a building's structure or about an entertainer or rock band. Without his first-hand knowledge, much of the minutiae about the Pier would be lost. He was always gracious, interesting, and had a wealth of fantastic stories. It has been a true pleasure talking to this giant among American showmen and I thank him ever so much.

My superb editors Neal Roberts and Leslee Ganss of Down The Shore Publishing made sure the text flowed and offered relevant suggestions that were both sound and encouraging. Both did a fantastic job. Ray Fisk of Down The Shore Publishing believed in this book almost immediately; thanks for all of your help and guidance and making my idea a reality.

I also thank Ed Hurst, a well-known legend on Philadelphia radio and television as well as dance host on Steel Pier from 1958 until it closed in 1978. The late Ed Davis was a prince of a man who broadcast from radio station WFPG on the Pier as well as hosting the live big band remotes from the Marine Ballroom. He spent much time with me discussing those days that he loved so much and is sorely missed.

Jim Craine, who literally grew up on the Pier from 1963 to 1973, as a part of the comedic divers in the Water Circus, among other things, always had time to tell some crazy jokes and offer Pier memories.

Sarah Detwiler Hart, widow of Philadelphia Flyers announcer Gene Hart, took a great deal of time explaining how she dove from a forty-foot platform into a pool of water on the back of a horse. Philadelphia musician Mike Pedicin told me what it was like to play on the Marine Ballroom stage, and Jeannemarie McGowan had numerous stories about her grandfather, Steel Pier publicity director Harry Volk, and the entertainers that would visit their home.

Thanks to Bob Graziosa, who appeared out of nowhere with an amazing story about the neon American flag that graced the Marine Ballroom proscenium. Historian Tom Allen gave me a vital African-American point of view when analyzing the unfortunate racial history of Atlantic City and Steel Pier.

Ratso from Philadelphia added local flavor in telling how he used to sneak onto the Pier, and other stories of 1960s Atlantic City that would make a great movie someday.

Many performers took the time to talk to me at length about their memories. Thanks to Frankie Valli, Smokey Robinson, Dick Clark, Al Alberts of the Four Aces, Chubby Checker, Connie Haines, Al Martino, Alan King, Joey Bishop, Artie Shaw and Lou Marks of the Fisher and Marks comedy team.

Thanks to my wonderful, beautiful wife Andrea, for her love and understanding. And to my father Izzy, sister Karen, Aunt Sunny, cousins, uncles, aunts, in-laws and friends; and to my mother Alice (who I know is looking down at all of this and is thrilled) thank you all for your love and support.

And, finally, to the thousands of musicians, performers, entertainers, technicians, electricians and architects that were the backbone of the Pier — without you, millions of people would never have had the privilege of experiencing one of the world's greatest attractions.

Bibliography

Books

Barnet, Charlie: *Those Swingin' Years,* Louisiana State University Press, 1984

Borgnis, Mervin E.: *We Had A Shore Fast Line,* Exposition Press, 1979

Butler, Frank M.: *The Book of the Boardwalk,* 1954 Association, 1953

Cassidy, David: *David Cassidy: Could It Be Forever? My Story,* Headline Publishing Group, 2007

Clancy, William D. with Kenton, Audree Coke: *Woody Herman— Chronicles of the Herds,* Schirmer Books, 1995

Clooney, Rosemary; Bartel, Joan: *Girl Singer,* Doubleday, 1999

Coxey, William J.; Kazempel, Frank C.; Kranefown, Sammy E.: *The Trains to America's Playground,* West Jersey Chapter of the National Railway Historical Society, 1988

Hamid, George A. and George A. Jr.: *The Acrobat,* ComteQ Publishing, 2004

Howard, Moe: *Moe Howard and the Three Stooges,* Citadel Press, 1977

Kent, Bill with Robert E. Ruffalo Jr. and Lauralee Dobbins: *Atlantic City – America's Playground,* Heritage Media Corp., 1998

LeVan, Russell G.: *Memories of Atlantic City, New Jersey – The Queen of Resorts,* Gateway Press Inc., 1998
_____: *This Is Atlantic City,* Ottumwa Printing Co., 1997

Levi, Vicki Gold; Eisenberg, Lee: *Atlantic City – 125 Years of Ocean Madness,* Clarkson N. Potter Inc., 1979

Levinson, Peter J.: *Trumpet Blues, The Life of Harry James,* Oxford University Press, 1999

McMahon, William: "So Young, So Gay: Story of the Boardwalk," *Atlantic City Press,* 1970   (transferred from periodicals---this is a book)

Pignone, Charles: *The Sinatra Treasures,* Bullfinch Press, 2004

Sinatra, Nancy: *Frank Sinatra – An American Legend,* General Publishing Group Inc., 1995

Simon, Bryant: *Boardwalk of Dreams,* Oxford University Press, 2004

Periodicals

Chinem, Nate: "Sir Duke," Philadelphia *City Paper,* April 22, 1999

Duffy, Glen: "Steel Pier's Magic Past Faces Uncertain Future," *Atlantic City Press,* August 24, 1978

Gardner, Paul: "Vallee Enjoying Actor's Holiday in Atlantic City," *New York Times,* August 21, 1962

Kent, Bill: "The Horse Was in Charge," *New York Times,* May 4, 1997

Klauber, Bruce: "And the Bands Played On," *Atlantic City* magazine, May 1991

Loughnane, Lee: ITG *Journal-International Trumpet Guild,* February 1998

Price, Karen: "From High-Diving Horses to Volleyball," *Pittsburgh Tribune-Review,* June 16, 2005

Rockwell, John: "Steel Pier Rocks to Scottish Rollers," *New York Times,* June 28, 1976

Rosenberg, Amy S.: "Rough-and-Tumble Times of an Acrobat and His Son," *Philadelphia Inquirer,* May 23, 2004

_____: "Striking Up The Band-Again," *Philadelphia Inquirer,* February 2, 2001

Thayer, Paul: "80 Years of Steel Pier," *Atlantic City* magazine, August 1981

Urgo, Jacqueline L.: "At the Steel Pier, Those Were the Days," *Philadelphia Inquirer,* March 1998

Atlantic City magazine
Atlantic City Daily Press
Atlantic City Jewish Times
The Atlantic City Press; The Press of Atlantic City (South Jersey Publishing Co.)
Atlantic City *Union*
Billboard
Boardwalk Illustrated News
Downbeat magazine
Metronome magazine
Philadelphia magazine
16 magazine
The New York Times
The Philadelphia Inquirer
The Washington Post
Time magazine

Web Sites

Badfads.com
BillyBragg.co.uk
BonnieBramlett.com
Brucebase.shetland.co.uk
Cromwellbutlers.com
IloveAC.com
ipowerweb.com
Petticoated.com
Steel-Pier.com
WSBTV.com

Index

About the Author

Steve Liebowitz has been researching Atlantic City entertainment history and the Steel Pier for many years. He has written articles for the Baltimore Sun, Baltimore Jewish Times, and Generations, the journal of the Jewish Museum of Maryland. He wrote about the old days of Wildwood, NJ in that Shore town's newspaper for six years. After writing and producing commercials for CBS Radio, he wrote, co-produced and co-hosted "The Rock & Leebo Show" and has now gone out on his own with his comedy sports program "The Leebo Show" heard in Baltimore.

A graduate of the Chicago Academy of Fine Arts, Steve is a student of old theaters and show business history and is involved in historic theatre preservation. He lives outside of Baltimore with his wife Andrea, where he dreams of living near an ocean and a boardwalk.

Down The Shore Publishing specializes in books, calendars, cards and videos about the Jersey Shore. For a free catalog of all our titles or to be included on our mailing list, just send us a request:

Down The Shore Publishing
Box 100, West Creek, NJ 08092

info@down-the-shore.com

www.down-the-shore.com

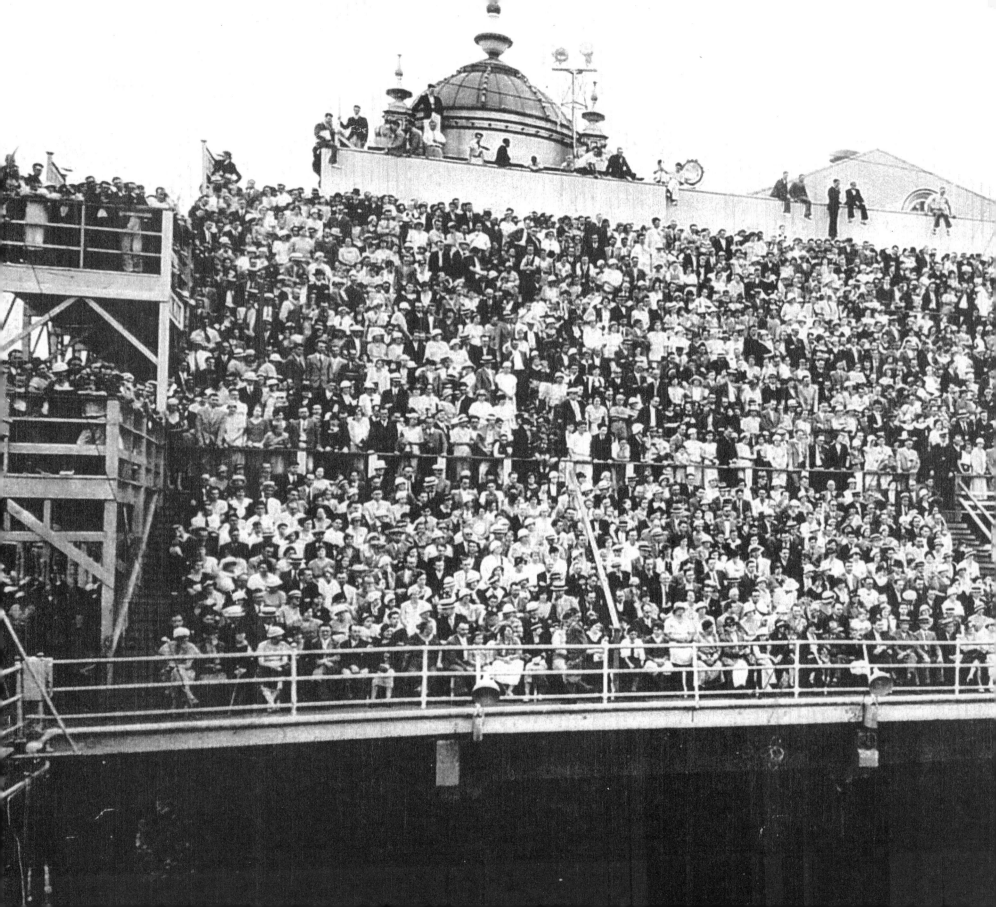